INTUITION: THE INSIDE STORY

INTUITION: THE INSIDE STORY

Interdisciplinary Perspectives

A Collaborative Project of the Academy of Consciousness Studies,

Princeton Engineering Anomalies Research Laboratory,

Princeton University

Edited by

Robbie Davis-Floyd and P. Sven Arvidson

Published in 1997 by
Routledge
29 West 35th Street
New York, NY 10001

Published in Great Britain by
Routledge
11 New Fetter Lane
London EC4P 4EE

The text was set in Centaur.
Printed in the United States of America on acid-free paper.

Library of Congress Cataloging-in-Publication Data
Intuition: the inside story / [edited by] Robbie Davis-Floyd &
P. Sven Arvidson.
p.   cm.
Includes bibliographical references.
ISBN 0-415-91593-7 (cloth). — ISBN 0-415-91594-5 (pbk.)
1. Intutuition (Psychology) 2. Intellect. 3. Mind and body.
I. Davis-Floyd, Robbie.   II. Arvidson, P. Sven.
BF315.5.I48   1997   96-37299
153.4'4—DC21   CIP

To Bob Jahn and Brenda Dunne,

Directors, Academy of Consciousness Studies,

in deep appreciation

Contents

FOREWORD

Intuition, the direct experience of things as they are. Elephants do it, fleas do it, birds do it, bees do it; why should not human beings do it? When we experience the world directly, beyond the filter of conception, we *live* that world. We are in the world and the world is in us. We can love the world, and the world can love us. When we experience only a world preprogrammed by our conceptual conditioning, we merely exist, as if in a dead world. And we destroy all life. The fact that the intellectual authorities of our world have denied intuition for so many generations is a mark of imbalance that, if it goes much further, could become mass insanity. No wonder so many people are crying for help. But when the cry comes from the voice of intuition, the only help the medical establishment generally offers is drugs or other methods to dull that voice.

The essays in this book argue, cogently and rationally, for intuition's natural presence and spontaneous insight in everyone's lives. And they argue, as well, for the importance of a true balance between intuitive experience and intellectual information-gathering and analysis. Joining intellect and intuition, head and heart, mind and body: this is the key to an authentic human life and a good human society. Loving-kindness toward others follows naturally when we are in harmony within ourselves.

The good news is that this is not just so much more unusable talk. Nor is it the case that intuition is only available to the lucky, or perhaps unlucky, few. We can *train* to join intellect and intuition, mind and body. As these essays show, we can hear the voice of intuition when the manipulative, controlling attitude of intellect's chatter is relaxed. There are methods, such as the increasingly well-known and understood method of mindfulness-awareness, that can help us relax our inner chatter, and listen to the voice of intuition with the still, calm clarity of true intellect.

How different our world might become if the education of scientists, doctors, academics, business professionals, and even lawyers included listening to the heartsongs of intuition as well as wielding the sharp sword of intellect. Education of this kind has been going on for some time in a few places where intuition's inside story is told and listened to, such as the Naropa Institute in Boulder, Colorado, and the Academy of Consciousness Studies at Princeton University. This latter program was initiated in the summer of 1994 at the Princeton Engineering Anomalies Research Laboratory. The editors and principal contributors to this volume and I participate in the Academy, which is another noble effort to bring together the deep knowing of intuition with the clarity of intellect. As a collaborative product of Academy members, this book is a welcome step toward restoring the balance of human life on this planet, and toward bringing about a good society able to celebrate all facets and talents of human and beyond-human nature.

JEREMY HAYWARD
The Naropa Institute

PREFACE

Robbie Davis-Floyd and P. Sven Arvidson

Each of the authors participating in this unique text regards their task not as a "chapter to write" but as a "story to tell." There is a difference: "chapters" are subject to more rigorous restraints and are far more likely to be dull and dry than "stories." Rather than maintaining traditional academic detachment, here the authors expose their character in the telling of their stories. We encouraged them to do so, even though this collection is academic by nature and design, because intuition is an intensely personal topic to which justice cannot be done in a detached way. We believe that intuition must be both experienced and analyzed to constitute the most fertile ground for academic exploration, and so we urged our contributors to delve into the experience itself as deeply as into the analysis of that experience. The result is a wide-ranging, experientially based, and academically grounded narrative reflection on the nature of intuition and its scientific and practical aspects.

All of the primary authors lived and studied together during a part of the summer of 1994 as Fellows of the Academy of Consciousness Studies at the Princeton Engineering Anomalies Research Laboratory at Princeton University, New Jersey (see chapter 7 for a description of the PEAR Lab and its work). The Academy's purpose is to advance the creation of an international interdisciplinary community of scholar/practitioners who address the interrelationships of consciousness and environment in the construction of reality, acknowledging the dynamic complementarity of science and spirituality. Recognizing the scientific method as a powerful approach to the acquisition of truth and the growth of wisdom and knowledge, members of the Academy engage in collaborative interdisciplinary research that respects the viewpoints of diverse cultures and traditions. The Academy seeks to cultivate an expanded metaphor of reality that embraces the subjective and interpersonal, as well as the objective and analytical, in a responsible way. This volume represents one of the ways that Academy members are making their findings available to the broader community.

Although the contributors to this volume are formally trained in diverse fields—physics, education, anthropology, psychology, philosophy, humanities, computer science, engineering, environmental studies, and midwifery—they share a unifying interest in widening the scope of consciousness studies. One of the tools that scholars can use to wedge open this emergent field of consciousness studies is an interdisciplinary approach to the phenomenon of intuition. Such interdisciplinary studies are increasingly valued today as a way to bridge the moats that divide academic disciplines, so that insight from many different perspectives can be applied to the study of a single phenomenon. Since this volume is the first of its kind, it represents a humble attempt to build those bridges. We believe the reader will find that this book creates a conceptual space around the phenomenon of intuition within which further work can be both conceived and carried out.

Many disciplines are rediscovering consciousness as an appropriate and worthy subject for academic investigation. As a result, the nature and experience of intuition is being discussed in many more disciplines than ever before. We offer here a thumbnail sketch of some of the exciting developments in various disciplines. The reader is referred to chapter 1 for a more comprehensive account.

Specialties within post-behavioristic psychology, such as cognitive science and neuropsychology, have recently rediscovered the phenomenon of consciousness. Consequently, the phenomenon of intuition has also been rediscovered, and the move is on to integrate intuition with well-documented findings from behavioral analysis. This newfound respect among psychologists for those who are willing to talk about consciousness and intuition is exemplified by the rediscovery of the works of William James, especially his *Principles of Psychology*. A surprising number of major articles and books in psychology cite James as the groundbreaking figure of the discipline. This marks a turning around and away from the psychology of B. F. Skinner and other behaviorists, whose work dominated the field for decades.

On many levels, the move in health care is more toward the human and less toward the machine. On the heels of feminist scholarship, practitioners are being taught to consider the ethics of care rather than merely the previously taught ethics of justice (and impartiality). Practitioners themselves are wondering where the truth of mechanism ends and the truth of intuition begins. Top medical residency and nursing programs are beginning to teach their students to treat the patient holistically. In the midst of this revolution, those who search find a dearth of honest and informative scholarship about what it means to rely on intuitive as well as technological diagnosis in treating the patient.

In philosophy, the deep questions of artificial intelligence, spirituality, and human sensation and meaning are turning on the question of consciousness and intuition. Many philosophers have renewed their interest in the works of Henri Bergson, Alfred North Whitehead, Edmund Husserl, and William James (all to some extent intuitionists), the status of mystic and aesthetic experience, the possibility of knowledge and types of knowledge, and phenomenologies of sensation and thought. These topics, ignored or treated analytically by the logical and linguistic philosophers of the 1950s, 1960s, and 1970s, are being embraced by their students. There are now professional philosophy conferences with intuition as the theme, as well as intriguing discussions of vagueness, fuzzy logic, and quantum mechanics as they relate to problem-solving, human insight, or intuition among those philosophers interested in artificial intelligence.

As educators have become more like facilitators and less like lecturers, a number of education scholars have become interested in the nature of intuition. After all, if what they do as educators is create situations in which learning as insight or intuition can occur, it makes sense that educators would be interested in discovering more about intuition. For example, much discussion at college-level conferences on teacher development concerns the learning style of the student. Here one can hear the phrase "intuitive or subjective style" used in comparison or juxtaposition to procedural, constructive, dualistic, relativistic, or other types of learning style.

The advent of quantum theory has shown scientists—in physics, chemistry, biology, and computer science—that there is something peculiar in the interaction between human, machine, and world. Like the medical practitioners, they have asked openly what constitutes insight, creativity, and method in science. If scientific knowledge involves the subjective perspective of the observer as an integral part of whatever bit of nature is being measured, as quantum theory implies, then it is not surprising that scientists want to know more about the role played by consciousness in the observer/observed relationship, and about how intuition operates in the process of scientific discovery.

This volume investigates intuition from all of the above disciplines, and from hybrid perspectives not anticipated by these categories. Each author was encouraged to tell the readers how he or she goes about investigating intuition and what experiences helped shape the author's unique approach. Therefore, each chapter begins somewhat autobiographically. We are proud to present a scholarly volume in this fashion. With the recognition in the late twentieth century of the pervasiveness of narrative or story in structuring the full spectrum of life-experience, from scientific thinking to spirituality, we think the reader will find this approach not only timely, but also refreshing.

Part I of this volume consists of chapters that plunge deeply into exploring the nature of intuition. Intuition is currently much in vogue, which makes it easy to forget that this concept has a long history. Marcie Boucouvalas's "Intuition: The Concept and the Experience," reviews that history and the extensive literature on intuition, in order to illuminate the similarities and differences in its conceptualization across disciplines. Building on this basis, she then explores the experiential dimensions of intuition from both scholarly and applied/practical perspectives.

Charles Laughlin's "The Nature of Intuition: A Neuropsychological Approach" begins with a description of the experience of intuitive insight. Laughlin probes the neuropsychology of intuition, claiming that the supposed dualism between intuition and intellect is false. He links intuition to unconscious information processing in the brain, contrasting the effects of left and right lobe processing and stressing their complementarity. Laughlin places intuition early in human evolutionary history, before the development of language, thus accounting for the difficulties we experience when we try to verbalize intuitive insights. He also presents a fascinating discussion of cross-cultural techniques for accessing intuition, noting that skillful access to intuitive processes is fundamental to contemplative training in many of the world's religions and spiritual traditions.

P. Sven Arvidson's "Looking Intuit: A Phenomenological Exploration of Intuition and Attention" asks "What is the shape of consciousness in intuition?" He points to the transformation of attention in the reorganization of the conscious field as a crucial issue in responding to such a question. Inspired by phenomenologist Aron Gurwitsch, Arvidson discusses various types of attention, ultimately linking insightful intuition with "synthesis." He examines the intuitive moment to see which reorganization processes describe its emergent structure, and which do not, and compares his findings with those of Bastick, Treisman, Posner, and other psychologists working on attention or intuition.

Joe Sheridan and Anne Pineault's "Sacred Land—Sacred Stories: The Territorial Dimensions of Intuition" draws a powerful set of connections between "the wild" of the external landscape and intuition, which is sourced from "the wild" we each carry inside. Locating humans *in* the land, they suggest that intuition is a type of intelligence whose origin and engagement happen best in the natural world. The intriguing and important implication is that there is a high positive correlation between the shrinking of the wilderness and the devaluing and disuse of wild ways of knowing. Pointing to the disappearance of the legitimacy of intuition as concurrent with the loss of our experience with biodiversity, the authors stress that "monocultures of mind or land are never justifiable if our goal is sustainable health in each."

Guy Burneko's "Wheels Within Wheels, Building the Earth: Intuition, Integral Consciousness, and the Pattern That Connects," takes a thoroughly interdisciplinary and postmodern approach to the phenomenon of intuition. Essentially, Burneko argues that consciousness has been trained to be less than it can be, and intuition as integral consciousness can give epistemological, ontological, and ethical life to "the pattern that connects." The implication is that in intuiting and integrating this "pattern that connects," one is not aware of some ultimate foundation, but rather existentially returns to the beginning: in Jean Gebser's words, to an "ever-present origin."

The five chapters in Part II explore the complex relationships between intuition, science, and the hands-on praxis of physics, medicine, and midwifery. Evelyn H. Monsay's "Intuition in the Development of Scientific Theory and Practice" examines what it takes to be an intuitive scientist or engineer, identifying prerequisites and techniques for the development of "physical" intuition. Physics and engineering are usually seen as epitomes of reason and analysis; in fact, much of the everyday work in these fields does depend on rational, formulaic thought and processes. However, it is most often true that real advancement in these disciplines requires the holistic, imaginative, and creative aspects of intuition. Whether major changes of paradigm, or solutions to more limited problems, sudden insights—received as ineffable images or as "deep knowing"—are frequently *experienced* first and then backfitted with a logical and mathematical basis. Monsay discusses the roles of both formulas and intuition in physical science and engineering, and examines the particular forms that intuition can take and has taken in the development of theory and of invention.

Building on Monsay's arguments, Brenda Dunne's "Subjectivity and Intuition in the Scientific Method" explores the historical dissonance between intuition and the doing of science and argues that explicitly incorporating both into scientific discipline is a necessity. Dunne considers scientific objectivity a myth and calls for a more productive approach to truth in science, one that recognizes that scientific investigation is at the same time an investigation of human consciousness. This shift in perspective will better accommodate the intuitive and creative aspects of scientific investigation that are now denied their proper status.

Bob Harbort's "Thought, Action, and Intuition in Practice-Oriented Disciplines" presents a way of differentiating between naturally developed modes of thought and intentionally learned ones. This distinction has important implications for the relationship of thought and action in practice-oriented disciplines such as medicine. He discusses intuition in light of theory, practice, intentionality, and human culture.

Robbie Davis-Floyd's "Intuition as Authoritative Knowledge in Midwifery and Homebirth" calls attention to midwives' utilization of and reliance on intuition as a guide to action and decision-making during homebirths. Davis-Floyd discusses the nature of intuition and the reasons for and consequences of the general devaluation of intuitive thinking by the wider society. She describes the separation-based technocratic approach to birth in the hospital, in which only externally obtained information is considered to be authoritative, and contrasts it with the connection-based holistic approach of midwives who attend birth at home. Skilled in the use of diagnostic technologies, these midwives nevertheless exhibit a remarkable willingness to rely on inner knowing even when it conflicts with technologically obtained information. Through the stories midwives tell about their experiences with intuition

Robbie Davis-Floyd and P. Sven Arvidson

during birth, Davis-Floyd searches for the roots of their respect for inner knowing; she finds those roots in women and their bodies and in the strong connections they form during labor and birth.

These connections are further explored by midwife Lucia Roncalli in "Standing by Process: A Midwife's Notes on Story-telling, Passage, and Intuition." Synthesizing analysis and experience, Roncalli tells the story of her passages through death and birth. Her years of experience attending people as they die counterpoint years of assisting women to give birth; in both arenas, intuition often played a powerful role in Roncalli's ability to truly serve those she attended. With fearlessness and honesty, the author narrates the many times she listened to her inner voice and the positive outcomes that resulted, as well as the one time she failed to listen. Although all external indicators were normal at that birth, the overwhelming "feelings of dread" that Roncalli kept experiencing did in fact presage obstetrical catastrophe. This correspondence taught her hard lessons about the essentiality of trusting herself and of developing a wider understanding of what constitutes authoritative "knowledge." Roncalli also uses her narrations to identify and distinguish between various types of intuitive experience.

By presenting both the breadth and depth of diverse perspectives on intuition, this volume hopes to convey more than just information. If the careful reader rediscovers or confirms that human consciousness is a delicious mystery, an intimate dance with one's self in which the partner's eyes are deep pools of unpredictable resourcefulness, then this book is well on its way to succeeding in its aims.

ACKNOWLEDGMENTS

We wish to acknowledge, with gratitude, the intellectual excitement generated by the initial 1994 meeting of the Academy of Consciousness Studies, which sparked the idea for this volume and continues to inspire our collaborative efforts. In this light, we wish particularly to acknowledge Robert G. Jahn and Brenda Dunne—to whom this book is dedicated—for organizing the Academy, for keeping it alive through their networking efforts, and for their ongoing research at the PEAR Lab. This research has established a powerful conceptual space in which anomalies, too often given short scientific shrift as unruly disturbances in the well-ordered scheme of creation, become essential tools for uncovering the fundamentals and interrelationships of the material and nonmaterial worlds.

We also wish to acknowledge the Fetzer Institute for providing the funds that made possible the initial meeting of the Academy of Consciousness Studies, and all of the members of the Academy for their enthusiasm, commitment, and ongoing contributions to the development of this exciting field.

We express our appreciation to the Department of Anthropology, University of Texas at Austin, for providing Robbie Davis-Floyd with a Research Fellowship in

Anthropology, and to the College of Mount St. Joseph for research grants supporting Sven Arvidson's work on this project. In particular, Sven Arvidson thanks the Humanities Department for providing technical support, and most especially his bride, Julie Arvidson, for being lovingly present during his work on this book, from inception to completion. Robbie Davis-Floyd is deeply grateful to her husband, Robert N. Floyd, and her children, Peyton and Jason, for their presence, their support, and their patience with her long and erratic working hours.

Robbie Davis-Floyd and P. Sven Arvidson

PART I

THE NATURE OF INTUITION

I

INTUITION

The Concept and the Experience

Marcie Boucouvalas

Some years ago when my daughter was four years old, she lay on the couch late one Saturday afternoon hot with a moderate fever and the beginning of a sore throat. I tended to her, thinking, "Well, another ear infection. We've been through this saga before. I must bring her in to see the pediatrician early Monday morning." Suddenly and unexpectedly an image invaded my mind's eye. Flashing red with warning, the words "scarlet fever" appeared. Quick as a gazelle I hopped to the *Medical Encyclopedia* and read voraciously on the symptoms of scarlet fever. With book in hand, examining my daughter, the "goodness of fit" between her presenting symptoms and the literature was alarming enough. I immediately called the pediatrician's office. It was late; they were leaving for the day. Upon describing in detail my daughter's signs they implored me to bring her in immediately as the very last appointment of a busy day. They waited. We arrived. The diagnosis? You probably guessed it: scarlet fever—perfectly treatable on Saturday—but by Monday would have entered a more advanced stage where some of the observable symptoms may have even disappeared!

Over the years I have gradually come to trust these experiences as valid sources of knowledge, although many are not nearly as dramatic as the one above. By now I have become somewhat accustomed to these kinds of messages, having learned much from those that I did not heed. (This topic is discussed in more detail with vivid illustration by Lucia Roncalli in this volume.) Still, the questions linger and the mystery of this kind of "knowing" and "knowledge" has sustained my motivation in pursuing the study of this territory over the years, while tending and attending to the discernment of valid intuitive information from impulses, projections of personality, and the like. I, like the other authors in this book, would like to invite you, the reader, to share this venture into the intuitive arena.

I am a student of life and have been a professor of adult learning/development and education since 1980. Prior to that I spent twelve years as a practitioner, working with adults as learners ranging from my involvement with the continuing education of physicians to human resource development efforts in a state department of corrections in our criminal justice system. Whether teaching about research "method" and working with student dissertations as in my present position, or working as previously with the learning enterprises in medical and legal/justice systems, I have continually been confronted with this prime epistemological question: What are valid sources of knowledge and how does one know what one knows? My background preparation is in the social sciences (psychology and sociology). My undergraduate professor of experimental psychology continually admonished me that the types of questions I raised were best left to the poets while I tended to developing and refining my scientific acumen.

So, academically and professionally I became a good experimental psychologist (and later a sociological field worker), but in my private life I continued to be informed and likewise guided by "knowledge" that did not always come to me through the culturally acknowledged rational process or through analytic thinking. About midway through my doctoral program, academic exploration of this territory became possible as I pursued my dissertation on "An Analysis of Lifelong Learning and Transpersonal Psychology as Two Complementary Movements Reflecting and Contributing to Social Transformation." The rational/analytic and what we are calling the intuitive began to integrate for me. This process continues to unfold as I further pursue my understanding of transpersonal psychology, which by now has become the transpersonal orientation permeating many disciplines (see, for example, Boucouvalas 1980, 1981, 1983, 1984, 1995). Essentially, the transpersonal orientation recognizes various levels, states, and structures to human consciousness and multi-modal epistemologies. I am writing here both from a conceptual/theoretical basis and from experience in embracing and investigating intuition as a well-documented way of knowing that warrants further exploration, especially during these transformational times.

During the technological explosion that defines the recent history of our species, increasingly sophisticated tools and instruments are proliferating to help us more deeply probe the mysteries of our internal and external worlds. Whether in an applied or basic sense, however, in our fields of practice or study, our "self" becomes one of the most important "instruments" of attunement and, when finely tuned, can provide data and information that technology may not be able to supply. The intuitive realm is an integral part of this "tuning in."

Marcie Boucouvalas

Accordingly, this chapter will illuminate and explore intuition as a current concept with a long history. Emergent areas of controversy, such as the sources of intuitive knowing and matters of gender, provide rich sources of questions, challenges, and issues for further pursuit, while a more practical discussion focuses on the experience of intuition and the way it is being addressed by individuals, groups, professions, and society-at-large.

Intuition: The Concept

A Long History

"There is constant reference in the present day to intuition," announced James McCosh in his treatise on intuition—a statement that could have been made by any of the authors in this book, or by you, the reader, or by a whole host of other contemporaries as we approach life in the twenty-first century. Indeed, interest is burgeoning both in scholarly as well as in applied/practical literature. McCosh's book, however, was published in 1882! One cannot help but wonder how our readers one hundred years hence will respond to our present literature. What would we want them to know about our times and our interest in intuition? Moreover, if intuition was "in vogue" during the nineteenth century, what has been its trajectory since then? What similarities and differences exist in the then and now of the concept?

McCosh drew upon both ancient and then modern philosophers to inductively investigate intuition and to assert that "there is an eye of wider sweep than the telescope and more searching than the microscope" (1882: 3). This claim resonates with Ovid's exhortation in *Metamorphosis*: "What nature denies to human sight she gives to the eyes of the soul." McCosh clearly established what he referred to as two schools of mind from his investigations: (1) knowledge from observation and experiences; and (2) ideas, principles, truths originating in native power or as seen in the inward light of the mind. But he was concerned that it was "an unfortunate time for giving forth such a work to the world" because "the two manner of principles . . . [were] struggling for mastery" (1882: 4). Today, these two schools of mind still define opposing positions as to what constitutes valid knowledge and, accordingly, what one is willing to accept as data. Nevertheless, there are some equally compelling differences between then and now. Some signposts are in evidence that modern society is moving beyond a purely either/or perspective on the issue of valid knowledge. The relativism of both ways of knowing is evident, for example, in the plethora of cross-cultural training programs that prepare executives and others to work abroad in different cultures, often in countries with languages, values, political systems, and so on, *vastly* dissimilar from their own. Additionally, evidence is just beginning to emanate from various sectors of the scholarly community of an emergent dialectical perspective on sources of knowledge and research paradigms. In other words, both sources of knowledge set forth by McCosh are beginning to be perceived as valid in their own realm and as complementary parts of a greater whole.

Our concern in this book is with his second "school of mind," specifically intuition. Nevertheless, we need to establish a perspective on the importance of balance between the modes that one might term outer and inner knowing. Balance is a point stressed in general by Lerner-Robbins (1993) and others, and more specifically by authors such as Dreyfus and Dreyfus (1984, 1986) with regard to our technological age and ways of knowing.

Phenomena such as intuition, which ebb and flow throughout history, whose spark may dim but not extinguish, speak to some aspect of humanity that can come to full fruition only in a time-appropriate, context-appropriate manner. When McCosh wrote in the 1880s, science (and along with it technological advances of an industrial era) were taking center stage. Auguste Comte had earlier developed his philosophy of positivism, which was taking root. In his "stages of knowledge," scientific knowledge (in the analytic sense) topped the hierarchy while theological knowledge was relegated to a lower realm. At the same time, Mendeleyev was developing the groundbreaking *Periodic Table of Elements*, and Wundt was establishing the arena of experimental psychology. These important events necessitated a societal spotlight on what McCosh dubs "outer knowing."

Perhaps now, with the validity and contribution of this "knowing" in place and the concomitant technological revolution well established, "outer knowing" can step back from the spotlight and take its place on stage with other ways of knowing while the spotlight now shines on the spectrum of epistemologies. "Outer knowing," with no need to further prove itself, perhaps can take its rightful place as a partner alongside "inner knowing." Now, we need to intensively probe and develop this arena, but with different lenses. Society, we trust, is readier now than in 1882 to take this leap.

Even earlier philosophers such as Plato, and later Russell, Bergson, Spinoza, and Eastern philosophical perspectives such as Zen (see Yamaguchi 1969), while sustaining different positions regarding the nature of intuition, all heralded its potential for the individual, for the benefit of the community, and for the further evolution of the species. Many volumes have been written on their works. The interested reader is referred to modern-day reviews such as those provided by Wescott (1968) and Bastick (1982), both of whom illuminate the movement of discussion on intuitive knowing from the philosophical to the psychological literature. Another equally applicable cache of literature is the phenomenological. Levinas (1973), for example, examines Husserl's theory of intuition, while authors such as Hanna (1993), employing a psychological framework, illuminate how the phenomenological method of both Husserl and Heidegger involve direct intuitive seeing. The phenomenological approach is telescoped by Arvidson's chapter in this volume.

Modern-Day Conceptualizations

Those searching for conceptual precision may become frustrated with this quest in the contemporary literature. A variety of terms are used interchangeably with intuition, such as "right brain thinking," "gut feeling," "hunch," and so forth. While informal dialogue might accommodate the interchangeability, intuition is a broader concept. Some terms represent process, others experience. Advancing our understanding of intuition necessitates recognition that it may manifest as a mental thought, an emotional feeling, a spiritual experience, or even in a visceral sense. (This conceptual conundrum is examined more fully in the chapter by Laughlin.)

In exploring the "mystery of intuition," Inglis (1987) keys on the concept of *dae-mon* referred to as early as Socrates as a force or a presence, a voice, a passion, an urge of certitude that impels one to action. This daemon, according to Inglis, takes the form of the Muses, who inspire the poet, artist, writer, and composer, and of the "Eureka effect" that serves mathematicians and scientists. Inglis reminds us that the very notion of *daemon*, chronicled throughout history by both modern civilizations and indigenous cultures, fell out of favor in the West around the nineteenth century as educated people began to embrace the advent of scientific "knowing." Concomitantly, the concept of *daemon* (Latin) and *daimon* (Greek) gave way to the English demon, interpreted as evil influences. In order for the evolution of the human species to progress, this schism is in timely receptivity for repair, as argued by Dunne in this volume.

Fundamentally, the different caches of literature tend to converge around the theme that intuition represents a way of direct knowing that seeps into conscious awareness without the conscious mediation of logic and the rational process. What is claimed here is a way of knowing outside the conscious rational/logical/analytic process. This is a thorny issue, though, because different positions exist on the source of the information/knowledge. While many hold the position that the source is a direct apprehension that lies outside sensory channels and analytic thought, others claim that such knowledge may indeed come through the senses first, but through subliminal or nonconscious awareness that is stored in the unconscious before coming into consciousness.

Some conceptualize intuition in cognitive terms (e.g., Day 1947), while others (e.g., the entire realm of transpersonal literature) focus on the contemplative and spiritual frameworks of conceptualization. Or, perhaps as the Jungian-based Briggs (1994) ponders, can flashes of intuition be accounted for by a species memory fueled by a collective unconscious?

The source of intuitive knowing may become a major issue area of concern. How will we choose to respond? Might we tend to gravitate toward and embrace one position and refute another? Or is it possible that several positions have validity—that intuitive knowing may have different origins? Some information may come to us through sensory channels at a subliminal level before manifesting in conscious awareness. Other information or knowledge might arrive through other than sensory channels or perhaps through means we may not even begin to understand at this point in the evolution of the human species. This kind of speculative inquiry as to the source of "intuitive knowing" may provide a fertile source of research activity for the emerging field of consciousness studies.

Another issue of modern-day conceptualizations focuses on whether, or in some cases how much, intuitive capacity is an element of personality as suggested by Larmiell et al. (1983) and by Jung and the popularized Myers-Briggs instrumentation based on his theories. This concept is also suggested by an ever-growing literature base (for example, Landry 1991, Murphy 1992, Nadel 1992, Rosanoff 1991, Vaughan 1979), a capacity that, with help, everyone can tap.

Other issues focus on gender and the purported "women's intuition." Research, although still embryonic, is beginning to evolve and focus on potential gender differences in brain physiology and genetics that may account for intuitive knowing. Various counter-positions abound on this heated issue (on extrapolating from pathological cases, see Collins 1993—a commentary to Murphy et al. 1993). Much of the literature focusing on the role of intuition in business and management (discussed in the next section) suggests that a semantic issue is involved: males prefer use of the terms "hunch" and "gut feeling" and often refrain quite strongly from using the term "intuition" to describe their own experiences. Frances Vaughan (1979) suggests that women evidence more valid intuitive experience than men in the emotional arena. At present, data are inconclusive as to whether a possible difference in brain physiology between the genders may account for differences in intuitive capacities.

EXPERIENTIAL DIMENSIONS

The experience of intuition varies from individual to individual. Vaughan (1979) offers a typology of ways in which intuition might manifest itself (she credits the development of this schema to a workshop on professional training in psychosynthesis that she had taken with R. Gerard). These "levels of awareness" include: (1) physical, (2) emotional, (3) mental, and (4) spiritual. "Awareness" refers to the level(s) at which the intuition is consciously perceived. "Physical" refers to bodily awareness, "emotional" to feeling, "mental" to images, ideas, and thoughts, and "spiritual" to the more mystical experiences independent of sensations, feelings, and thoughts. For example, the "lived world" of these spiritually experienced intuitions (see Battis 1981) is qualitatively different than the intuition that manifests itself at a physiological level as a migraine headache or a warm energy flow.

While most literature currently focuses on intuition as an individual experience, researchers such as Martha Crampton (1995a, 1995b) are experimenting with and exploring the phenomenon of group intuition. Concentrating on the concepts of energy and openness, Crampton convened what she terms an "evolutionary council"—a handful of selected individuals immersed in intuitive research and practice to explore the concept of group intuition on both a scholarly and experiential basis.

During August 1995, with a grant from Lifebridge Foundation, a small group gathered in Loveland, Colorado. Each participant was a seasoned professional and specialist in a particular approach or approaches to facilitating the collaborative process. Illustrative of the approaches represented were, for example: Bohm dialogue, community-building, council process, systems energetics, an art-centered approach, and intuitive art consulting. Uniting the group was a deep belief in and commitment to the importance of the emerging field of consciousness studies and the role that the consciousness factor plays in linking individuals and groups. It is difficult, of course, to capture the dynamics and "results" of this experiential activity on paper. This gathering was for Crampton (1995c) a first step in a journey to "create a model and process for use in think tanks and for groups addressing various aspects of cultural and social change." The work of each participant has become far more enriched. As a result of this pilot, the next step planned is to move forward in a research manner. The design of such a venture is currently in process.

Intuitive experiences are relevant to both the professional and personal spheres. In fact, under continued investigation is the role intuition plays in expert versus novice performance of professional responsibilities (see, for example, Dreyfus and Dreyfus 1986; Harbort, this volume). Other literature sources focus on the experience of intuition and the role it plays in relationships and communication (Johnson and Daumer 1993), organizations (Agor 1983, 1989a, 1989b, 1991), and society-at-large (Goldberg 1983 and others).

To bring many disciplines and professions together in dialogue, the Institute of Noetic Sciences (IONS) has established the Intuition Network, through which members and others can join discussions via in-person national conferences, intuition cruises (where all activities and sessions on the cruise revolve around the theme of intuition), and electronically through a well-organized computer conference system on the topic. The Network, originally a two-year project of IONS, is now incorporated as an independent (but affiliated) nonprofit venture.

To IONS, a focus on intuition represents a movement toward balance or wholeness, a theme illuminated throughout this chapter and also discussed by Burneko and Sheridan in this volume. As stressed by Winston Franklin (1996), executive director of IONS, "we all seem to know inherently that we are not complete with total reliance on the rational or logical." Intuition represents "the dimensions within each of us [that] all of us both recognize and cherish." Consequently, IONS has been proactive in serving as a vehicle through which individuals can coalesce into interactive groups. These groups hold promise for ultimately recreating the balance between the rational and the intuitive.

The intuitive influences on inventive scientists, mathematicians, and literary personages have been recognized for years as part of the creative process (for a fresh approach, see Monsay, this volume). More recent is the advent of discussions on the intuitive experience in other professions and its cultivation. From an education/learning stance, Dreyfus and Dreyfus (1984, 1986) have concerned themselves

Marcie Boucouvalas

with "knowledge engineering" whereby computers are being programmed to act and "think" like the experts in various professions whom they are attempting to mimic. These scenarios have prompted the authors to research and illuminate the unique role that human intuition plays in expert knowledge, a role they claim is difficult to replicate in the computer (see also Harbort, this volume). They would hold the position, though, that professionals can actively cultivate intuition. Baghadoost (1993) illuminates, via a literature review, how this is accomplished in the field of mathematics, and Van Dalen (1993) to a greater depth examines mathematical intuition from a phenomenological perspective. Likewise, applied articles abound on cultivating mathematical intuition (for example, Peck and Connell 1991, Garafolo and Durant 1991, and others). For use by educators and others, Rockenstein (1985) has developed a taxonomy of educational objectives for the intuitive domain to complement those already developed years ago for the cognitive, affective, and psychomotor domains of learning.

As might be expected, discussion of the experience of intuition in the therapeutic and counseling literature is growing (see, for example, Keith 1987, Little 1991, Lomas 1993) and an entire conference was recently devoted to the theme of "Empathy and Intuition" (1993); there is also increased discussion of intuition in the literature on nursing (for example, Kenny 1994–95, Leners 1990, Miller 1995, Polge 1995, Polishchuk 1993). As a physician, Miksanek (1993) unravels and examines his very own vivid experiences with intuition in his practice of medicine. The recurring theme of knowledge that would complement and supplement diagnoses sustained by rational problem-solving over the years prompted him to increasingly trust intuitive information and to include both reference and deference to it in teaching interns, residents, and other medical students. In fact, the medical profession appears to be witnessing an emerging receptivity to the role that intuition can play in providing quality medical care. Professionals such as Winter (1993, 1995) have been well received in their conduct of workshops to assist physicians in developing their intuitive faculties (see also Davis-Floyd, this volume).

It appears, however, that the largest body of literature on the experiential dimension of intuition and its cultivation is burgeoning within the arena of business administration and management. As the "new frontier" in management (Parikh 1994), this literature ranges from serious research and concomitant application items (Cappon 1994a, Lank and Lank 1995) to practically oriented guides relevant to the indispensability of intuition to productivity and good business (LeBoeuf 1995, Schultz 1994), often drawing and learning from the experiences of highly successful and unusually innovative entrepreneurs.

Exercises to develop one's intuition are even being developed and offered (Watts 1993). While the potential inherent in the training of intuitive capacities is acknowledged as amenable to teaching and learning interventions (Robinson 1985, Sherman 1994), intuitive capacities are equally sought now in the hiring process as an important management skill (Foster 1994). The Marine Corps's new "command and control vision" stresses intuition as a central key to victory (Goodman 1995). Bell Atlantic Corporation (1994) has begun to list intuition as an important quality on job descriptions, and the role of intuition in the successful research and development process (Glaser 1995) has been highlighted, replete with a measurement system developed by Agor, who likewise developed the Brain Skill Management program that helps organizations identify intuitive talent (Agor 1991). The question of measurement, in fact, is a topic that is now equally reaching the popular press through researchers such as Cappon (1994b), who spent years developing an instrument to measure one's capacity for intuition. Like McCosh (cited earlier), Cappon differentiates between two broad types of intelligence: intuitive (for inductive knowing) and analysis (for deductive knowing). Complementarity is a key. As he explains, "If logical reasoning and scientific analysis have brought knowledge to the crown of human intelligence, then intuition—and its inseparable twin, creativity—form the jewel in the crown" (1994b: 35). Cappon stands steadfast in his position that intuition can be measured, not just by conventional paper and pencil or oral methods, but also by laser disc technology, which he is completing, and by virtual technology, which remains his vision. In general, the role intuition can play in administrative acumen is being heralded, based in large part upon a recognition of the increasingly complex problems inherent in today's organizations. Its applicability even to superintendents is being explored (Brown 1990).

Breakthrough thinking, fueled by intuitive energies, often occurs when managers take that proverbial "leap of faith." Morris (1990) has rendered a penetrating analysis of how a sample of eleven human resource development managers accessed intuition at the moment of solution for an ill-structured problem. This research has illuminated the roles that interpersonal relations and listening play in intuitive knowing. Seven of the eleven managers were engaged in interpersonal dialogue when the intuitive moment of solution alighted. Also, all eleven "co-researchers" kept meticulous journals as part of the research process, thus enabling insights into the experience of intuition such as its qualities of self-evidence, internal consistency, perseverance (i.e., resistance to alternate interpretations), etc. The research provided the additional insight that intuition is employed when individuals either do not have enough data or an overload of information is at hand. What happened at an individual level has now led Morris to study learning organizations. Where living conditions are not framed entirely by rules, intuition can be cultivated (Morris 1995). As a counterbalance to these supportive streams regarding the role of intuition in business and management, an emerging voice warns of the dangers inherent in relying too heavily on intuitive leads (see, for example, Business Decisions 1995, Kihm 1993, Shoemaker and Russo 1993). At issue, it seems, is the meaning given to the term "intuition." Some rigorous attention is needed to the differentiation and discernment between valid intuitive knowledge and contenders such as impulses, projections, biased perspectives, and the like. Rosanoff (1991) has provided some guidance for popular press readers; however, this is an arena that likewise warrants the attention of researchers of consciousness studies.

Toward the Future

Intuition, as we have seen, has a long and intriguing history that resonates with modern-day conceptualizations cutting across many disciplines and fields. The term itself, while comfortable and meaningful to some, raises the suspicion of others who might prefer the terms hunch, gut feeling, and so on. "Intuition" seems to lend a bit more assuredness to the knowledge, whereas "hunch" carries with it a tenuousness. Both terms are clearly rooted in a nonrational way of knowing, but since the rational has more established stature, perhaps use of the term "hunch" may be more preferable for some in that it does not make as much of a commitment to the credibility of the knowledge. The question of how much one can rely on intuition underlies and fuels much of the concern regarding its function as a valid source of knowledge. The chapter by Davis-Floyd illuminates this issue clearly. We are invited into the "lived world" of midwives, many of whom are often informed by the intuitive mode. We witness their own wrestling with the issue as they try to figure out when the "inner voice" is intuition as differentiated from other signals, such as fear and the voice of the rational mind.

Even if one accepts the validity of intuition, questions beckon. Is the source of the knowledge outside of and beyond the senses, located in a capacity of the human species that we do not yet fully understand? Or does it originate in the senses at a less than conscious level of awareness? Another question that recurs in the literature: Can intuition be taught? Or is it an element of personality, gender, or a capacity of a particular type of intelligence? An element of discernment seems to be called for so as not to confuse valid intuition from impulses, projections, biases, and the like. Some characteristics that can serve as guideposts have been generated by authors such as Rosanoff (1991)—for example, persistence (it continues to recur over time and seems resistant to alternate reasoned interpretations) and assuredness (there exists a certainty at a very deep level of knowing beyond one's ego). Of course, this is an area that abounds with fertile research questions for further inquiry.

As researchers, however, we would want to make sure that we are embracing inquiry in its fullest sense, not just as a series of methods and techniques applied externally to one's being, but with equal attention paid to fine-tuning one's "instrument" (i.e., one's own "self"), which necessitates a deep understanding of our ways of knowing and being-in-the-world. It is worth investigating, for example, the manner in which Native American scholars include intuitive understanding as part of their research "method" (Barden and Boyer 1993). Also noteworthy in that vein is the establishment of the Worldwide Network of Indigenous Science by Pamela Colorado (1992). In addition, the chapter in this volume by Sheridan and Pineault, who are both descendants of indigenous peoples, offers keen insight into the Native American orientation to knowing in and from the land, and suggests that a taming of the wild may have paved over our capacity for intuition. How much and what kind of intuitive knowing seems involved in which kinds of research and what role does it or can it play?

I would like to suggest the meaningfulness of the work of Roberts (1989) in this regard. Writing from a transpersonal perspective that acknowledges a variety of levels, states, and structures to human consciousness, he proposes a vision of an educated person that has direct relevance to research in the intuitive realm. Given the premise that the mind and body function in a variety of states, that different capacities and incapacities exist in each state of consciousness, that there are many ways of voluntarily entering each state and maximizing what can be learned there, an educated person becomes one who can select the appropriate state, enter it, and use or develop the "resident" abilities. It is conceivable, then, that our current research designs have analogues in different states of consciousness.

Basically, we are all still pioneers and pilgrims on the pathway of better understanding human consciousness. The intuitive realm is one that has apparently been functional since the dawn of humanity and, although the topic is outside the domain of this book, perhaps intuition constitutes the purview of animals as well. Humans, however, have the reflective capacity to explore their various ways of knowing. In our age of diversity and concomitant complementarity, it seems essential to transcend the either/or way of thinking that previously juxtaposed in an antithetical manner the rational/analytic and intuitive modes of knowing, in order to embrace the notion of balance. To the degree that we can accomplish this feat we will leave a legacy for future inquirers that provides multi-modal epistemologies for research while expanding the context for our own professional and personal functioning in the world.

References Cited

Agor, Weston H.

1983 (August) "Tomorrow's Intuitive Leaders," *Futurist*, 17: 49–53.

1989a (November–December) "Intuition and Strategic Planning: How organizations can make productive decisions," *Futurist*, 23(6): 20–23.

1991 "How Intuition Can be Used to Enhance Productivity in Organizations," *Journal of Creative Behavior*, 25(1): 11–19.

Agor, Weston H. (ed.)

1989b *Intuition in Organizations: Leading and Managing Productively*. Newbury Park, CA: Sage.

Arons, Michael

1993 (Summer) "Instinct, Intuition, and Supraconscious: De-alienating reflections," *Humanistic Psychologist*, 21: 158–179.

Baghadoost, Mansureh

    1993 "The Improvement of Mathematical Intuition: Literature Review." Master's Thesis, University of Dayton.

Barden, Jack and Boyer, Paul

    1993 "Ways of Knowing: Extending the boundaries of scholarship," *Tribal College: Journal of American Higher Indian Education*, 13(3): 12–15.

Bastick, Tom

    1982 *Intuition: How We Think and Act.* New York: John Wiley & Sons.

Battis, Peter Collin

    1981 "Intuitive Experiences among Advanced Practitioners of Spiritual Disciplines: A Qualitative Study." Doctoral dissertation, Boston University.

Bell Atlantic Corporation

    1994 (April 15) "Bell Atlantic's Hunt for a CIO," *Datamation*, 40(8): 36.

Boucouvalas, Marcie

    1980 "Transpersonal Psychology: A working outline of the field," *Journal of Transpersonal Psychology*, 12(1): 37–46.

    1981 "Transpersonal Psychology: Scope and challenge," *Australian Journal of Transpersonal Psychology*, 1(2): 136–151.

    1983 (March) "Social Transformation, Lifelong Learning, and Transpersonal Psychology: The fourth force," *Lifelong Learning: The adult years*, 6(7): 6–9.

    1984 (June) "Transpersonal Psychology: Guiding image for the advancement of international adult education," *Graduate Studies Journal* (University of the District of Columbia), 2: 17–35. (Edited version appeared in G.J. Conti and R.J. Fellenz [eds.]. *Dialogue on Issues of Lifelong Learning In A Democratic Society*, 48–58. College Station, TX: Texas A & M University.)

    1995 "Transpersonal Psychology: Scope and challenges re-visited." In E.M. Neil and S. I. Shapiro (eds.). *Embracing Transcendence: Visions Of Transpersonal Psychology*, 1–25. Stafford Heights, Australia: Bolda-Lok Publishing.

Briggs, Dennis and Mosher, John

    1994 (September) "Formative Causation," *Fate*, 47(9): 46–48.

Brown, Allen Roger

    1990 "The Use of Intuition in the Decision-Making Processes of Public School Superintendents." Doctoral Dissertation, Texas A & M University.

"Business Decisions by the Numbers," *Area Development Sites and Facility Planning*, 38(1): 1995 63–66.

Cappon, Daniel

    1994a *Intuition and Management: Research and Application.* Westport, CT: Quorum Books.

    1994b (September) "A New Approach to Intuition: IQ2," *Omni*, 16(12): 34–43.

Collins, J.

    1993 (November 13) Female Intuition? (comment) *Lancet*, 342(8881): 1188–89. Comment on Murphy et al., *Lancet*, November 13, 1993, 342(8881): 1197–1200.

Colorado, Pamela

    1992 "Wayfaring and the New Sun: Indigenous Science in the Modern World," *Noetic Sciences Review*, 22: 19–23.

Crampton, Martha

    1995a (May) Personal Communication

1995b (August) Evolutionary Council Laboratory Group/Think Tank. Loveland, CO.

1995c Personal Communication (telephone dialogue, October 7, 1995). (Communications with Crampton may be addressed to: 215 West 88th Street, Apt. 6B, New York, NY 10024.)

Day, Sebastian

 1947 *Intuitive Cognition: A key to the significance of the later scholastics.* St. Bonaventure, NY: Franciscan Institute.

Dreyfus, Hubert L. and Dreyfus, Stuart E.

 1984 (Summer) "Putting Computers in their Proper Place: Analysis versus intuition in the classroom," *Teacher's College Record*, 85: 578–601.

Dreyfus, Hubert L. and Dreyfus, Stuart

 1986 *Mind Over Machine: The power of human intuition and expertise in the era of the computer.* New York: The Free Press.

Empathy and Intuition (Proceedings of the American Academy of Psychoanalysis 36th Annual Meeting, Washington, DC, May 1992) 1993 *Journal of the American Academy of Psychoanalysis*, 21(4): 477–654.

Foster, Peter

 1994 (May) "By-the-Book Brilliance," *Canadian Business*, 67(5): 78–79.

Franklin, Winston

 (Executive Vice President, Institute of Noetic Sciences) 1996 Personal Communication (February 1996)

Garafolo, Joe and Durant, Kingsley

 1991 (November) "Where Did That Come From? A frequent response to mathematics instruction," *School-Science-and-Mathematics*, 81(7): 318–21.

Glaser, Milton

 1995 (March/April) "Measuring Intuition," *Research-Technology Management*, 38(2): 43–46.

Goldberg, Philip

 1983 *The Intuitive Edge: Understanding and developing intuition.* Los Angeles: Tarcher.

Goodman, Glenn H.

 1995 (April) "The Synthesis of Uncertainty," *Sea Power*, 38(4): 75–80.

Hanna, Fred J.

 1993 "Rigorous Intuition: Consciousness, being, and the phenomenological method," *Journal of Transpersonal Psychology*, 25(2): 181–97.

Inglis, Brian

 1987 *The Unknown Guest: The mystery of intuition.* London: Chatto and Windus.

Johnson, Pamela R. and Daumer, Claudia Rawlins

 1993 (Summer) "Intuitive Development: Communication in the nineties," *Public Personnel Management*, 22(2): 257–68.

Keith, David V.

 1987 "Intuition in Family Therapy: A short manual on post-modern witchcraft," *Contemporary Family Therapy: An International Journal*, 8(1&2): 11–22.

Kenny, C.

 1994 (December)–1995 (January) "Nursing Intuition: Can it be researched?" *British Journal of Nursing*, 3(22): 1191–95.

Kihm, Steven G.

 1993 "More Harm than Good," *Public Utilities Fortnightly*, 131(11): 74–77.

Landry, Linda

1991 "A Study of the Experience, Use, and Development of Intuition." Doctoral Dissertation, University of Massachusetts. *DAI (A)*, 52(2): 476.

Lank, Alden and Lank, Elizabeth A.

1995 "Legitimizing the Gut Feeling: The role of intuition in business." *Journal of Managerial Psychology*, 10 (5): 18–23

Larmiell, James T., Foss, Michael A, Trierweiler, Steven J., and Leffel, Michael

1983 "Toward a Further Understanding of the Intuitive Personologist: Some preliminary evidence for the dialectical quality of subjective personality impressions," *Journal of Personality*, 51: 213–35.

LeBoeuf, Michael

1995 *Fast Forward: How to win a lot more business in a lot less time*. New York: Putnam.

Leners, Debra Woodward

1990 "The Deep Connection: An echo of transpersonal caring." Doctoral Dissertation, University of Colorado Health Science Center. *DAI (B)*, 51(06): 2818.

Lerner-Robbins, Helene

1993 *Trusting Intuition: Finding balance.* San Francisco: Harper-Collins.

Levinas, Emmanuel

1973 *The Theory of Intuition in Husserl's Phenomenology* (Andre Orianne, trans.). Evanston, IL: Northwestern University Press.

Little, Janet Sue

1991 "The Intuitive Counselor: A study of development and training for the use of intuition in counseling." Doctoral Dissertation, University of Massachusetts. *DAI (B)*, 52(2): 168.

Lomas, Peter

1993 *Cultivating Intuition: An introduction to psychotherapy*. Northvale, NJ: Jason Aronson.

McCosh, Rev. James

1882 *Intuitions of the Mind: Inductively investigated* (3rd ed.). London: Macmillan.

Miksanek, Tony

1993 (February) "An Independent Diagnosis," *Discover*, 14(26): 28–29.

Miller, V. G.

1995 (June) "Characteristics of Intuitive Nurses," *Western Journal of Nursing Research*, 17(3): 305–316.

Morris, Linda E.

1990 "Strategies and Tactics to Access Intuition: A look at the moment of solution." Doctoral Dissertation, Virginia Polytechnic Institute and State University.

1995 Development Strategies for the Knowledge Era. In Sarita Chawla and John Renesch (eds.). *Learning Organizations: Developing cultures for tomorrow's workplace*. Portland, OR: Productivity Press.

Mott, Vivian Wilson

1994. "A Phenomenological Inquiry into the Role of Intuition in Reflective Adult Education Practice." Doctoral Dissertation, University of Georgia.

Murphy, Decian G. M. et al.

1993 (November) "X-Chromosome effects on Female Brains: A magnetic resonance imaging study of Turner's Syndrome," *Lancet*, 342: 1197–1200.

Murphy, Michael

1992 *The Future of the Body: Explorations into the further evolution of human nature*. Los Angeles: Tarcher.

Nadel, Laurie

1992 *Sixth Sense: The whole brain book of intuition, hunches, gut feelings and their place in your everyday life.* New York: Prentice-Hall.

Parikh, Jagdish

1994 *Intuition: The new frontier of management.* Cambridge, MA: Blackwell.

Parrott, C. A. and Strongman, K. T.

1985 "Intuitive Problem Solving: Individual differences in ability and subjective experience," *Journal of Creative Behavior,* 19: 140.

Peck, Donald M. and Connell, Michael L.

1991 "Using Physical Materials to Develop Mathematical Intuition in Fraction Part-Whole Situations," *Focus on Learning Problems in Mathematics,* 13(40): 3—12.

Phillips. Alan M.

1969 "The Theory of Intuition in Plato's Republic." Doctoral Dissertation, Michigan State University.

Polge, J.

1995 "Thinking: The use of intuition in making clinical nursing judgments," *Journal of the New York State Nurses' Association,* 26(2): 4—8.

Polishchuk, Lul.

1993 Znachenie Instuitsil u Psikhiatril [The Importance of Intuition in Psychiatry]. *Zh Neuropatol Psikhiatr Im S S Korsakova,* 93(3): 99—101.

Roberts, Tom

1989 "Multistate Education: Metacognitive implications of the mind-body psychotechnologies," *Journal of Transpersonal Psychology,* 21(1): 83—102.

Robinson, Anne D.

1985 (May) "How to Have a Safe Trip to the Cutting Edge," *Training and Development Journal,* 39(5): 45—48.

Rockenstein, Zoa Louise

1985 "A Taxonomy of Educational Objectives for the Intuitive Domain." Doctoral Dissertation, University of Georgia.

Rosanoff, Nancy

1991 *Intuition Workout: A practical guide to discovering and developing your inner knowing* (2nd ed.). Lower Lake, CA: Asian.

Schultz, Ron

1994 *Unconventional Wisdom: Twelve Remarkable Innovators Tell How Intuition Can Revolutionize Decision-Making.* San Francisco, CA: Harper-Collins.

Sherman, Stratford

1994 (August 22) "Leaders Learn to Heed the Voice Within," *Fortune,* 130: 92—100.

Shoemaker, Paul J. H. and Russo, J. Edward

1993 (Fall) "A Pyramid of Decision Approaches," *California Management Review,* 36(1): 9—31.

Van Dalen, D.

1993 R.L. Tieszen, "Mathematical Intuition: Phenomenology and mathematical knowledge," *Husserl Studies,* 18(3): 249—260.

Vaughan, Frances E.

1979 *Awakening Intuition.* New York: Doubleday.

Watts, George

1993 "Exercise for Bringing Head and Heart Together," *Training and Development Journal* 47 (11): 17–19.

Wescott, Malcolm R.

1968 *Toward a Contemporary Psychology of Intuition: A historical, theoretical, and empirical inquiry.* New York: Holt, Rinehart and Winston.

Winter, Teresa

1993 *Intuitions: Seeing with the heart.* Saco, ME: Tor-Down Publishing.

1995 (August) Personal Communication, Saco, Maine.

Yamaguchi, Minoru

1969 *The Intuition of Zen and Bergson* (Comparative intellectual approaches to Zen: Reasons of divergence between East and West). Tokyo: Enderle.

Marcie Boucouvalas

2

THE NATURE OF INTUITION

A Neuropsychological Approach

Charles Laughlin

> The mystery of the universe is its comprehensibility.
> —*Albert Einstein*

Anthropologists are always running into intuition and its products during their fieldwork experiences among the peoples they study. I am an ethnographer and in my various fieldwork situations I have been forced by the data I have collected to reflect upon the nature of intuition. During the time I spent with the So of Northeastern Uganda, I was introduced to "dreamers" who routinely reported divinatory material to the elders who in turn took the reports seriously and acted upon the portends expressed in the dreams. Among the Tibetan lamas I worked with, I found that many of the meditative techniques they use are intended to evoke and mature intuitive realizations about the properties of consciousness. And among Navajo healers, diagnoses of disease are often derived by way of a judicious merger of empirical observation and intuitive insight. So diverse are the situations we run into as anthropologists that our discipline is forced to borrow freely sometimes from our sister disciplines in order to better explicate our subject matter—in my case borrowing freely from phenomenology and the neurosciences.

The need for an interdisciplinary perspective is nowhere clearer than in the case of intuition. The word "intuition" is a fairly fuzzy term that refers to a range of types of knowing. The root of the English word derives from the Latin *intuitus* meaning roughly "the act of achieving knowledge from direct perception or contemplation." In the field of cognitive psychology, Daniel Kahneman and Amos

Charles Laughlin

Tversky (1982) suggest that intuition refers to at least three types of phenomena: (1) judgments made about things that are consonant with a person's worldview, (2) a person is unaware of the rules and procedures used to reach judgments about things, and (3) there is a lack of analytical and computational methods used to reach judgments about things.

The Experience of Intuition

Intuition typically labels a type of experience in which the answer to a question, the solution to a problem, guidance in following some goal, a creative impulse resulting in the emergence of some image, idea, or pattern, springs into consciousness whole-cloth, as it were—seemingly out of nowhere. William James (1890: 45), considered by many to be the father of psychology, left us an interesting description of the achievement of intuition in his *Principles of Psychology*:

> If pure thought runs all our trains, why should she run some so fast and some so slow, some through dull flats and some through gorgeous scenery, some to mountain-heights and jewelled mines, others through dismal swamps and darkness?—and run some off the track altogether, and into the wilderness of lunacy? Why do we spend years straining after a certain scientific or practical problem, but all in vain—thought refusing to evolve the solution we desire? And why, some day, walking in the street with our attention miles away from the quest, does the answer saunter into our minds as carelessly as if it had never been called for—suggested, possibly, by the flowers on the bonnet of the lady in front of us, or possibly by nothing that we can discover? If reason can give us relief then, why did she not do so earlier?

Perhaps by way of illustration I might share a personal experience of intuitive insight, one of many that have occurred in my life. I was once driving along a highway and chatting with a companion. As I glanced at the side of the road I chanced to notice a strange object. It was a tapestry about ten by fifteen feet in dimension apparently made out of old tires. It was an object so novel to me I was momentarily curious about what it was and what it was used for. The curiosity passed and I went back to the discussion with my companion and thought nothing more about it. A bit further on we entered a construction zone and there was a sign on the side of the road warning us that explosives were being used and that we should not broadcast with radios. I continued the conversation with my friend as we drove past the construction zone, and then suddenly, seemingly out of nowhere, I knew what the tapestry of old tires was used for—to cushion the force of dynamite blasts on the construction site. One moment I was talking with my friend about something totally unrelated, the next I knew the function of that object that, for me, was completely novel, about which I had been briefly curious, but that I had given no conscious thought to since that brief moment of curiosity. And I knew its function with absolute certainty, yet a certainty ungrounded in any observations of the use of the tapestry. I subsequently discovered that this is indeed the function of such tapestries and have seen them in use many times since then. But what I realized at the time was that here was an intuitive insight, the product of unconscious cognitive processes that had been working on the problem while "I" had been chatting gaily away about unrelated things, that was experienced as absolutely certain, but that despite the sense of certainty might well have proved to be wrong.

I offer this perhaps trivial example to illustrate how common and everyday the experience of intuition can be, at least for many people. I offer it also to exemplify many of the features of the experience of intuitive "leaps" or "aha's" reported in the literature on the topic. For instance, Adelbert Ames, the remarkable perceptual physiologist and philosopher, is said to have

> had the habit of putting a problem to himself in the evening just before he went to bed. Then he "forgot" it. The problem never seemed to disturb his sleep. But he often "found" the next morning on awakening that he had made progress on the problem. And as soon as he got to his office he would pick up his pencil and pad of paper and begin to write. He always said he didn't know just "what would come out." (Cantril 1960: viii)

We have all had some experience of "seeing" through to the solution to some problem. The "seeing" is an apprehension through sudden awareness of an activity that has always been operating and there to "see." This sort of knowing is fundamental to the functioning of awareness and occurs in all of us all the time.

Despite its common occurrence, intuition is poorly understood and poorly studied by psychology. One of the best current studies of the topic is that by Tony Bastick (1982) in which he isolates a number of the characteristics of the experience. These include confidence in the process of intuition, the sense of certainty of the truth of insights (Husserl calls this the "apodicticity" of insight; see Laughlin 1994), the suddenness and immediacy of the awareness of knowing, the association of affect and numinosity with insight, the nonanalytic (nonrational, nonlogical) and gestalt nature of the experience, the empathic aspect of intuition, the "preverbal" and frequently ineffable nature of the knowledge, the ineluctable relationship between intuition and creativity, and the fact that an intuitive insight may prove to be factually incorrect. The insight about the function of the blasting tapestry was characterized by most of these features with the exception of empathy and ineffability, and this was due to its trivial nature.

Intellect versus Intuition: A False Dichotomy

It is apparent to anyone who is in touch with one's own source of creativity and discovery that there is no creativity in science—indeed, in any domain of creative activity—that does not entail intuition (See Monsay in this volume; see also Koestler 1959, Hayward 1984: 29–33, Weil 1972, Vaughan 1979, Westcott 1968, Bastick 1982,

Poincare 1913, Jung 1971, Slaatte 1983). In light of that fact, why is it that some critics of intuition insist upon an absolute dichotomy between reason and intuition, and claim that intuition has little or no place in science (see, e.g., Bunge 1962, Lyons 1986, Weissman 1987, Piaget 1975)?

The answer to this question lies in the historical association of intuition with metaphysics and religious knowledge (see Morris and Hampson 1983: 25–40). Religion and metaphysics together became the nemesis of science. They appeared to stand as a hindrance to the free exploration of reality and as a source of notions about the world unavailable to empirical verification. They both appealed (it was argued) to private, esoteric, and ineffable knowledge that, however productive of personal wisdom, was seen by scientists to be inaccessible to public scrutiny (see Laughlin, McManus, and d'Aquili 1990: chap. 12 for a critique of this belief). In reaction to the presumed metaphysical and theological claim of ineffability, positivist science demanded that in order to be taken seriously, explanations of the world had to be couched in publicly shared natural language and be tied to observational procedures guaranteeing verifiability.

Somewhere in the process of formulating the positivist project, the intuitional baby was thrown out with the metaphysical bath water. Science continued to depend upon the intuitive processes of mind for its creative impulse, but simply ignored or denied the role of insight in a welter of rational justification (see Hanson 1958). Scientific discovery became interpreted in the culture of science as due solely to rigid compliance with a thoroughly nonproblematic, unmysterious, rational scientism. Theories, considered to be the product of a conscious, rational, and linguistically expressible activity, came to be considered as logically tied to acts of objective observation by sets of rationally determined "correspondence rules."

There was no room left in this version of the process of scientific discovery for intuitive insight. It did not seem to bother most positivists that virtually no creative scientific discoveries are actually carried out in accord with the positivist protocol, least of all in the social sciences, which nonetheless struggled valiantly to legitimize their activities in positivist terms.

The Key Problem: Verifiability

We must not lose sight of the original problem the positivists wished to solve: the cleaning up of a science littered with unverified and unverifiable notions about the world. This concern is valid. However, no philosopher of science of whom I am aware and who is critical of the positivist account would advocate a wholesale return to metaphysics or a theology of priestly received wisdom. The problem is not solved by rationalizing the essential intuitive source of creative knowledge, but rather by studying the way science proceeds when it is successful at being creative.

My colleagues and I have argued elsewhere (Laughlin, McManus, and d'Aquili 1990: chap. 12) that science and mature contemplation have many points in common—the latter being the practice of mind-states most conducive to the acquisition of intuitive insights about the self and the world.[1] When we actually examine how science and contemplation are carried out, as well as how each community views the other, it is clear that both perspectives are to some extent esoteric and depend upon intuitive insight for their creativity. Moreover, both in fact produce theories tied to observations, and both find it necessary to train practitioners in the requisite ways of thinking and observing before they are able to fully participate in their respective disciplines.

In the case of both science and contemplation the issue of verifiability of intuitively derived insights is a valid concern, and is not easily solved. How one verifies notions like "black holes" (a scientific concept) and "emptiness" (a concept in Buddhist phenomenology) is not a straightforward matter, but requires training and skill at relating ideas and observations in a manner that allows the one to cross-check the other.

It seems to me that an empirical aspect always accompanies even everyday experiences of intuitive insight. In the trivial example of the blasting tapestry given above, the insight was accompanied by a sense of certainty, and yet there was the awareness that the insight might prove wrong. "Prove" in what sense? Prove by reference to another domain of experience, namely asking someone in the know or hanging around construction sites until one sees the tapestry in use. In fact I later did confirm the use of the tapestry with someone who had direct knowledge of blasting techniques.

Intuition, Unconscious Cognition, and the Brain

In more recent years, attempts have been made to explain the process of intuition by reference to neurophysiological research (e.g., Bogen 1969). It is known, for example, that the two hemispheres of the human brain carry out complementary functions: the left lobe primarily mediates language production, analytic thought, lineal and causal sequencing of events, while the right lobe primarily mediates the production of images, gestalt or "holistic" thought, and spatiotemporal patterning (Bogen 1969, Bogen et al. 1972, Sperry 1974, 1982, Levy 1972, Levy-Agresti and Sperry 1968, Gazzaniga 1970, Bryden 1982, Milner 1980, Ley 1983). Simplifying somewhat, one could say that the left lobe distinguishes parts of wholes—sees trees, so to speak—and the right lobe integrates parts into wholes—sees the forest. This analytical and integrative processing is occurring prior to and, as it were, "behind" the actual experience that is registered in consciousness. Although the experience may be of a perceptual gestalt, both processes will be involved in producing the experience, although the intentionality of an experience may emphasize one function over the other.

Some researchers have used these findings to suggest that we humans have two modes of consciousness, one corresponding to what we call "reason," associated with left lobe functioning, and another called "intuition," associated with right lobe functioning (see e.g., articles by Ornstein and Galin in Lee 1976). Some theorists in anthropology have gone so far as to suggest two different types of culture defined upon these dual modes of knowing. Warren TenHouten (1978–79) has called these two modes of thought "propositional" and "compositional" and has argued that they lie on a continuum with a third mode of knowing, the "dialectical," lying in the middle as an integration of the left and right lobe cognitive functions. Years ago, P. A. Sorokin (1941) suggested that all societies oscillate over time like a pendulum between two extreme poles, one having cultures characterized by rational knowledge and materialistic values, and the other by intuitive knowledge and spiritual values. He said that the most enlightened societies are those at the "golden mean" between the two extreme poles. But, as this oscillation is unconscious to people in the society, no society is able to hang onto the midpoint for long.

Whereas there is no doubt some use to be made by distinguishing the experience of intuition from the experience of ratiocination—for example, in distinguishing the kind of insight one attains in meditation as opposed to solving a set of differential equations—I believe it is a fundamental error to consider them either as oppositional modes or as due simply to left and right lobe functioning. It is certainly erroneous to characterize Western science as associated solely with ratiocination and Eastern mysticism solely with intuition—a tendency all too evident in the current New Age literature, where intellect frequently becomes the "bad guy" foil to intuition's "good guy." Culturally speaking, this polarity is merely the opposite bias to that of positivist science, where, as we have seen, intellect wears the white hat and intuition the black hat, or no hat at all. This dualism leads to a distorted understanding of the acquisition of knowledge, as well as both science and mysticism. For example, Buddhist psychology becomes frequently associated with holistic teachings about "totality" while, say, Buddhism's more analytic teachings such as the *patthana* section of the *Abhidharma*, or the *Great Discourse on Causality* (*Maha-Midana-Suttanta*) are ignored.

My view is that ratiocination (including intellect, reason, logic) refers to cognized models of cognitive processes that are culturally reified and couched in terms of normative rules (see Rubinstein, Laughlin and McManus 1984: 34, Beth and Piaget 1966, Tiles 1991). Intuition, however, refers to our experience of the products of transcendental, operational cognitive processes that occur while usually disentrained to the neural network producing consciousness (Kissin 1986). And these unconscious, operational processes are mediated by neural networks in both lobes, not merely in the right lobe. Moreover, I suspect that these unconscious cognitive processes are thoroughly *neurognostic* (i.e., they are genetically determined in their initial structure and function; see also Changeux and Dehaene 1989); this would account for the universal, pan-human attributes frequently evident in the experience of intuitive insight. Practitioners of *zazen* are encouraged by various techniques (e.g., the *koan*[2]) to suspend the rational faculty and directly access intuitive sources of knowledge (Chang 1959). It seems likely that they manifest the more balanced hemispheric functioning characteristic of intuitive processing when they enter the *samadhi* states.

A source of confusion relative to the synthetic or analytic quality of intuitive operations is the suddenness and completeness of the products of intuitive operations when they first enter consciousness. As previously noted, intuitions commonly appear as a whole, whether or not the processes that produced the results involve synthesis or analysis, or whether they have occurred serially or as parallel processes.

Speaking metaphorically, it is as though the solution to a problem were being processed at the bottom of a murky river, and the results written out on a blackboard that is then released to float upward to the surface. "I" (the empirical ego) become aware of the solution in a sudden flash of insight as the blackboard breaks the surface. "I" experience the realization of the solution reached in this manner differently than I do when "I" have worked out the solution using formal rational processes. I can perceive the analytical faculties operating in the latter, but not in the former. "I" naively appear to have control over the latter, but not the former (actually mature contemplatives come to have some measure of control over access to intuitive processes as well; see Laughlin, McManus, and d'Aquili 1993).

LANGUAGE, EVOLUTION, AND INTUITION

The association of natural language with scientific knowledge and theory in the positivist account is a clear tip-off to the etiology of the isolation of intellect from its intuitive foundations, and the closure of positivistic, formalized procedures. Biogenetic structuralism, our own school of anthropology, has argued that language evolved as a sign system for the transmission of vicarious experience and the control of individual cognized environments in their service of adaptive sociality and action (Laughlin and d'Aquili 1974: 95–96, Rubinstein, Laughlin, and McManus 1984: 26). These relations are crucial to understanding the nature, evolution, and development of the intuitive processes.

The Cognitive Extension of Prehension

An evolutionary advance in cognitive complexity and social cooperation is clearly evident in the hominid line—at least by the stage of *Homo erectus* (roughly a million years ago). This advance was due not to increased reliance upon tool-use, but upon developments in the capacity of the hominid brain to mediate cognized relations in both space and time that were progressively less stimulus-bound (we called this development the "cognitive extension of prehension"; see Laughlin and d'Aquili 1974: chap. 4). That is, the brain could now cognize a world significantly more extensive than the perceptual field, and causally more complex than temporal immediacy. This extended spatiotemporal "chunking" of associations allowed the production of a society comprised of categorical relationships no longer dependent upon direct, face-to-face social encounters.

Images and behaviors became embedded in spatially more extensive maps and bound into temporally more complex "plans" (Miller, Galanter, and Pribram 1960, Pribram 1971). Despite the temptation to place technology and economic strategies at center stage in explaining the evolution of the brain (e.g., Passingham 1982: 166ff), neural evolution was minimally linked to technology, the latter being more an artifactual expression of advances in cognitive competence caused by other, non-technological factors (Laughlin and d'Aquili 1974). The factor being addressed here is the emergence of neurobiological structures capable of associating events distant in space and duration.

This evolutionary advance in cognitive capacity, if it had occurred separately from those neurophysiological processes mediating interlocution, would potentially have produced the formulation of divergent individual cognized environments among group members to the detriment of sociality and cohesive group action. But, of course, the nervous system evolves all of a piece, and its symbolic processing along with it. Not only was there an advance in the neurocognitive capacity to elaborate meanings beyond immediate perceptual space-time, there was also an advance in the capacity to express (describe, instruct about, augment, remark upon, etc.) the cognized environment. In other words, not only did evocative symbolism evolve, but also the cognitive capacity evolved to fulfill meaning in action, and express meaning in communication.

To fully appreciate the argument here it is crucial to keep in mind that *the expressive mode of symbolism is a behavioral elaboration of the fulfilling mode.* An organism anticipates the fulfillment of meaning; that is, the neural structures that produce the meaning of an object will cause the organism to seek that object to arise in the sensorium—the sensorium being the entire sensory system (Neisser 1976, Changeux and Dehaene 1989: 73). This desire for fulfillment will result in behavior as simple as scanning with the eyes, or as complex as a chimpanzee trudging off to find a termite hill, twig in hand. Such behavior in part functions to control perception so that the desired object or event arises in the sensorium (Powers 1973). Sometimes these behaviors will take on a signaling (expressive) function. Expressive behavior may function as well to fulfill anticipated sensorial events, as when a male bird attracts a mate or repulses a rival with his call. Fulfilling operations and behaviors manipulate the individual and its world, while expressive operations and behaviors may also manipulate the individual's conspecifics (group members).

The Evolution of Language-As-Technology

Thus, with the advent of the cognitive extension of prehension both the evocative and the fulfilling modes of symbolic operations evolved to become more elaborate, and there likely was a vigorous selection in favor of expressive faculties, especially noticeable in the archaeological record around the beginning of the Upper Paleolithic (approximately 40,000 years ago), and producing a balance between neurocognitive evolution as manifested in individual development and social cohesion.

Communication was no longer merely an augmentation of immediate experience, but became capable of transmitting vicarious experience. Communication became a medium for sharing information about resources and events encountered while separate from conspecifics, and synchronizing individual cognized environments within a total worldview that facilitated more complex collective action.

This transformation of communication and sociality among the early hominids has been admirably worked out in *optimal foraging theory* (Kurland and Beckerman 1985). Indeed, Parker and Gibson (1979, 1982, Parker 1985) have also argued persuasively that language began to develop among the early hominids in precisely this way—as an augmentation of technology for the joint exploitation of food resources by the group. Language expanded the range of subsistence strategies beyond that of individual foraging by making possible the indication of hidden foodstuffs and other resources, recruitment of cooperative ventures like game drives and the processing and transportation of materials, and so on (Parker 1985: 25).

Adaptation and Intuition

Language evolved as a neurocognitive act specialized for socially adaptive purposes. Neither language, nor its concomitant conceptual structures, evolved to understand and express the products of the entire cognitive system and its operations, but rather to make conscious and express versions of knowledge abstracted to service adaptation in a very social creature. To arbitrarily limit legitimate knowledge in science to that which the brain's linguistic/conceptual structures can express is to tacitly select for knowledge in its most superficial social and adaptive guise and to cut off the process of knowing from its much grander scope—that is, from the transcendental processes upon which knowledge in its broader creative sense depends.

On the other hand, to cleave to the ineffable and away from socially shared forms of knowledge is to select for a solipsistic stance that is understandably an anathema to science. Neither extreme is necessary, of course. Both the transcendental, operational structures of the being (including the intuitive faculties), and the linguistic-conceptual structures that model and express the operational structures have evolved as a unit and should be interpreted within a framework that accepts the functions of each (Slaatte 1983: 142, Salk 1983: 80).

Not knowing in any ultimate sense how we come to know what we know via intuitive processes, we must build in socially meaningful cross-checks to veridicality and truth. After all, I could have been wrong about the function of the blasting tapestry. It might have been used to shore up crumbling earth banks along the road. There must be ways built into the movement from knowledge to experience that allows empirical verification. However, there must be full appreciation that those social mechanisms by means of which we query the truth of intuitive knowledge must never so constrain exploration that access to the greater transcendental processes of knowing is lost.

Neither cleavage to the ineffability of truth, nor limiting knowledge to formal scientistic epistemologies will wash for any domain of empirical exploration, least of all for the exploration of consciousness. While it is quite common in science to disclaim the value of "mysticism," the fact is that the further one explores into the areas of uncertainty relative to knowledge, the more one's results seem "mystical" or "occult." The only way a scientist can avoid the "mystical" aspects of scientific discovery is to stay well away from socially recognized domains of uncertainty. But then that scientist's ideas and results will likely contain nothing new or interesting.

When we study consciousness, our brain is querying its own essential structures. The structures we wish to know about are the very structures whose organizations mediate the knowledge we seek. The act of consciously knowing about consciousness is the act of the brain mirroring its own organizations, cognizing about its own cognizing. And, the act of cognizing changes the organization of the tissues being explored. An apt Eastern metaphor is of the snake eating its own tail: in coming to know its own essential organizations, the organizations themselves develop and change.

Thus self-knowing is literally neural structures growing-into-knowledge. Being able to express that knowledge is always secondary to the intuitive processes involved, for *conceptualized and expressed knowledge is always transposed[3] knowledge*. Yet such expression is essential in order to cross-check for delusory interpretations. As Ludwig Wittgenstein put it in the *Tractatus* (1921: 1), " . . . what can be said at all can be said clearly, and what we cannot talk about we must pass over in silence." In evolution, erroneous intuitions were penalized by extinction; in science they are penalized by disconfirmation and social sanction.

Modern neurophenomenology depends upon a unified blending of the transcendental source of intuitive knowledge with the socially constrained expression and verification of that knowledge. Intuition is the transcendental source of inspiration, and socially shared individual experience is the field of verification of that inspiration—an evolutionarily ancient combination of individual and social biological processes that merely appear historically new in their roles as "neurophenomenology" and "science."

At Play in the Fields of the Lord

It is important to emphasize that extreme stress inhibits creative insight (see Daniels 1973 cited in Bastick 1982: 91, Schroder et al. 1967, Harvey et al. 1961). The relationship between perceived stress and cognition is a complex one and may be modeled using an inverted U-curve (see Rubinstein et al. 1984: 32, McManus 1979, Laughlin and Brady 1978: 43). Briefly put, the individual cognitive system operates at its best, at its most creative and its greatest complexity, under an optimal range of perceived environmental press. This is how we would define positive stress, or "eustress" in Selye's (1956, 1974) terms. Below that level of perceived stress, there is a decrement in complexity and creativity evidenced in cognitive responses, a decrement also evident when too much perceived stress (negative stress, "noxity," or "distress" in Selye's terms) impinges on the system. Eustress challenges the system to peak performance, distress tends to drive the system toward concreteness and habitual responses. Severe necessity is definitely *not* the mother of invention, to paraphrase Barnett (1953: 91).

The association of intuitive leaps in insight and play is common knowledge. And the activity of play follows the same curvilinear relationship (Laughlin 1990, Laughlin and McManus 1982). Play is also inhibited by distress, not only among humans, but also in all social mammals exhibiting play behaviors. The organism must feel secure but interested in the world in order to spontaneously play. The two phenomena, play and intuition, are thus related. The neurocognitive growth facilitated by play involves intuitive learning, and intuitive insights frequently arise as a consequence of "playing around" with a problem. Both are manifestations of the intrinsic, neurognostically structured cognitive imperative that drives the *intentional processes* (those processes that organize meaning about the object of consciousness) of the brain to construct adaptive meaning about the object of consciousness. And this growth is most optimal when the world is perceived as interesting and challenging, but not demanding abrupt responses and threatening dire consequences for failure. In other words, this growth is optimal when the system is in a "metanoic"[4] state (Laughlin 1990).

As Karl Girgensohn empirically demonstrated way back in the 1920s (see Wulff 1991: 554–59), the attainment of intuitive knowledge about the self and the world while in metanoic states provides the core of all religious systems, including their ritual practices and their institutional symbolism. It is from intuitive insight alone that the universal properties of totality, systemic interaction, and dependent existence arise. Only through intuition do we come to certainty about the essential unity of the world and all things in the world.

Ergotropic-Trophotropic Tuning and Intuitive Insight

There is a body of theory and research in the neurosciences that offers a compelling explanation for the relationship between stress and cognitive functioning. But curiously this view has had little play in the literature so far. I am referring to the work of Ernst Gellhorn and his associates (1967, Gellhorn and Loofbourrow 1963, Gellhorn and Kiely 1972) on the neurobiology of emotion and arousal. Based upon the pioneering work of W. R. Hess (1925, 1957), Gellhorn argued that the entire neuroendocrine system is polarized into two complementary systems: one, the *ergotropic* system, mediates excitational processes that facilitate adaption to the world; the other, the *trophotropic* system, mediates the relaxational, vegetative growth processes of the body. Whole ranges of states of consciousness are determined by the balance (or *tuning*) of these two systems (Gellhorn and Kiely 1972). This bicameral view of the human nervous system has been applied to an account of a variety of alternative states of consciousness, including ritual trance (Lex in d'Aquili et al. 1979) and meditation/contemplative states (Davidson 1976, Fischer 1986, Laughlin et al. 1986, Laughlin, McManus, and d'Aquili 1990: 307–23).

Roland Fischer (1971, 1986) in particular has pointed to research associating expectation-interpretive operations and behaviors with the ergotropic, or excitational system, and hypometabolic operations with the trophotropic, or relaxation system. He has related these metabolic-arousal associations to a continuum of mind-states mediated by differential ergotropic-trophotropic tuning, some of which are more open to intuitive awareness than normal waking consciousness.

Two Hypotheses

We need to go further than this. Given what I have said above about the evolution-ary-adaptive function of conceptualization and linguistic transmission of vicarious experience, it make sense to hypothesize that *the systems mediating linguistically-conceptu-ally based thought evolved as part of the ergotropic repertoire of the hominid neuroendocrine system for the purpose of consciously formulating and transmitting adaptively significant, vicarious experience among group members.* Being driven from a relatively heavy ergotropic tuning, concep-tually-linguistically based ratiocination produces a predominance of anticipatory operations over sensorial manifestations. That is, ergotropically driven thought shifts experience toward a predominance of projected meaning and symbolic fulfillment (what Jean Piaget 1971 would call "over-assimilation" of sensory input into relatively static models), and away from a predominance of sensorial novelty and symbolic evocation (Piaget's "accommodation").

These anticipatory processes include both left lobe mediation of ratiocina-tion and right lobe mediated fantasy and imagination as well. As any beginning meditator knows, it is discursive thought and fantasy that commonly distract the mind in its pursuit of centeredness and tranquillity, and as the tranquillity of the mind and body deepens, discursive thought and fantasy fall away of their own accord. Once quiet, the consciousness has much easier access to the intu-itive faculties.

On the complementary pole are those processes associated with trophotropic systems, including intuitive processing of meaning configured upon sensory objects and events. I would therefore hypothesize that *the systems mediating intuitively based knowledge or meaning evolved as part of the trophotropic repertoire of the hominid neuroendocrine sys-tem for the purpose of developmentally reorganizing the cognized environment relative to the zone of uncertainty.* Being driven from a relatively heavy trophotropic tuning, intuitive processes produce a predominant receptivity relative to sensorial manifestations. That is, trophotropically driven intuitive cognition shifts experience toward the pre-dominance of sensorial novelty and symbolic evocation (in Piaget's terms, "over-accommodation" by models to sensory input) and away from a predominance of rational projection and symbolic fulfillment ("assimilation").

It follows from everything I have said so far that there exists a range of possible strategies for coming to know the being and the world. These strategies range on a continuum from ergotropically driven adaptive knowing and the types of knowledge that may be socially transmitted, to trophotropically driven intuition and the types of knowledge appropriate to maximizing novelty in experience. If projection and anticipation are the goals of knowing in the moment, then ergotropically loaded strategies are appropriate. But if maximization of novelty and creativity are the goals, then trophotropically loaded strategies are appropriate.

Hypo- and Hyperintentionality

The ergotropic-trophotropic model of the metabolic-arousal functions of human consciousness, however ingenious for explaining the range of energy states in different states of consciousness, is in itself insufficiently complex to explain the full range of alternative states of consciousness of which the brain is capable. In order to complexify the model a bit, we must note that the essential intentionality of experience is mediated by a dialogue between prefrontal processes in the neocortex oriented and configured upon sensorial objects (the "prefrontosensorial polarity principle"; see Laughlin, McManus, and d'Aquili 1990: chap. 4). The prefrontal cortex is that part of the brain just above the eyes on both sides. If that part of the brain is destroyed, a person will still be conscious, but his or her system of knowledge will be dramatically changed. For example, he or she will be utterly insensitive to the future consequences of their actions or knowledge (Bechara et al. 1994).

The intensity of participation of the prefrontal cortex in constructing experience may range from minimal, or *hypointentional*, through normal *intentional*, to maximal, or *hyperintentional*, and the quality of experience will change along that dimension. Under hypointentionality, experience will be characterized by scattered attention, "dulled-out," "floaty," bored, uninvolved mind-states, lack of awareness, and so on. At the polar hyperintentional extreme, experience will be marked by absorption in the object, energetic interest, intense curiosity, and so on. Normal intentionality ranges between these two extremes.

Combined with the range of left and right lobe processes that may be entrained to consciousness, the three dimensions—ergotropic-trophotropic tuning, hemispheric asymmetry of function and intentionality—may be combined to describe a fairly broad range of states of consciousness experienced by the contemplative and understandable within our limited knowledge of the neuroendocrine system.

Prefrontal cortical processes are known to have intimate reciprocal connections with those subcortical areas, such as the limbic system and the brainstem reticular activating system, that control arousal. The prefrontal cortex is also connected to those cortical and subcortical areas, such as the posterior parietal visual attention processes, the frontal eye fields, and the superior colliculum ocular orientation processes, that control attention. The prefrontal cortex would seem to exercise considerable control over selection of objects of interest and the investment of energy in studying those objects, regardless of whether the objects are constituted via pre-dominantly left lobe or right lobe processing. For example, it is an apparent paradox that in certain states of consciousness (e.g., lucid dreaming and insight meditation) the body may be in a state of hypertrophotropic tuning (virtual paralysis, or "sleep") while at the same time experience is marked by energetic perception and study of the object of perception.

Habitual relations obtaining among processes of the three dimensions modeled above will define recurrent structures that limit the attributes of any state of con-sciousness. For example, an object (say a dog, spider, chasm, etc.) may evoke a pho-bic reaction when it penetrates to and evokes imagery buried in unconscious right hemisphere memory, anxiety mediated by limbic structures and aversive behavior mediated by motor cortex. Clearly, there are constraints on the nature of experience imposed by the state of the neuroendocrine system and the precise entrainment of the neural networks mediating experience.

The combinations of entrainment possible within the field defined by these three dimensions are many and complex, but produce predictable domains of expe-rience, many of which are readily recognized by the mature contemplative. It is pos-sible to experience a state of consciousness marked by deep tranquillity and lack of interest in any object, mediated by extreme trophotropic tuning and hypointention-ality. On the other hand there may be deep tranquillity accompanied by intense interest in some object, mediated by trophotropic tuning and hyperintentionality. The interest during such states of consciousness may range widely among all the various sensory modes, or may encompass some multi-modal object, like the con-cept of object itself, or some abstract quality of objects in all modalities, such as impermanence, spatial extension, or movement.

CONCLUSION

The processes in our nervous system that produce our world of experience form a complex, multi-layered, and distributed network of untold millions of cells inter-acting in trillions of ways—myriad ways that are heavily influenced in their pat-terning by culture and by personal development (Edelman 1987, 1989, Changeux 1985, Changeux and Dehaene 1989). Most of the knowing that goes on in this wel-ter of processing is unconscious. Comparatively little knowledge is derived initially from conscious ratiocination. Indeed, the very nature of our brain, and its modes of producing our world of meaningful experience, are inherently intuitive. Our brains are constantly feeding forward into a world of anticipated experience and testing those expectations against a fulfilling field of perception. Most of this process of anticipation, recognition, and cognition is intuitive. Thus, in order to accurately portray our species as an animal richly endowed with symbolic consciousness and the social transmission of meaning (i.e., culture), it is necessary to acknowledge the central importance of intuitive processes in the production of knowledge.

NOTES TO CHAPTER 2

1. By mature contemplation I mean the developmental stage in the career of a contemplative at which the mind may be cleared and access to intuitive insights is rapid and straightforward. For the mature contemplative, the intuitive faculty will answer questions as rapidly as they form in consciousness. Individuals rarely are capable of this mature stage of contemplation without training and discipline.

2. A *koan* is a question posed by the teacher that is designed to evoke an intuitive insight. Examples of *koans* are "Thinking neither of good nor of evil, at this very moment, what is my Original Nature?" "Who was I before I was born?" "What is the sound of one hand clapping?"

3. The concept of "transposition" is borrowed from C. S. Lewis (1965) *Screwtape Proposes a Toast*, Glasgow: William Collins and Sons, and has been developed at length elsewhere (see Laughlin, McManus, and d'Aquili 1990). The term essentially means that information is lost during the process of symbolic expression, information that is regained only if it is already modeled and penetrated during the act of evocation. Metaphorically speaking, symbolically expressed knowledge is to the total field of intuitive knowledge as a guitar version of Beethoven's Fifth Symphony is to the full orchestral version.

4. A metanoic state is a state of consciousness most conducive to transformation and development.

REFERENCES CITED

Barnett, Homer G.
  1953 *Innovation: The Basis of Cultural Change*. New York: McGraw-Hill.
Bastick, T.
  1982 *Intuition: How We Think and Act*. New York: Wiley.
Bechara, Antoine, Antonio R. Damasio, Hanna Damasio, and Steven W. Anderson
  1994 "Insensitivity to Future Consequences Following Damage to Human Prefrontal Cortex." *Cognition* 50: 7–15.
Beth, E. and J. Piaget
  1966 *Mathematical Epistemology and Psychology*. Dordrecht, Holland: D. Reidel.
Bogen, J. E.
  1969 "The Other Side of the Brain: The Appositional Mind." *Bulletin of the Los Angeles Neurological Societies* 34: 135–62.
Bogen, J. E. et al.
  1972 "The Other Side of the Brain IV: The A/P Ratio." *Bulletin of the Los Angeles Neurological Societies* 37(2): 49–61.

Bryden, M. P.
  1982 *Laterality: Functional Asymmetry in the Intact Brain*. New York: Academic Press.
Bunge, M.
  1962 *Intuition and Science*. Englewood Cliffs, NJ: Prentice-Hall.
Cantril, H.
  1960 *Morning Notes of Adelbert Ames*. New Brunswick, NJ: Rutgers University Press.
Chang, G. C. C.
  1959 *The Practice of Zen*. New York: Harper and Row.
Changeux, Jean-Pierre
  1985 *Neuronal Man: The Biology of Mind*. Oxford: Oxford University Press.
Changeux, Jean-Pierre and Stanislas Dehaene
  1989 "Neuronal Models of Cognitive Functions." *Cognition* 33: 63–109.
Daniels, U. P.
  1973 "The Effect of Perceived Locus of Control and Psychological Stress on Intuitive Problem Solving." Unpublished doctoral dissertation, York University, Toronto, Ontario, Canada.
D'Aquili, Eugene G., Charles D. Laughlin, and John McManus
  1979 *The Spectrum of Ritual*. New York: Columbia University Press.
Davidson, J. M.
  1976 "The Physiology of Meditation and Mystical States of Consciousness." *Perspectives in Biology and Medicine* 19: 345–79.
Edelman, G. M.
  1987 *Neural Darwinism: The Theory of Neuronal Group Selection*. New York: Basic Books.
  1989 *The Remembered Present: A Biological Theory of Consciousness*. New York: Basic Books.
Fischer, Roland
  1971 "A Cartography of the Ecstatic and Meditative States." *Science* 174: 897–904.
  1986 "Toward a Neuroscience of Self-Experience and States of Self-Awareness and Interpreting Interpretations." In *Handbook of States of Consciousness* (ed. by B. B. Wolman and M. Ullman). New York: Van Nostrand Reinhold.
Gazzaniga, M. S.
  1970 *The Bisected Brain*. New York: Appleton Century Crofts.
Gellhorn, E.
  1967 *Principles of Autonomic-Somatic Integration*. Minneapolis: University of Minnesota Press.
Gellhorn, E. and W. F. Kiely
  1972 "Mystical States of Consciousness: Neurophysiological and Clinical Aspects." *Journal of Nervous and Mental Diseases* 154: 399–405.
Gellhorn, E. and G. N. Loofbourrow
  1963 *Emotions and Emotional Disorders: A Neurophysiological Study*. New York: Harper and Row.
Hanson, N. R.
  1958 *Patterns of Discovery*. Cambridge: Cambridge University Press.
Harvey, O. J. et al.
  1961 *Conceptual Systems and Personality Organization*. New York: Wiley.
Hayward, Jeremy
  1984 *Perceiving Ordinary Magic*. Boston: Shambhala New Science Library.
Hess, W. R.
  1925 *On the Relations between Psychic and Vegetative Functions*. Zurich: Schabe.

1957 *Functional Organization of the Diencephalon.* New York: Grune and Stratton.

James, William

1890 *The Principles of Psychology* (1981 edition). Cambridge, MA: Harvard University Press.

Jung, Carl G.

1971 *Psychological Types.* Princeton, NJ: Princeton University Press.

Kahneman, Daniel and Amos Tversky

1982 "On the Study of Statistical Intuition." *Cognition* 11: 123–41.

Kissin, B.

1986 *Conscious and Unconscious Programs in the Brain.* New York: Plenum.

Koestler, Arthur

1959 *The Sleepwalkers.* New York: Penguin.

Kurland, J. A. and S. J. Beckerman

1985 "Optimal Foraging and Hominid Evolution: Labor and Reciprocity." *American Anthropologist* 87: 73–93.

Laughlin, Charles D.

1990 "At Play in the Fields of the Lord: The Role of Metanoia in the Development of Consciousness." *Play and Culture* 3(3): 173–92.

1994 "Apodicticity: The Problem of Absolute Certainty in Transpersonal Anthropology." *Anthropology and Humanism* 19(2): 1–15.

Laughlin, Charles D. and Ivan A. Brady

1978 *Extinction and Survival in Human Populations.* New York: Columbia University Press.

Laughlin, Charles D. and Eugene G. d'Aquili

1974 *Biogenetic Structuralism.* New York: Columbia University Press.

Laughlin, Charles D. and John McManus

1982 "The Biopsychological Determinants of Play and Games." In *Social Approaches to Sport* (ed. by R. M. Pankin). Fairleigh Dickinson University Press.

Laughlin, Charles D., John McManus, and Eugene G. d'Aquili

1990 *Brain, Symbol and Experience: Toward a Neurophenomenology of Human Consciousness.* Boston: Shambhala New Science Library.

1993 "Mature Contemplation." *Zygon* 28(2): 133–76.

Laughlin, Charles D., John McManus, Robert A. Rubinstein, and Jon Shearer

1986 "The Ritual Transformation of Experience." *Studies in Symbolic Interaction* 7 (Part A) (ed. by N. K. Dengin). Greenwich, CT.: JAI Press, 107–36.

Lee, P. R.

1976 *Symposium on Consciousness.* New York: Penguin.

Levy, J.

1972 "Lateral Specialization of the Human Brain: Behavioral Manifestations and Possible Evolutionary Basis." In *The Biology of Behavior* (ed. by J. A. Kiger). Corvallis: Oregon State University Press.

Levy-Agresti, J. and R. W. Sperry

1968 "Differential Perceptual Capacities in Major and Minor Hemispheres." *Proceedings of the National Academy of Science* 61: 1151–54.

Ley, R. G.

1983 "Cerebral Laterality and Imagery." In *Imagery: Current Theory, Research, and Application.* New York: Wiley.

Charles Laughlin

McManus, John
  1979 "Ritual and Ontogenic Development." *In the Spectrum of Ritual* (ed. by E. G. d'Aquili, C. D. Laughlin, and J. McManus). New York: Columbia University Press.
Lyons, W.
  1986 *The Disappearance of Introspection.* Cambridge, MA: MIT Press.
Miller, G. A., E. H. Galanter, and K. H. Pribram
  1960 *Plans and the Structure of Behavior.* New York: Holt, Rinehart and Winston.
Milner, B.
  1980 "Complementary Functional Specializations of the Human Cerebral Hemispheres." In *Nerve Cells, Transmitters, and Behavior* (ed. by R. Levi-Montalcini). Vatican City: Pontificia Academia Scientiarum.
Morris, P. E. and P. J. Hampson
  1983 *Imagery and Consciousness.* New York: Academic Press.
Neisser, U.
  1976 *Cognition and Reality: Principles and Implications of Cognitive Psychology.* San Francisco: Freeman.
Parker, S. T.
  1985 "A Social-Technological Model for the Evolution of Language." *Current Anthropology* 2(5): 617–39.
Parker, S. T. and K. R. Gibson
  1979 "A Development Model for the Evolution of Language and Intelligence in Early Hominids." *Behavioral and Brain Sciences* 2: 367–407.
  1982 "The Importance of Theory for Reconstructing the Evolution of Language and Intelligence in Hominids." In *Advanced Views in Primate Biology* (ed. by A. B. Chiarelli and R. S. Corruccini). New York: Springer.
Passingham, R. E.
  1982 *The Human Primate.* San Francisco: Freeman.
Piaget, Jean
  1971 *Biology and Knowledge.* Chicago: University of Chicago Press.
  1975 *Insights and Illusions of Philosophy.* New York: World Publishing Co.
Poincare, H.
  1913 *The Foundations of Science.* New York: Science Press.
Powers, W. T.
  1973 *Behavior: The Control of Perception.* Chicago: Aldine.
Pribram, Karl H.
  1971 *Languages of the Brain.* Englewood Cliffs: Prentice-Hall.
Rubinstein, Robert A., Charles D. Laughlin, and John McManus
  1984 *Science as Cognitive Process.* Philadelphia: University of Pennsylvania Press.
Salk, Jonas
  1983 *Anatomy of Reality: Merging of Intuition and Reason.* New York: Columbia University Press.
Schroder, H. M., M. Driver, and S. Streufert
  1967 *Human Information Processing.* New York: Holt, Rinehart and Winston.
Selye, H.
  1956 *The Stress of Life.* New York: McGraw-Hill.
  1974 *Stress Without Distress.* Toronto: McClelland and Stewart.

Slaatte, H. A.

　1983 *The Creativity of Consciousness: An Empirico-Phenomenological Psychology.* New York: University Press of America.

Sorokin, P. A.

　1941 *The Crisis of Our Age.* New York: E. P. Dutton.

Sperry, Roger W.

　1974 "Lateral Specialization in Surgically Separated Hemispheres." In *The Neurosciences: Third Study Program* (ed. by P. J. Vinken and G. W. Bruyn). Cambridge, MA: MIT Press.

　1982 "Some Effects of Disconnecting the Cerebral Hemispheres." *Science* 217: 1223–26.

TenHouten, Warren

　1978–79 "Hemispheric Interaction in the Brain and the Propositional, Compositional, and the Dialectical Modes of Thought." *Journal of Altered States of Consciousness* 4(2): 129–40.

Tiles, Mary

　1991 *Mathematics and the Image of Reason.* New York: Routledge.

Vaughan, F. E.

　1979 *Awakening Intuition.* Garden City, NY: Anchor Books.

Weil, A.

　1972 *The Natural Mind.* Boston: Houghton Mifflin.

Weissman, D.

　1987 *Intuition and Reality.* Albany: State University of New York Press.

Westcott, Malcolm R.

　1968 *Toward a Contemporary Psychology of Intuition.* New York: Holt, Rinehart and Winston.

Wittgenstein, L.

　1921 *Tractatus Logico-Philosophicus* (1961 edition). London: Routledge and Kegan Paul.

Wulff, David M.

　1991 *Psychology of Religion: Classic and Contemporary Views.* New York: John Wiley.

3

LOOKING INTUIT

A Phenomenological Exploration of Intuition and Attention

P. Sven Arvidson

The only philosopher I have ever "met" is Socrates. I am often introduced as a philosopher. I have advanced degrees in philosophy. I belong to a philosophy department and teach about philosophy in order to make my living. Strictly speaking, though, I am not a philosopher. A philosopher is one who, like Socrates, wakes up in the morning reflecting on universal human questions, discusses them relentlessly with others, and continues questioning until bedtime. If this strikes the reader as too demanding a lifestyle, well, I agree. That is why I would not call myself a "philosopher." Although I admire it, this is not what I actually do every day. I spend a lot of time with my family, and though I am often ambitious in many ways, sometimes I am just plain lazy! Socrates, it appears, paid little attention to his family, was not ambitious in the ordinary sense, and had seemingly inexhaustible energy for friendly disputation.

Like Socrates, however, I enjoy discussing universal human questions with others. As a professor of philosophy, part of my profession is to discuss with students and others "The meaning of Life," or such questions as "Who am I?" or "Is there a God?", etc. I also enjoy writing responses to these questions. This paper is one of those responses. In philosophy, responses are not "answers." If it is good philosophy, a response to a universal human question has the result of advancing the question, as a question.

How does one respond to the question of intuition? Socrates himself never cared to ask or respond to this question, although Plato asks and responds to it in his own way. It is a smaller question than "What is the meaning of Life?" But in our times it is an extremely important question. The notion of intuition has been involved in a cultural tug of war throughout this century. It would be a mistake, however, to suppose that the question starts with William James or Henri Bergson. It is at least as old as Plato's groundbreaking "Divided Line" and "Allegory of the Cave" in the *Republic*. Actually knowing The Good is certainly not an affair of the analytical mind, although analysis may lead up to that moment.

The most revealing way to respond to a question about the nature of human consciousness—a question like "What is intuition?"—is to simply describe what is happening in consciousness when an intuition occurs. This method of description has a history in philosophy and psychology, and it is now called phenomenology (see Spiegelberg 1982; Embree 1989). Phenomenology claims that with the right attitude, the researcher can articulate what is going on in consciousness. So if I am sufficiently attentive to the phenomenon of the world as it presents itself in consciousness, I should be able to add something important to the conversation about what intuition is.

Yet the stream of consciousness is messy, a "blooming, buzzing, confusion" as William James says. So how does one organize one's observations? My solution (which, not surprisingly, has the effect of narrowing the scope of the question of intuition in this chapter) is to start by recognizing a pattern that infuses every conscious experience, namely, a figure/ground or theme/thematic-field pattern. We recognize this structure in art, but do not realize that our conscious experience would have to be something very strange if it were not organized in terms of figure and ground, or, more generally stated, theme and thematic-field. So what I do here is describe an actual event that happened in the classroom, an event that would likely be called intuition by current researchers. Then I explore the role that this seemingly universal patterning of theme and thematic-field plays in the experience. Phenomenology, then, articulates the organization and shifts of organization that define particular kinds of experiences. One way to discuss this organization and its reorganization is in terms of attention.

This paper addresses intuition from the point of view of consciousness and attention. The question is this: If we grant that in every way of knowing there is a characteristic shaping and reorganization of consciousness, such that, for example, falling in love is different than embarrassment, what is the shape of consciousness in and near the moment of intuition? Even the most comprehensive studies of the phenomenon of intuition have not discussed intuition in terms of the phenomenology of shifts of attention. The issue here is not one of analysis or probability, or whether such knowledge or feelings actually turn out to be true, or what percentage of intuitions are reliable indicators of reality. The question is much more simple and descriptive. Namely, what is the transformation of the shape of the field of consciousness in the moment of intuition; what is the nature of the reorganization of consciousness that takes place? In a discussion of various types of attention, the intuitive moment is examined to see which reorganization processes describe its emergent structure, and which do not. The findings are then discussed with an eye to the possibility of future research on intuition and attention.

There are many ways to approach the phenomenon of intuition. One can examine its cognitive or affective components. One can examine the processes that lead up to intuition, e.g., the "internal" processes of emotional frameworks or the "external" processes of a classroom environment. One can examine the sociological dimensions, in science, anthropology, and religion. There are, of course, many more possible approaches. I admit at the outset, then, that this study is simply one way to approach this intriguing phenomenon of human being. As such it is not necessarily better or worse than other approaches, merely different, and one that strikes me as a useful way of furthering the question.

EXAMPLES: TEACHING THE *REPUBLIC*

The first order of business is to state in a preliminary way what I mean by intuition. The type of experience that I will discuss here is often called insight. It is a sudden solution to a problem, a solution that appears all at once, complete, and is markedly distinct from the processes that may have led up to it. There are many other possible aspects of intuition, as Tony Bastick's comprehensive study, *Intuition: How We Think and Act* (1982), has shown. But this general description is sufficient for my present purposes. One of the questions that I will be concerned with here is the difference between what Bastick calls the "Eureka" experience and the "Clicking-in" experience. Both refer to a sudden reorganization of what is presented in the field of consciousness, but, as Bastick points out, they are differentiated at least by the processes that lead up to their appearance. It is unclear, however, whether he thinks they are different in their essential structure. In the course of this study I will respond to this question.

The "Eureka" experience involves a sudden insight into the solution of a problem that is preceded by a period of inattention to the problem. The "Clicking-in" experience involves a sudden insight into the solution of a problem that is preceded by a period of concentration on solving the problem. (The term problem is to be taken in a wide sense, not simply a mathematical one.) Although Bastick categorizes both of these as intuition, and rightly so, he points out different intuitive processes at work in each, namely, "recentring" and "drifting," respectively.

My analysis of intuition occurs at a different level than Bastick's. I am interested in the attentional shift that describes the structure of the subject's ongoing awareness and how attention works in the structure of the product itself. Bastick (1982: 253) is more interested in the processes, especially "emotional sets" that make probable an intuition. What I propose to do, then, is to examine the structure of intuition in the "Eureka" and "Clicking-in" experiences by identifying the shifts of attention in the field of consciousness and the structure of what is presented. In this way I will suggest a structure of the shape of consciousness in these moments of intuition, while examining from another level whether these two types of intuition are phenomenologically distinct. I will conclude that these two "types" of intuition are not distinct insofar as the shape or structure of the moment of presentation is concerned, although they are distinguished with respect to the processes that precede their occurrence.

Consider the following. Early in my teaching career, I was teaching Plato's *Republic* at a small college to a class of about forty-five undergraduates. We had read four other dialogues by Plato and in teaching each one I had stressed the importance of the first sentence in Plato's dialogues. But the *Republic*'s first sentence did not seem to be crucial like the others. I mentioned this to a friend, who suggested its importance. He said that the beginning phrase spoken by Socrates, "I went down to the [port city] . . . " probably had something to do with the Allegory of the Cave later in the work. But of course! The connection emerged spontaneously. The opening line foreshadows and parallels the descent of the philosopher-king (represented by Socrates) back down into the cave to help make the cave-dwellers and himself better. Suddenly it was crystal clear how the beginning (the first sentence) and the pinnacle of the dialogue (represented by the Cave Allegory) were connected: the dialogue was now presented to me as a coherent whole, with the first sentence and the Cave Allegory as interdependent formative constituents of the gestalt or theme.

Although my insight here was cued by the other's suggestion, it was no less mine. This is an example of the "Clicking-in" type of intuition. I had worked on this problem intently, believing that Plato's first sentence in the work held a key secret. My belief represents what Bastick would call the "drifting" of an "emotional set." In other words, I felt that I was going in the right direction, even though my main clues were only the previous instances of first sentences being crucial to understanding a dialogue as a whole. Then in the midst of trying to solve the *Republic* problem, my friend gave me the big clue I needed. Note, however, that the solution he uttered *was not equal to my solution*. In my solution the whole was given, everything seemed to fit into place. He did not put that into my present experiencing by his utterance. His utterance was part of the process that enabled me to be presented with the solution in my own field of consciousness and in my own way. In other words, it is incorrect to say that he caused the insight. This would imply a direct mechanical connection between what he intended the shape of my consciousness to be, and its actual restructuring. It is more correct to say that my conversation with him was part of the conditions that allowed the insight to occur.

One might object that this example does not describe intuition at all. What is described is simply a solution to a problem, just as we solve many problems, large

P. Sven Arvidson

and small, every day. As we shall see, however, there are various ways to solve problems. The sudden appearance of a solution—an immediate, novel, and striking synthesis of what was previously unrelated or only loosely related—a solution that is comprehensive and immediately given as true, as a perfect fit, and that cannot be reduced to the "steps" of reasoning that preceded it, is utterly different phenomenologically than solving the problem of how to construct a child's bicycle by following the step-by-step instructions. Intuition in philosophy and everyday life has many, and often conflicting, meanings, and they cannot be unraveled here. So I should stress that other studies may examine intuition in a much broader way than this one does. I investigate here the *formal structure* of conscious presentation at and near the moment of these "types" of intuition.

Now consider a related story of intuition that illustrates the "Eureka" experience. Later, in class, after I had spent virtually the whole period on the Allegory of the Cave in the *Republic*, I asked the students to turn back to the first page of the dialogue and read along with me the first line. Then I reminded them that we had seen how crucially important all of Plato's other first sentences were, and that several classes ago I noted to them that I could not find a similar importance in the first sentence. So the puzzle was previously presented. I am reasonably certain that these students (though bright traditional non-majors) were not losing sleep over this puzzling phenomenon. I am also reasonably certain that they paid attention to it when it was first presented, since they had already had an investment of four Platonic dialogues and since a hefty assignment was in the offing. Still, given the length and difficulty of the *Republic*, it is doubtful that many (any?) students turned *back* and read that first sentence again on their own later, pondering its meaning.

When I told them the secret that the first sentence held, the whole room decompressed. The collective sigh was visible and audible. It hit them hard. They had been trying to make sense, off and on, of this long, seemingly rambling, ancient text and here was a major breakthrough for them; the whole text cohered at least momentarily. Although I can't speak for what they went through, I feel safe in saying that it was insight or intuition. Now what is presented intuitively in both cases could be very much the same. But their experience seems different in at least one important respect from my own. In mine, I was specifically attending to the problem of how the first sentence fits in with the whole for a relatively continuous length of time previous to my intuition of the solution (I admit my obsessiveness about these kinds of riddles). I was *expecting* an insight. My students had read the first sentence previously, and had been struggling for an hour with the Cave Allegory, but they had not recently attended intently for any length of time to the significance of that first sentence and its connection to the *Republic* as a whole. In fact, I did not give them a chance to worry about it again since I simply told them the significance (a very non-Socratic teaching move!). So although our insights may have been similar, I was intending to have it; theirs was more of a surprise (even if they were intending to be "educated" about Plato, such intense insights do not happen every class day).

One might complain that such intuition is inventive and cannot involve someone else telling the subject the solution. This is true, but it is no complaint against what I am describing. As stated before, regardless of the presentation of the information, the insight or intuition cannot be *made* to happen in someone's consciousness. What is created is the condition for its emergence (this *is* Socratic).[1]

INTUITION AND ATTENTION

I will use the field-theory of consciousness articulated by Aron Gurwitsch to develop these descriptions of intuition and suggest which modifications of attention are involved. Gurwitsch was a phenomenological philosopher interested in Gestalt psychology. His most important works, *Studies in Phenomenology and Psychology* (1966) and *The Field of Consciousness* (1964), attempt to use both phenomenology and Gestalt psychological principles to articulate invariant structures of consciousness. The field of consciousness, rather than the consciousness of the field, was his main interest. The field of consciousness is all that is presented or intended at any moment, while the consciousness of field is the presenting or intending activity. This distinction is made only for purposes of phenomenological analysis. When discussing the structure of the field of consciousness, one is concerned with the organization of presented phenomena. Gurwitsch found that all that is presented in consciousness is organized along three dimensions: theme, thematic-field, and margin.

Consider the following. I attend to the globe on my desk, wondering if it is too big for the space. The globe is presented as thematic. It is the focus of my attention and occupies the center of my field of consciousness. The desk, the pictures, the plant, are also presented, but not as thematic. These background items are part of the thematic-field. They are part of the relevant context for the globe. Meanwhile, the faint stirring of hunger, or the car in the lot outside the window, are irrelevant. Although co-presented, these items are marginal with respect to the globe as thematic and its presented background (the thematic-field).

The *theme* is the focus — that which engrosses the subject's attention and forms the center of the presented field. It is like the figure in figure/ground perception. The theme is a gestalt that is organized by the coherence of its constituents for each other, a functional significance of internal relatedness that marks it off as bounded from the thematic-field, like a figure is marked off from a background. In other words, the theme is presented at once as simple and unitary (e.g., a globe), even though it could later be analyzed into its constituent members (e.g., golden-brown, heavy, dented, aged). It is also presented as independent from the background context (the thematic-field), even though the context is related to it.

The *thematic-field* presents the relevant context or background for the theme. Its constituents are organized by a unity of relevance for each other and also for the theme. That is, the items in the thematic-field are not central but are important or relevant to the centrally presented theme. The most relevant thematic-field items are presented as (perceptually, but not necessarily physically) close to the theme, and the least relevant are presented as farther away, extending indefinitely. For example, the framed pictures sitting on the desk that make up a part of the thematic-field are physically farther removed from the globe, but are at the moment more relevant to my musings concerning the positioning of the globe (and hence closer to the theme) than the physically closer paperweight. Even so, all thematic-field items are presented as relevant to the theme, no matter how clearly or vaguely they are presented. Again, I am only vaguely aware of the positioning of the desk in the room, but it happens to be relevant, even if vaguely so, to the globe given in the context (thematic-field) of its position on the desk. The items that are presented as *irrele*-vant to the theme are marginal.

In the *margin*, the third dimension of the field of consciousness, items are merely co-presented with the theme and thematic-field but are otherwise not relevant to the presented possible lines of context or relevance dictated by the theme. In the example given, I may be marginally aware of the birds chirping outside the window, but it is not relevant to the theme as given (of course, at some point, the chirping itself could become a new theme, with a new thematic-field).

There are a number of possible modifications that can occur within this three-domain patterning of theme, thematic-field, and margin. However, here, I am primarily concerned with shifts in thematic consciousness, which means that the margin will not be discussed. Note at the outset that thematic consciousness is not consciousness of a bare theme. Thematic consciousness means theme and thematic-field. According to Gurwitsch, a theme must always appear in a thematic-field (could one have figure without background?). The attentional modifications to be discussed are serial shifting, elucidation, singling-out, and synthesis.[2]

Serial Shifting

While studying a mathematical problem, I can shift from one part of the problem to the next, and then to the next step, and so on. This serial shifting from one theme to another related to it involves a movement of a gestalt from being a part of the thematic-field, to being the theme, and then to being a part of the thematic-field again. For example, in figuring taxes, while Step Two is presented as thematic (e.g., my Net Income), Step One may present itself as relevant but not thematic. Step One (my Gross Income) was thematic but is now part of the thematic-field. Step Three (my Deductions) may also be part of the thematic-field. When Step Three is presented as thematic, Step Two now becomes part of the thematic-field, probably more relevant and hence closer to the theme (which is now Step Three) than Step One, but both are part of the relevant context or thematic-field for Step Three, and so on. We commonly call the type of thinking referred to by this modification of attention "analysis." Notice that my Gross Income, my Net Income, and my Deductions may all be presented at the same time. But the dimension of consciousness to which each

P. Sven Arvidson

belongs may be different. To be presented in consciousness is not necessarily to be presented as focal. The thematic-field presents what is relevant to the theme, but it is organized differently than the theme. Later, I will show that much current research neglects this difference in organization.

Clearly, intuition is something different than analysis, although analysis may lead up to it. For example, while serially shifting through the presentations of the steps of a mathematical problem, a sudden reorganization of the field may occur such that the solution is presented all-at-once, "jumping over" intermediate steps. Something similar appears to be the case in "Clicking-in." The attentional modification of serial shifting is not part of the structure of intuition. It is included here as foil, showing what intuition is not.

Elucidation

It might be the case that the thematic-field is presented as somewhat obscure, with only vague lines of relevance or context traced out from the theme. Then, either gradually or suddenly, the thematic-field becomes elucidated. The vagueness is clarified and the theme is reoriented in a fully meaningful way. For example, suppose I am on a "blind date" and I have some vague idea about who the person across the table from me is. She is presented to me as a nice girl, friendly, with green eyes. Suddenly or slowly, I get a clearer picture of who she is. This clarification or elucidation affects the presented theme (i.e., my date as she is presented to me); it situates or gives light and perspective to the theme. She is still presented as focal, the theme is not new, but its relevance or meaning is clarified.[3]

If this clarification occurs suddenly, it may be a very moving experience. Indeed, it may be called intuition by some. It does not, however, describe the phenomenon of "Clicking-in" or the "Eureka" experience for which we are looking. This is because elucidation describes a field of consciousness where the presented theme remains essentially the same, while the thematic-field changes. In the intuition experiences we are interested in, the theme itself undergoes a radical change; in short, *achievement involves replacement*, the new theme that is suddenly presented was absent previously. In my experience of the *Republic* described earlier, the final product of intuition was not this or that section of the book, or the first sentence. It was not anything that was given as theme previously. In elucidation, however, the theme stays the same.

In elucidation, the center of the presented field (i.e., the theme) may suddenly be recontextualized, but it is still the same theme. For example, I may be attending to the first scene of a strange contemporary play. Not having seen it before, I wonder what significance the opening lines have. As the scene unfolds, I represent to myself the opening lines of the actor. Perceptual lines of relevance are traced out, vague possible connections are presented. Suddenly, I am present to the significance of the actor's opening lines. The thematic-field has become elucidated and what were previously obscure and prenumbral perceptual lines of determination of context

P. Sven Arvidson

are now clearly formulated, giving the originally presented theme (the actor's open-ing lines) a fuller contextual relevance.

Why is this not the same as the intuition I described earlier? Again, the difference is the type of reorganization involved. In the intuition that involved the first line of the *Republic*, the newly presented theme was not the first line, although the first line was a formative constituent of the new theme. The new theme was the *Republic* as a whole. However, in the case of the play, there was not a new theme pre-sented (it is still the actor's lines), only a newly elaborated thematic-field. Although the theme is not new, it is presented in a new light or orientation. This modification of attention, elucidation, is not a part of the structure of intuition in the "Clicking-in" or "Eureka" experiences.

Singling-out

Singling-out involves the modification of attention whereby that which was previ-ously a constituent of a theme is now a theme itself. Adopting a simple example described by Gurwitsch (1966: 241), consider the shift from thematically attending to a row of lines, to attending to the left-end line (see Figure 1).

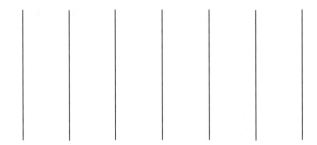

Figure 1

This is often referred to as "zooming-in" or "focusing" or "selecting." But the way that psychologists and philosophers use these terms is problematic because what is presented is thought to remain the same, while the only change is the sub-jective orientation. This view holds that the same row of lines is presented in all its detail, while the only thing changing is that I pick one of the lines out instead of another, or instead of all of them. In fact, it is not simply a matter of narrowing down the perceptual field while all else remains the same. In singling-out, *a new theme is presented*. One is tempted to say that the constituent (the left-end line) has become the theme and there is really no significant change thereby. However, this new theme (the left-end line) has a different functional relationship to its thematic-field (e.g., the other presented lines) and a different functional relationship in terms of its own internal structure, that is, between its constituents (e.g., its length, width, color intensity, etc.). In short, the left-end line is no longer functioning as a constituent but is now a theme, and so has different internal and situated relations.

Singling-out the left-most line from a row of lines creates a new theme with new relations. Notice the difference between being a member of a thematic presentation (i.e., a constituent) and being a theme. For example, after singling-out, the other lines may be presented as the thematic-field for the left-end line as the new theme. In this transformation, the "left-end" line is no longer the originally appearing left-end line; it is now central in consciousness, whereas before it was part of the context.

Singling-out is not part of the structuring of intuition. Singling-out shows, however, the kind of radical modification of the theme needed to account for the "Clicking-in" and "Eureka" experiences. But singling-out is a change in the opposite direction than what intuition demands. Synthesis, a modification in the reverse direction from singling-out, is the essential attentional modification involved in the type of intuition described here.

Synthesis

Synthesis involves the reorganization of the theme so that what was previously thematic is now a constituent in the new theme. For example, in Figure 1, the left-end line that was previously singled-out can recede from central status and become a member of the row of lines. The row itself becomes the new theme. We have moved from the singular to the bigger group. What was previously presented in the thematic-field has been transformed; it is now presented as thematic or central. Or a musical passage that was salient, that was singled-out as thematic, can become a harmonious member of an overall orchestration. The bigger orchestration, which was the thematic-field, is now given as the theme. The salient musical passage, which was a theme, is now a constituent in the new theme — the orchestration. The new theme in each case includes the previous theme. But now that previous theme (e.g., the salient passage) is a mere constituent in the new theme.

Sometimes synthesis is referred to as "zooming out." This locution is misleading, however, since it implies that everything else stays the same except the subjective perspective on what is presented. In the attentional modification of synthesis, nothing remains what it was insofar as its function is concerned. There is a new theme (the row of lines, the overall orchestration) with a new functional coherence between its constituents. For instance, in the *Republic* example, the *Republic* was given as a theme for me, but the place of the first sentence within it was not set. The first sentence was not incorporated into the theme in the way it was later. The theme was not the new theme born of the modification of synthesis. In the replacement of the old theme with the new theme, the importance of the first sentence and the *Republic* as a whole was conserved but reorganized. The formative constituents of this new theme were the first sentence and the Allegory of the Cave. Neither of these *was* the theme, but each contributed to the formation of the whole. Although these two constituents may not be the only members of this new theme, they are the most conspicuous constituents, the formative ones around which the others organize or reorganize their function for the whole.

P. Sven Arvidson

The case of my students' intuition is similar. We are supposing that previous to the new theme, they were not attending to the first sentence for any length of time, although I had previously pointed out the problem and was doing so again. If their experience is described as the modification of attention called synthesis, then the previous thematic presentation might have been either the first line as presently pointed out, or the Allegory as discussed for the previous hour (or indeed they might have been daydreaming about the forthcoming party that night). The synthesis involves pulling both the Allegory and the first sentence together in a *new* theme that did not include either of them in the way that they are now presented. The attentional modification of synthesis is involved in the essence of the intuitive moment in the "Clicking-in" and "Eureka" experiences.

The field of consciousness that I have been describing has a correlate in the consciousness of field. The relative clarity of the thematic-field (this is descriptive of the field of consciousness) is correlated with the feeling or attitude of wholeness and completeness of the insight (this is descriptive of the consciousness of field). In the type of intuition discussed here, the thematic-field is not obscure but fully clarified, at least all but the remotest parts of it. This relatively full clarification of context and relevance is the (field of consciousness) correlate to reports of crystal clearness, wholeness, and completeness in the final moment of intuition. This is analogous to the elucidation of the theme that was earlier rejected as the way intuition is presented in the field of consciousness. But it is not elucidation as there defined because here the theme is new (achievement involves replacement), and the clarification occurs synchronically with the emergence of the theme. In elucidation as an attentional shift, no new theme is given.

The following is offered as a phenomenological description of attention and the field of consciousness in types of intuition called "Clicking-in" and "Eureka" experiences. With respect to the *moment* of intuition, their structures are indistinguishable. This intuition is the sudden reorganization of the field of consciousness, through the modification of attention called synthesis, in which the previous theme is replaced with a new theme. Synthesis is the rapid emergence and momentary stabilization of thematic consciousness involving the replacement of one thematic presentation by another, and the transformation of what was previously presented as thematic into a constituent of the new theme. Intuition is also unique with respect to other everyday experiences since lines of demarcation of context or relevance from the new theme to the new thematic-field are instantly, and relatively fully, clarified.

BASTICK

I have mentioned already that the analysis here differs from Bastick's in some respects. I have also indicated that there are some problems with the traditional

P. Sven Arvidson

view of attention as it might relate to intuition. It is appropriate to close by being more precise about these issues.

My study here differs from Bastick's approach in two main ways. First, he (1982: 252) describes the intuitive process and not the intuitive product. Bastick is interested in "emotional sets" that are the underpinnings for the occasion of the attentional modifications I have described. In other words, he is concerned with what leads up to the intuition, what makes it possible, not with the attentional transformations of consciousness in the moment of the presentation of the intuitive product. He defines intuition as the state of the system at the end of the intuitive process. After reading his work closely, I see no reason to object to his treatment of the matter. It is consistent with the approach taken here. The only possible disagreement, and it is a significant one, is if Bastick is claiming that the processes that lead up to the intuition *define* the shape of the intuition itself. It is unclear if this is implied by his statement of the intuitive product being the state of the system at the end of the process. I have endeavored to show, among other things, that the intuitive moment is not a function of the processes that may lead up to it. The achievement of intuition is the *replacement* of one theme by another, and is therefore new with respect to what came before it.

The other way that Bastick's approach differs is that the present study is narrowly focused on attentional modifications in the field of consciousness, while his (almost four-hundred-page) study considers much more than just perception. Again, I have few complaints about his treatment of the matter from that more global level.

PROBLEMS OF METAPHOR IN ATTENTION AND INTUITION

Although Bastick does not discuss attention and intuition, one might look to other psychologists for clues about how to describe intuition in terms of attention. Indeed, in any decent university library one can find a huge amount of research, most of it recent, on the psychology of attention. But when it comes to describing intuition and attention there is a dearth of research. I would like to suggest one reason why.

I do not think that traditional psychological approaches to attention would be able to succeed if they attempted to describe how attentional modifications work in intuition. The reason is that the metaphors used in theorizing and generating research on attention in psychology are misleading and not resonant with the phenomenological findings. For example, the metaphor of attention as a "spotlight" has been used by Posner (1980), Treisman and Gelade (1980), and others to theorize about how attention works and to measure its qualities.[4] The main problem with this approach was suggested earlier when discussing "zooming out" and "zooming in." The selection or focusing process is thought to fully account for the reorganization in the field of consciousness, the items presented otherwise remaining the same. However, there is a substantial change possible in what is presented. For example, in synthesis and singling-out, the theme is completely reorganized and is situated in a new thematic-field. Simply saying (or implying) that the focus changes while everything else remains the same misses important possibilities of attentional modification. Also, in order to save some form of realism in their philosophical systems, some philosophers (Aronson 1984; Harré 1986) theorize a two-part process in the formation of the theme (although they do not use this field theory language). One part of the theme is beneath consciousness, a pre- or subconscious orienting response. The other is the conscious emergence of the theme. Hence, attention is thought to be a two-step process: orientation and selection (focusing). The problem with this description is that it makes the theme into a two-part presentation, when phenomenologically it is not presented as two-part. In other words, by not attending to what is presented and how it is presented, these thinkers in psychology and philosophy describe a presentation that is not presented. Recently, Aronson and Harré (Aronson et al. 1994) have brought their ideas more in line with how perception works.

The metaphor of attention as a "spotlight" entails the following organization of the field of consciousness: what is focal is emphasized and what is not under the focal spotlight of attention is de-emphasized (Cohen 1993: 4). This emphasis/de-emphasis organization, however, misses the essential connections between that which is focal (the theme) and that which is not (the thematic-field and margin). In short, presented relevance (the thematic-field as context) is not taken into account as a dimensional structure of the field.[5]

Some theorists (Mangun and Hillyard 1988; Lind 1980) recognized that "noticing" what fell within the spotlight and "not noticing" what fell outside its boundaries did not fit with differences of organization of what is presented. What they proposed, then, was that attention is more broadly distributed, so that there is a gradient across the field. Still, the notion of a gradient does not capture the different organizational dimensions of theme and thematic-field. Numerical difference does not account for the difference between the near or far area outside of the theme and what is thematic. The "closeness" and "distance" are differences in degree *of* relevance, but this very notion of presented relevance (with respect to the theme) is exactly what is missed by the spotlight metaphor.

In 1980 Anne Treisman collaborated on what is now a leading theory of spatial attention in psychology. The Feature Integration Theory explicitly uses the metaphor of attention as a spotlight. In essence, it claims that the spotlight of attention selects a certain spatial area within which focal attention can provide the "glue" that combines and holds together features, thereby presenting objects. What is interesting is that in 1993 Treisman changed the metaphor dramatically to an "attentional window." So instead of attention spotlighting and gluing together what is illuminated, attention is the broad or narrow opening that *suppresses* some information and allows other information to be selected so that focal attention can work serially within the frame. She writes (1993: 22), "In this view, the problem for perception is one of suppressing all *but* the correct picture of the scene, not one of building up a single correct picture." This change of metaphor, which allows her theory to account better for presented conjunctions that do not have to be "glued," appears to be a response to possible gestalt-based objections to the spotlight metaphor. Still, this improvement does not go far enough. There is no discussion of *dimensional* differences of organization in what is presented, i.e., the presented difference between the theme and the thematic-field and the margin. The switch from spotlight to window is still inadequate because it is simply a unidimensional conversion: from whichever side the light shines, it shines through the same hole. A radical rethinking is needed. The problem here is that in searching for microprocesses, using micromeasuring instruments, one gets a microview of the modifications of attention, neglecting the larger qualitative differences in the field of consciousness.[6]

The usual phenomena studied by attentional psychologists—orienting response, divided attention, effortful attention, sustained attention—are all explained in terms of selective attention. I have discussed selective attention here as singling-out, but have endeavored to avoid these researchers' problem. The problem here is similar to the problem with the spotlight metaphor, and it is not just psychologists who are at fault. In short, the problem is that according to these accounts the differentiation within the field of consciousness is between what is selected and unselected, what is illuminated and unilluminated, what is noticed and unnoticed. If this is the only distinction, then the theory of attention has not progressed since 1899 when William James (1983: 19) described the field of consciousness as presenting that which is focal (selected) and that which is marginal (unselected).[7] Treisman (1993: 23) writes, "What varies across tasks is how broadly or narrowly focused the attention window is." But how can this change account for the radical change in what is presented evidenced by synthesis or singling-out? In these cases there is a new organization even though the same "elements" are involved. The description of this change in the content or organization of the theme cannot be captured by a broadening or narrowing spotlight or window representing the modification of the standard case of attention as selectivity.

Many of these theorists are stuck in the narrow corridor of research that is deemed valuable if it produces a *measurable* response from a subject. How could interesting phenomena such as intuition possibly fit into a paradigm that considers microseconds of eye movement standard phenomena for research? What is needed in order to describe such phenomena as intuition, depression, ecstasy, boredom, is a way of describing experience that is not necessarily tied to *measurable* results even though it may be compatible with these results. Aron Gurwitsch introduced such a description of attention sixty-five years ago, and I have used it here to suggest how narrow the research corridor of psychology has become. A radical change in theoretical foundation is needed to allow meaningful discussion of intuition and other complexities of human consciousness.

A final problem to be discussed, related to the others, is the persistent notion of the cognitive bestowal of organization on previously unorganized stimuli or data. As has been shown, traditionally, that which is "spotlighted" and focused is thereby organized. Hence, the concept of the presentation of the object involves a processing of stimuli or elements in order to build up a whole. This is the legacy of the empiricism of David Hume (1888). There is promise, however. For example, even in Treisman's first formulation of the Feature Integration Theory, there are some "pre-attended" conjunctions that do not need to be "glued" together. But in order for an object to be presented as thematic (i.e., "focal"), cognitive processes need to bestow organization by focusing these presented relations. In the latest version of her theory, Treisman appears to reevaluate the necessity of bestowing organization on what is presented. Still, although conjunctions between "pre-attended" features are made by either an "externally directed window of attention" or by "inhibitory control" by cognitive maps tied to features, it seems that the function of focal attention (not "pre-attentive" processes) is still to finalize objectification by *adding on* organization to what is so far conjoined.

The achievement of presenting an object as thematic is not to be accounted for by the cognitive processes leading up to it. What was presented is replaced by a new presentation at the moment of achievement. In effect, we do not make the field reorganize by a focusing of attention that bestows on it a cognitively processed organization, thereby putting the pieces together to make an object. At some point the theme is presented as a gestalt, inherently organized, replacing what was previously presented independently of the processes that led up to this reorganization.

With the persistence of misleading metaphors, it is doubtful that the current work by researchers on attention can reveal much on the phenomenon of intuition. This paper in part proposes a radical reinspection of the metaphors used for describing consciousness, so that it is possible to discuss certain experiences, such as intuition, from the perspective of attention. Intuition is an incredibly complex, valuable, and legitimate human experience, even if it cannot be measured in a way that may please today's cognitive or neuropsychologist. It would be useful and appropriate for these researchers to reexamine phenomenological thinkers such as Gurwitsch, since they can provide guidance on how to grapple with interesting but "messy" phenomena of human consciousness, without sacrificing rigor.

Notes to Chapter 3

Acknowledgments: I would like to thank the College of Mount St. Joseph for a summer grant to aid in writing this chapter, and Robbie Davis-Floyd for valuable editorial suggestions. Some ideas in the final section were previously presented in Arvidson (1996).

P. Sven Arvidson

1. As any teacher knows, this occurrence of an "Aha! Experience" by a majority of a class simultaneously is very rare and quite rewarding. I remember distinctly how its power caught me off guard. I have since tried a number of times to duplicate the event by duplicating the processes leading up to it, but have been largely unsuccessful. For the deciphering of Plato's first line I thank Michael Taber.

2. The following is informed by Gurwitsch's work (1966). Other attentional modifications discussed there but not here are "restructuration" and "enlargement."

3. This is a different case than what Laughlin (in this volume) describes with the chalkboard analogy, since there it is the theme that is unclarified, not the thematic-field.

4. For overviews of attention research see Johnson and Dark (1986) and Kinchla (1992). For a discussion of metaphors in attention research see LaBerge (1995). Recently, some researchers have been trying to bring context into focus in their work. Ballesteros and Manga (1993) present contextual scene analysis, which can be a marked improvement on "cueing" and "flanker effect" analysis. Churchland, Ramachandran, and Sejnowski (1994) present work linking neurology to "global attention." Rafal and Robertson (1995) give the most sophisticated presentation of how context works in attention that I have seen with respect to experimental psychology, although their theoretical underpinning is weak because of the neglect of the subtleties of attentional transformation that Gurwitsch describes.

5. Gurwitsch (1966: 202) writes, "Thematic consciousness does not consist, as one usually asserts of attention, in a beam of light being cast upon a certain content while a chaotic confusion of other contents fills the regions of shadow and darkness. We must beware of taking literally the metaphor of the 'illuminating light' of attention. Beyond that the correctness of this analogy remains very much in question. In general, the distinction between 'noticed' = 'illuminated' and 'unnoticed' = 'unilluminated' parts of consciousness misses essential phenomenological structures." For Gurwitsch, such a description in terms of illumination does not capture the essential descriptive feature of the phenomenon of attention: namely, the structural features of the field of consciousness, and in particular, the relation between the theme and thematic-field. For Gurwitsch, it is this relation that must take center stage in any discussion of attention.

6. N. R. Hanson (1958: 16) remarks, "If one must find a paradigm case of seeing it would be better to regard as such not the visual apprehension of colour patches but things like seeing what time it is, seeing what key a piece of music is written in, and seeing whether a wound is septic."

7. See Arvidson (1992) for a discussion of this formulation by James.

REFERENCES CITED

Aronson, Jerrold
  1984 *A Realist Philosophy of Science*. New York: St. Martin's Press.
Aronson, J., Harre, R., and Way, E. C.
  1994 *Realism Rescued: How Scientific Progress is Possible*. London: Duckworth
Arvidson, P. Sven
  1992 "The Field of Consciousness: James and Gurwitsch," *Transactions of the C.S. Peirce Society*, 28(4): 833–56.

1996 "Toward a Phenomenology of Attention," *Human Studies*, 19: 71–84

Ballesteros, S. and Manga, D.

1993 "The Influence of Irrelevant Information in Visual Perception." In Ballesteros, S. (ed.). *Cognitive Approaches to Human Perception*, Hillsdale, NJ: L. Eribaum.

Bastick, Tony.

1982 *Intuition: How We Think and Act*. New York: John Wiley and Sons.

Churchland, P. S., Ramachandran, V. S., and Sejnowski, T. J.

1994 "A Critique of Pure Vision." In Koch, C. and Davis, J. L. (eds.). *Large Scale Neuronal Theories of the Brain*. Cambridge, MA: MIT Press.

Cohen, R.

1993 *The Neuropsychology of Attention*. New York: Plenum Press.

Embree, L.

1989 "The Legacy of Dorion Cairns and Aron Gurwitsch: A Letter to Future Historians," *Analecta Husserliana*, 26: 115–46.

Gurwitsch, Aron

1964 *The Field of Consciousness*. Pittsburgh, PA: Duquesne University Press.

1966 *Studies in Phenomenology and Psychology*. Evanston, IL: Northwestern University Press.

Hanson, N. R.

1958 *Patterns of Discovery: An Inquiry into the Conceptual Foundations of Science*. London: Cambridge University Press.

Harré, Rom

1986. *Varieties of Realism: A Rationale for the Natural Sciences*. Oxford: Basil Blackwell.

Hume, David

1888 *A Treatise of Human Nature*. (Ed.) L. A. Selby-Bigge. Oxford University Press.

James, William

1983 *Talks to Teachers on Psychology and to Students on Some of Life's Ideals*. Cambridge, MA: Harvard University Press.

Johnson, W. A. and Dark, V. J.

1986 "Selective Attention," *Annual Review of Psychology*, 37: 43–75

Kinchla, R. A.

1992 "Attention," *Annual Review of Psychology*, 43: 711–742.

LaBerge, D.

1995 *Attentional Processing: The Brain's Art of Mindfulness*. Cambridge, MA: Harvard University Press.

Lind, R.

1980 "Attention and the Aesthetic Object," *Journal of Aesthetics and Art Criticism* 39(1): 131–142.

Mangun, G. and Hillyard, S.

1988 "Spatial Gradients of Visual Attention: Behavioral and Electrophysical Evidence," *Electro-encephalography and Clinical Neurophysiology* 70: 417–428.

Posner, M. I. et al.

1980 "Attention and the Detection of Signals," *Journal of Experimental Psychology* 109: 160–174.

Rafal, R. and Roberston, L.

1995 "The Neurology of Visual Attention." In Gazzaniga, M. (ed.). *The Cognitive Neurosciences*. Cambridge, MA: MIT Press, 625–48.

P. Sven Arvidson

Spiegelberg, H.

1982 *The Phenomenological Movement.* The Hague: Martinus Nijhoff.

Treisman, A. M.

1993 "The Perception of Features and Objects." In *Attention: Selection, Awareness, and Control: A Tribute to Donald Broadbent*, A. Braddeley and L. Weiskrantz (eds.). Oxford: Clarendon Press.

Treisman, A. M. and Gelade, G.

1980 "A Feature Integration Theory of Attention," *Cognitive Psychology* 12: 97–136.

P. Sven Arvidson

4

Sacred Land—Sacred Stories

The Territorial Dimensions
of Intuition

For Carl Urion—the light in the West

Part I: Intuition and the Wild

Joe Sheridan

I became interested in intuition because I inherited certain talents from my mother's side of the family, the Harrisons. I understood from an early age that being in physical proximity with someone or some place was a foundation for knowing them when either they or I had gone away. In my family history, there was a remembered sense of why my ancestors chose to settle on the Georgian Bay (off Lake Huron). It had to do with the feel of the place: for the wandering West Coast Irish, the Georgian Bay felt much like the land they'd left behind on the Dingle Peninsula. I think the reason why the great Canadian folklorist Edith Fowke found such intact culture where I come from is because that Dingle Peninsula sensibility could survive best buffeted by a powerful body of water whipped by harsh winter winds. Like begets like.

Somehow that land intuition became a cultural and interpersonal quality, certainly among the Georgian Bay mothers. Perhaps it was because their sons and husbands and fathers spent so much of their time on dangerous waters unguided by compass or sextant, yet with a dead reckoning that only the fishermen seem to   57 understand. How to get oneself to a spot of water beyond all land coordinates and get home again with little more than five highly attuned senses is a talent quite in keeping with those intuitive qualities of the onshore women. Once in contact, always in contact.

These qualities of intuition first appealed to me as I used them on the water and in the bush, and were the reason why the dogs we kept were always members of the family. I left the Georgian Bay under the same conditions as my economic refugee forebears, and sought an education. I interviewed tramps about their resonance with land; that undergraduate thesis won me a scholarship with the legendary D. K. Wilgus at U.C.L.A.'s Folklore and Mythology Program, where I looked at the memory of land in Anglo-American folksong traditions. I worked as a folklorist with the Winnipeg Folk Festival, and my interest in land was again piqued by the elegant symmetries of mind and place among the Salteaux peoples of the Canadian Plains. Then I tried to understand intuition and its role in environmental education under Donald Oliver at the Harvard Graduate School of Education, and with Neil Postman at New York University. I concluded my doctorate under the great Crow anthropologist and linguist Carl Urion at the University of Alberta, where I attempted to demonstrate the assertion of Cree elder Raven Mackinaw that "wilderness and storytelling are the same thing," and to show how this assertion could rewrite environmental education. At York University, where now I teach education and environmental studies, I am working toward a renewed environmental and sustainability program chiefly concerned with returning location to information.

In this chapter, I approach intuition by looking at environmental factors that can assist in its discovery, use, and maintenance—and so its validation as real. If we begin at the beginning, the origins and empirical validity of intuition can provide an explanation of how we are able to experience its powers. How far back we must go with these memories may have something to do with how long it takes for us to recognize intuition for what it is. Nascent capacities for intuitive thought may not be easily recognized, for they are not as likely to be questioned as they are to be realized. Children's intuitive thought and its ready engagement with their participatory consciousness are evident in play, relationships with animals, and in their enthrallment with the natural environment (Egan 1988). As these powers are experienced they become taken for granted, and can come to be seen as completely normal. In this regard, intuition can be seen as both a place and a process. Allow me to explain.

In *The Ecology of Imagination in Childhood* (1977), Edith Cobb explained the relationship between direct experience of biological nature and subsequent stimulation of the creative capacities of human intelligence as they become manifest in the child. This qualifies her as a conservationist, in that she regarded biodiversity as essential to the living of a healthy and complete life of the mind. I believe she may also be interpreted here to mean that she conceived of mind as a place. That is, the mind of the child is the place into which goes the experience of the processes of nature and those noticed things that comprise the natural environment. Thereafter comes the participatory consciousness that allows the child to experience self and nature as undivided. Thus we may assume that exposure to biological diversity and biosystems complexity nurtures an intuitive strength in response. The experience of that response is the child's familiarity with intuition.

The process of noticing and apprehending the natural world through lived experience lays a foundation for subsequent noticings and apprehensions. The point is that we get better at our engagement with biodiversity as we explore the places where we live. This skill has a mental and emotional as well as a biological value. The things we think with and our ability to notice patterns therein are necessarily related. That is to say, thinking with all of the things that catch a child's eye creates a mental landscape that sees the connections between these things and perceives an order or logic of interconnection. Cobb's inference can be understood to mean that eco-logic is nascent and developing as verbal intelligence grows relative to an experience of place. World knowledge and word knowledge mutually inform one another. Once eco-logic is in place through lived experience in biodiverse environments, the child develops an earth-centered ability for creative thought. Creative thought, or the ability to see a variety of patterns between things, is where intuition intersects, in this regard. My co-author and I believe intuition may be the resonance with those patterns.

Conventionally, an informal explanation of intuition would rest on a genealogical rationale— intuition comes from mom or dad or their heritage. Just ask a Fey Irish mother how she knows where her children are even when they're not to be seen. But such explanations are complicated as adequate answers by their anthropocentrism. That one has intuition solely because one is Irish or Ojibway is the genetic equivalent of claiming, "The butler did it." Subsequent explanations from this foundation require us to roll back the matter of origins to the sacred dimensions of time and place and take responsibility for an interpersonal relationship with intuition, thereby making the answer as much a matter of location as relation, so to speak. How far back we go is an issue of importance because as we shall see, it is an essential step in grounding our own origins.

Investigators find a degree of comfort with the elbow room afforded such an inquiry in a developing field like consciousness and intuition studies, as it allows us to consider whether folk explanation possesses and demonstrates empirical validity between the professed origins of intuition and its fruits.

Undertaking a chronological and geographical explanation of how intuition began requires a cross-cultural basis that widely admits to intuition as coming from somewhere. No adequate explanation of intuition is separable from an explanation of human origin (see Laughlin, this volume). As a cross-cultural standard, that origin may be a springing forth from the ground/land—at least here in Turtle Island (North America). This is rarely taken into account. We cannot usefully discuss intuition outside of the ecology of natural, terrestrial domains, which makes the study of intuition a fundamentally organic inquiry and experience.

That said, we are obliged to discuss it as a spatiotemporal phenomenon consistent with human presence in the natural world. In effect, intuition is an element in the discussion of what it is to have intelligence on the planet, since intuition is a source of intelligence in both animals and humans. Advocates of a holistic understanding of intuition will be heartened by the research of J. E. Lovelock (1979, 1988) and Lynne Margulis and their attribution of an intelligence to the planet itself. (We suggest that this "earth intelligence" is not so distant from intuition itself.) The primal dimensions of intelligence are also advocated as applicable to the universe by cosmologist Brian Swimme (1984), whose book title *The Universe is a Green Dragon* expresses a conceptualization of the mythic elements comprising universal intelligence.

No mention of this area of reasearch and its experiential dimensions would be complete without reference to the seminal works of Paul Devereux (1982, 1989, 1990, 1992a, b, c, 1993, 1994, 1996, Devereux et al. 1979,1989, 1992, 1994, 1996), whose intercultural studies have greatly added the dimension of place to the study of intelligence. Devereux has been using the study of ancient ceremonial sites and landscapes as a "royal road" for attempting to understand traditional relationships between mind and the natural environment. He sees monuments as "fossils of consciousness" or nodes set up in mind states different from the monophasic mentality that pervades modern culture—hence the problem the modern mind has in fully interpreting ancient sacred places. He sees "prehistory" as precisely analagous to the unconscious, and history as the equivalent to the modern waking mind—indeed the concepts of prehistory and history are simply the reflections of these different levels of consciousness. In this model, then, ancient sacred places are like fragments of dreams we struggle to remember and make sense of, and need to be approached in that mode of mentation. The West lost this "dream-like" or mythic sense of place in classical times, when the old Greek word for the imaginative and evocative dimensions of place, *chora*, became divorced from the physical and utilitarian sense of place, expressed as *topos*. Devereux feels that unless we can re-mind ourselves about this archaic sense of place, more grandiose ambitions about ecology and environmental psychology will founder. To Devereux, "intuition" is a state of communication, individually expressed in an interaction between the conscious and unconscious mind, through the medium of dreams, visions, and feelings. In the transpersonal sphere, this dynamic is expressed individually, socially, culturally, in a mythic relationship between mind and nature—a meeting between the interiority of things: soul-to-soul with *anima mundi*.

Growth Rings

Any suggestion that intuition is exclusively primal, and so is somehow a-cultural, signals the conceit of a modernist whose elementally misanthropic opinion of ancestors implies that primal people, because they achieved ecological integrity, were not cultural. To suggest that intuition, like the rest of primal nature, is disappearing because it is not being valued, codes intuition as an endangered quality akin, perhaps, to the qualitative difference between a forest and a tree farm. If this is so, the extent to which we view intelligence as a domestic quality becomes the extent to which its primal qualities are endangered precisely because they are wild. It may be appropriate to view intuition as a type of intelligence whose origin and engagement happen best in the natural world.

For example, consider the growth rings of a tree. Assuming that the genesis of intuitive thought begins in childhood and, if underutilized, diminishes in importance as the child grows, there still remains within every human the presence of that earlier capacity, just as there is evidence of the sapling in the girth of an old growth tree. This example requires us to see our own origin and subsequent place of being in the natural world. If we can do this, we have a context for seeing modernist intelligence as domesticated intelligence, and for recognizing that, however powerful domesticated intelligence may be, it is not apart from intuition.

Domesticated Minds

Domesticated intelligence is made easier to recognize by the ready availability of urban surroundings. Domesticated surroundings legitimate domesticated minds because they prioritize those understandings and fixations that are largely alienated from wild nature, be that wilderness a forest or a psyche. Or to conflate that statement, in domesticated surroundings intelligence is seen as socially manifest, whereas intuition may be more nearly liminal with those cultural and natural habitats as they comprise our ancestral past. But seeing intuition as solely vestigial misses the point that it is integral to our beings, just as wild nature once was—and effectively still is.

So long as we have or can find ways to employ intuition in our lives, so long as we give it empirical credence, then we may understand how it is implicit in an ecology of the sensorium. Part of how intuition gets overlooked can be explained by the very absence of a somatically integrated intelligence in living modern life. Contemporary life privileges and burdens the visual and the cerebral as the primary senses of our conduct; thus the intuitive can easily become obscured or ignored in electronic urban culture.

As a further condition, it may be important to specify that wild temporal and spatial environments remain a part of us just as growth rings in a tree are always part of that tree. As Cobb noted, mind and place are co-evolutionary—one is the source of the other. Intuiting a sacred place on earth requires resonance with a sacred place in our minds.

The Nature/Culture Split

We take it as self-evident that seeing a divide between nature and culture is artificial, because it motivates an attitude to the natural that is corrosive. We suggest that such exclusion of the natural from the cultural can create unhealthy, unnatural, and

incomplete environments with immediate disastrous long- and short-term consequences for humans and their surroundings. An equation that separates nature from
culture fails to recognize the contiguities between self and nature, to the point
where we create multitudinous false dichotomies that distinguish between intuition
as an intelligence that populates the planet and the intelligence we call our own. In
so doing, we have made our minds into natural aliens (Evernden 1985) and become
solipsists whose minds are the domiciles we inhabit as agoraphobics unwilling to
accept the consequences of and responsibility for ourselves in the larger context of
Mother Earth. We are much akin to a cultural adolescent able to see the apron
strings of one mother but unwilling to cut them to know the mother's Mother, the
Earth. Seeing ourselves as natural aliens, even within a postmodernist framework, is
an unacceptable cosmology if we seek a compelling narrative of the human place in
nature. Nevertheless, such an outlook continues to influence our internal and mental environment to further create disenfranchised perspectives on the place of mind
in nature. One can hardly hope to build a holistic sense of intelligence from these
cold ashes of Cartesian divorce.

Intuition As a Planetary Phenomenon

Seeing intuition as a planetary phenomenon of mind made manifest in its creatures
allows us to be in nature and allows nature, in turn, to be in us (Maturana and
Varela 1988). Disallowing that symbiosis impacts not only our concept of what
intelligence is but also, at the same time, disallows our inclusion in the natural order
that is our very origin. However basic this insight, the potential such an exclusion
holds for environmental vilification is sorrowful.

A healthier ecological premise is needed to inform a definition of mind or intelligence that preserves the idea of the earth as both intuition's origin and the milieu
required for its continued existence. This premise would require us to understand
the primal nature in our immediate environment, in order to establish a potential
for re-creating or maintaining a convivial relationship between our minds and the
places where we live. To accomplish such re-creation, we would argue for restoration
of natural environments of mythic and intuitive proportions—in short, for intentionally planting a forest or returning a landscape to a condition where the primal
mind could again make stories from intuiting the meaning or spirit of the place.
That spirit, we believe, exists in that place and is stronger than the concrete and
asphalt apparitions of affluence that hide it.

If there is resonance and reciprocity between the integrity of the natural systems
that surround us and our own intuition, then we have created for an ecology of
intelligence an ethic akin to Aldo Leopold's when he stated, "A thing is right when
it tends to preserve the integrity, stability, and beauty of the biotic community. It is
wrong when it tends otherwise" (1952: 224–225). In the case of an ecology of intelligence, we can point to the disappearance of the legitimacy of intuition as concurrent with the loss of our experience with biodiversity. In either case, monocultures

of mind (Shiva 1993) or land are never justifiable if our goal is sustainable health in each.

Ethic of Mind

Thus arises the possibility of describing a principle. Just as the environment that we inhabit in ourselves needs to be resonant with those biological systems within which we also live, so we are locally secure when our cultural models reflect the local. Then, we are required to think in locally evident ways. Locally grounded cultural models enable us to maintain that sense of security that accompanies knowing where we belong, for we are ultimately local beings. Because the natural world falls into places, and because these places, in their totality, form a planetary system, it makes sense to see the intuitive not only as *having* a place, but also as *needing* a place. When those places have ecological stability, with humans playing their part to ensure that stability, intuition may have as many faces as the biodiversity that makes up the planet. Recognizing that everything is connected to everything else, we can say that all of creation also comprises an earthmind (Devereux, Steele, and Kubrin 1989). Ignoring the natural world when describing intelligence is thereby an act of repression and an affront to the possibility of an ecology of intelligence (and vice versa).

Inside/Outside

To gain a sense of this earthmind, we must recognize that earth is as much in us as we are in/of it. We eat it in vegetable matter as it is absorbed into the soil our bodies dissolve into as we return to the earth when it is our time. The water that comprises the majority of our being is the medium that allows our cells to be fully replaced in our bodies every seven years (Benton-Banai 1988, Egan 1979). My point here is that although intuition is generally not culturally recognized nor socially accounted for, merely recognizing its presence in daily life would amply demonstrate its existence. As we moved out of the predominantly natural environment, we lost sight of intuition only to rediscover it as putatively abnormal within the modern, urban milieu. Conventional definitions of intelligence do not include an adequate description of intuition because of a conceit whose essence is as false as it is venal. The lived mistake is that our notion of intelligence negates the empirical proof that satisfies and sustains an Irish mother at sundown. This conceit holds that there is an authentic division between intuition and intelligence. We argue that one without the other motivates a divisiveness that creates the epistemological ethic implicated in environmental destruction. By devaluing intuition we, at the same time, devalue those environments most conducive to its survival.

If intuition could find a validation that is empirically sound and experientially realized, this error would encounter far fewer advocates. Such an accounting might undo the injurious thematic of estrangement between modernity and antiquity and between us and the multitudinous realms within senate nature. But rather, let the

Joe Sheridan and Anne Pineault

burden of proof be shifted to the Cartesian notion of isolated domains. We would ask instead that those who wish to maintain the division first be made to support its existence.

What follows, I hope, is a proposition for the recovery of an ultimately healthy principle. If we are, in large measure, the sum of the things we think with, then we must be sensitive to the organisms that make up the places where we live. How those organisms can teach us what those places mean comes first from being sensitive to them, and then from understanding the meaning of interacting with them. Of course, the capacity for this kind of thinking builds on a corresponding belief in the validity of these interactive organisms as manifestations of a self-organizing intelligence. As children, we think and play with the organisms we find in the places where we live; the more we are outdoors, the more likely we are to interact with them. Being with these organisms outdoors means building better foundations for knowing and prizing what they can teach us. Biodiversity and biophilia are, in effect, what builds our intelligence both about and within the natural world.

Starting with the participatory consciousness of our earliest years, and moving toward that other place of dependency and intimacy in our old age, we see how our belonging in that place where we live changes. And we reflect on the many meanings that have accrued to that favorite tree of our youth over the years. In that way, we know our minds to be connected to places, and we know that the mind is also a place. Seeing the mind in this spatial and ecological sense allows us to understand why we need natural places to think with, and how thinking with them is a sacred communion. The unidimensional qualities of many of the media we think with (like print, for instance) create minds whose reference points have little to do with places in the natural world. Learning to think in the multidimensional ways appropriate to understanding mind spatially and ecologically may make us a little agoraphobic at first. But that fear of the outdoors can also be seen as the first step in overcoming our fear of having a mind that looks like and thinks like the land.

Restoration: We Are What We Intuit

The subject of this chapter has been not only what intuition *is* but also how what we do with it informs how we understand it. So it is reasonable to ask how we value ourselves as places and processes and how this creates a simultaneity that is both an ethic and a measure of our ability to restore ourselves and the places where ourselves happen—and to be mindful of the health that such an accomplishment would provide. Such a unity may throw us at first, but if we wanted an idea of what seventy thousand years of having mind in nature and nature in mind looked like, the late Linda Akan made a compressed statement that is a good place to start. Speaking as a Salteaux woman, she wrote:

> If one were to try to give a metaphorical description of some of the features of First Nations thought, one might say that they go to school in dreams,

write in iconographic imagery, travel in Trickster's vehicle, and always walk around. (1993: 213)

As a cultural foundation, Akan's summary of the implications of resonance between our beings and our surroundings may be uncomfortable for the modernist who fears the relations between the intuitive and the mythological. Yet, if we are to again make intuition a safe and valued part of our culture, it is necessary to recognize that intuition's return as an integral aspect of our intelligence may be best achieved in surroundings convivial to its substantiation, development, and exercise. This suggests that we are wild creatures whose exclusive domestication does not honor our identity. We would furthermore infer that the wild is a quality both of people and places, and that the difference between a tree farm and a forest is that quality. Our nervous systems can become the equivalent of a tree plantation instead of, say, a Druid's grove. Having surroundings convivial to the development of intuition is one of the surest ways to bring intuition back to health.

We suggest that restoration of wild places is convivial to the restoration of a renewed role for the symbiosis of wild intelligence made manifest in mind as in natural landscape. A renewed role for intuition in our lives would mean a renewed role for the natural environment, both in our daily life and in our ability to re-conceive of the meaning of intelligence as a symbiosis of the real and the symbolic. Our claim is that just as natural places have been obliterated by pavement, lawns, televisions, and strip malls, so too has domination extended to mind and being. Our concern is not so much for who may have ownership or autonomy within those monocultural environments, but rather to suggest that those environments are absolutely unfavorable ways of being.

However, we are not saying that people or places cannot recover from these conditions. We believe that there is an integrity in nature, our own included, more powerful than pavement and poured concrete. We admit that its strength is endangered and that Mother Earth may be losing both patience and the ability to be patient. Our point is that replanting those environments to again teem with the creatures of nature and their interconnections will return to our culture an intuitive sense of how to again think with the intelligence of those places and their creatures (including us)—and of how to watch as that symbiosis restores and renews and teaches us, through our participation within it, what it means to be integral to an environment of self-organizing intelligence made possible through restored biodiversity.

Power of Place

To understand what the power of place (Alexander Pope called it the "genius of place") may offer the study and practice of intuition, the writings of University of Alberta professor and Cree scholar Stanley Wilson (1994) make a significant starting point. He recounts his experience of attending an education conference in

Georgia and speaking Cree with his wife Peggy on the grounds of a college there. Initially, he was overcome with a feeling of elation he had never before experienced, then later fell into the grip of a debilitating depression. And so, on his return to Saskatchewan Indian Federated College, he sought the advice of Lionel Kinunnma, a Lakota-speaking Minnecujo. Lionel's response accounts for only one aspect of Professor Wilson's multifaceted encounter in Georgia. In Stanley's words this is what happened:

> He listened very intently to my story. When I was finished he told me that I had had what they refer in Lakota *ta as wanbli iwan yanks pi*. It roughly translates into English as "They are as watching Eagles." The Eagle referred to the way older people gain a telescopic perspective of time/life/energy. A person attaining this level of perception gains a different concept of life including the spiritual structure of life. This energy was always there when we became two-legged (perhaps that is what is referred to as molecular structure). We humans emerged from the spirit-only-time and we can still connect to that time under the right circumstances. A person doesn't need to go vision-questing. When everything is in the right place it will happen if the person is attuned to it. Lionel likened it to a parking lot full of cars all lined up except one. When it too becomes lined up a person can see through all the windows past the cars and see whatever was previously blocked out by the irregularly placed car. It seems that only older people report having these visionary experiences because younger people are usually too preoccupied with other interests. Those who have such experiences but don't talk about them are practicing self-oppression. . . .
>
> "You had a ten thousand year old experience," he told me. "A long time ago most of the northern part of the American continent was covered with ice. Your ancestors moved ahead of the ice southward. For generations they lived and died in that area. It was only after the great ice fields melted they began to move northwards again. Since most of the human body is composed of water, when we die that moisture returns to the atmosphere. In essence the atmosphere is sacred, as it is made up of moisture of our ancestors. Since generations of your ancestors have been supplying that area with life-giving moisture, their presence has become part of the total ecosystem. . . ."
>
> So what Lionel was telling me about was that something during my walk about on that campus in Georgia triggered ancient memories contained within the biological cells of my bones, my marrow, my skin cells passed on for generations by my ancestors. And that there was a communication between what I was genetically made up of and whatever traces of the ancestors were present at the site. (Wilson 1993)

Stanley Wilson's point is that his ancestors were literally *in* the land; because he spoke a tongue that had not been heard there for more than a century (since the Trail of Tears holocaust), his ancestors were most happy to see him until they finally got around to communicating about the many who had been murdered and evicted by colonial troops.

Intuition and Turtle Island

If intuition studies can learn from indigenous tradition lessons about what it means to be in Turtle Island, the first lesson may be the need to allow intuition to hear the spirit of the place. If you try to do so, prepare for an intelligence that accords interconnection between all those things that make up everything, to again know the territory in its richness. To concentrate on its maps to the exclusion of its dynamic Weltanschauung is the essence of our error. To do the thinking of Turtle Island is to learn how to regain that balance. Stanley Wilson and Linda Akan ask that we recognize that the walk of life in Turtle Island is one of affection and openness. These do not derive from information, but from the exploration of the nooks and crannies that make up the places of the land and the mind, according to each a quality of intelligence because each is made up of the other. With that appreciation, the "other" dwindles in its identifiable separateness, and in its place comes a quality of heart, an ethos of love, and an environmental ethic that reverses the validity of the idea that we are separate from nature. Fear of the wild and natural places comes together as fear of self, for self too is a wild place. In the dual fear of both, we watch this culture moving increasingly into domestication, creating a technosphere that allows us to arrange the world so that the natural is increasingly less experienced. Rootless and separated from the wisdom of the land, we pour our efforts into round-the-clock, nanosecond refinement of an intelligence beset by agoraphobia, feverishly cramming spiritless digital images of the world into virtual reality technologies convivial to no ancestor whatsoever.

Should intuition become a divining rod that fathoms what it means to be on the earth, to again be indigenous, it will have to admit that land and stories are its inseparable articulations. Going the distance from an egocentric to an ecocentric perspective advantages the possibility of rebuilding natural diversity, and so demonstrating a biophilia that wishes equally to build a culture and an intelligence cognizant that success can be gauged by the quality of its surroundings. What Cobb, Leopold, Akan, and Wilson offer is a beginning to the process of what is jointly a cultural and an ecological restoration. While Francisco Varela reminds us that this place we seek to restore is not one place and not two places either, his directive is clear: become part of it (Dooling and Jordan-Smith 1989).

If walking this talk is to be demonstrated by anyone aware of the issues, I believe Anne Pineault would be a key figure in the solutions and remedies we can propose. What follows is the scoping of the problem of intuition from the perspective of a country-raised Mic' Maq artist and graduate student in environmental studies now living in a southern Ontario city. In her thinking about her own displacement from traditional rural life, she has sought to adhere to and restore cultural traditions that permit her to maintain an ecocentric life undaunted by urban distractions. Let us follow her record of a traditionalist's life in the big city.

Part II: Intuition As Old Growth and Narrative of Self

Anne Pineault

When Joe Sheridan and I first began our discussions about intuition, we discovered that we had both had an intuitive feeling that we would be meeting each other. In those discussions, we realized that we had never really accounted for such qualities as we possess, such as, for example, distant seeing and receptivity to feelings we associated with places we had come to regard as sacred or special. Joe had resonated with the Big Horn Mountains in Wyoming and was compelled to go there, and those feelings and that place led him to Carl Urion in distant Edmonton, Alberta. Similar things have happened to me and I cannot regard them as random coincidences, in part because my cultural background (and I think Joe's too) has a way to explain these patterns. This explanation has to do with understanding the first principle of ecology, which Joe mentioned in the preceding section: *everything is connected to everything else.* So we think in circles, and realize that each tiny thing in the center sends out ripples that touch distant perimeters—and vice versa. My research in the Faculty of Environmental Studies at York University allows me to continue to subscribe to this paradigm, and to develop my art along lines that are in keeping with my sacred traditions.

In preparation for my part in writing this chapter, I consulted the Oxford dictionary and found intuition defined as "an immediate insight or understanding without conscious reasoning." The important part of this sentence is "without conscious reasoning." The immediate assumption is that intuition is generated from a place that is "apart" and therefore beyond our control. It can never be measured, controlled, or classified and as such, remains suspect within scientific communities.

When I make this statement it is not to dismiss the various peoples who are attempting to study this phenomenon, or to silence their voices by legitimating science. It is simply to reiterate that which is already known. We all remain suspect when we attempt to find scientific validation for our simple "truths." When I was approached to contribute in this article I needed to access my own "truth" very quickly. My initial response was negative. I agreed only when I was able to clarify that I would be able to write from a personal perspective.

This agreement presented a unique set of problems that I found difficult to assess. Primarily, what was my personal perspective ? How do I perceive my own understanding of intuition? When was I first aware of this phenomenon and what do I have to say about it ? What feeds these intuitive responses and from where do they arise?

Perhaps the most important distinction between Western thought patterns and First Nations understanding of intuition lies in the latter's rootedness in space and not time. The linear construction that dominates the historical approaches of the Western tradition is not at the center nor is it the focus of Native consciousness. This is not to say that Natives are not aware of the concept of time or that Western traditions ignore space. Yet, it is within this specific cultural difference that I find a starting point from which to begin the journey to my understanding of intuition. Other First Nations people may not agree with me. As I made clear earlier, I am simply speaking from a personal perspective.

Primarily, I believe that the First Nations perspective on intuition is based in the inherent teachings, which are land based and contain the inherent concepts or tools needed to understand the functioning of participating consciousness within a land-based philosophy. These teachings do not question or put forth a tentative ideology that *perhaps* there is an inherent consciousness. They firmly instill the fact that there *is* a participating consciousness and that we are a part of it and not separate from it. In the teachings, I recognize and acknowledge my position and how "I walk" on Turtle Island. When I speak about "my walk," I distinctly wish it to be perceived as the essence of my being and how it interacts with the other forms of consciousness in this measurable plane, which most humans consider to be the interactive world.

For endless time our ancestors have lived with and on this plane. They have walked it, and understood through the teachings of the Medicine Wheel that on one level of the multi-layered teachings, the four directions hold together in the same equal balance the four colors of humans (red, black, white, yellow) and the four nations—the human nations, the animal nations, the bird nations, and the plant nations—encompassing all that is created. In this understanding, we do not find "man" positioned at the apex, with all other forms of life in a subservient position. Humans are required to relinquish their dominating position and enter into an equal partnership with the rest of creation. In this way we are required to recognize the presence of all things/beings in creation. The understanding contained within the teachings is that the Great Mystery will answer our prayers, providing we follow the teachings that state that we are to respect all of creation, that we are only part of creation's extended family.

When one consciously walks in the path of the ancestors and attempts to understand and participate in their land-based memory and their ancient ways, we find peoples who spent their lives becoming experts at survival. They found a way to communicate and exist with Nature rather than trying to tame or dominate it. When we participate fully in the exchange we also understand that the spirit lives, that the ancestor spirit is alive within us, as well as surviving in the soil, leaves, and rocks and within the rest of creation. One of the strongest indicators of this process is to be found in the ceremonies that have been handed down through the oral tradition and the teachings of the Elders for countless generations. The ceremonies become a metaphor "naming" how one must approach the land: with silence, attentiveness, patience, respect, and a sense of timelessness. This metaphor attends to the energy patterns of other beings, wherein, at a certain juncture or positioning, a vector allows for meaningful communication or immediate insight without conscious thought. Therefore, one must sanction oneself to be conscious of an unconscious state in order to experience the transition. In this way, we experience and learn that we are constantly in a state of becoming and moving with or through the teachings of "all" participating consciousnesses in Creation. We also awaken to our ethereal position and come to the realization that the measurable plane, so well defined by the scientific paradigm, is simply one strand in the web of creation.

If modern physics maintains that all matter is energy shaping itself into particular patterns, is it so difficult to accept that we are simply one of the patterns? Is it such a radical departure from everyday thinking to believe that we are interconnected in inexplicable ways to others through land-based memory, DNA structures, participatory consciousness, or other patterns we are not yet conscious of in our evolutionary development?

One of the most common criticisms I encounter is the ever popular comment that we as First Nations peoples should bring our thinking into the twentieth century. "We," according to popular consensus, "are caught between Tradition and modernization." When I examine the multi-layered social, political, economic, and spiritual pressures placed on First Nations structures, I must agree with this criticism. Perhaps the words of Chief Dan George in 1967 give an understanding of the challenges of the transition we must make:

> I was born a thousand years ago. Born in a culture of bows and arrows. But within the span of half a lifetime, I was flung across the ages to the culture of the atomic bomb. And that is a flight far beyond a flight to the moon.

On the other hand, if I look carefully at the global environmental and spiritual transition of the recent past and the state the world is in at this particular point, I see few reasons to abandon my traditional outlook to become one of the *wasicu* (modern settler peoples).

It appears that many people are searching for the reasons connected to their season of discontent. I am constantly in dialogue with people who are puzzled, lost, and in tremendous pain and alienation. They remain in holding patterns, much like a jet circling an airport, waiting for an emergency to be cleared up under them so they may land. There are children being reared by more than a significant number of the population who are functioning under the mind-numbing effects of Prozac, alcohol, cocaine, and crack, to name a few, as well as the artificial reality set forth by electronic media. Young people in today's society are waiting with bated breath for the electronic age to take them away from the actuality of their parents' guilt and confusion. They speak of the electronic superhighway with all the fervor and elation of propagandists' raising adoring fists to the vigil of a Nazi redeemer. They view the electronic age as being the source of "power," and the entelechy within those systems as guiding their path to a new environment both sterile and pure. This abstraction almost demands on their part a transition to a technologized state of being, a longing for and intense desire to become the cyborg. The effects of this escapism are marked by an innate fear of aging, the too-familiar empty rituals of meaningless body alterations through cosmetic surgery and multiple piercings.

As a mother and one who believes in the accountability and responsibility of each of my actions affecting the next seven generations, I must consciously examine these concepts carefully and attempt to find a balance within the "generation gap." I do not advocate the removal or negate the significant value of the electronic age—I am perhaps as guilty of harboring an underlying excitement in that regard as the rest of the millions of users. Nor do I wish to discredit the advances made within the medical model. I merely wish to reiterate the necessity of recognizing the inherent pitfalls of one more time constantly looking at a visionary landscape (linearity) without recognizing that it is only one of many landscapes (spatiality). The starting point is understanding the inherent internal landscape, which will ground us firmly and become the fulcrum for generating generational balance.

Therefore, I choose to continue to understand the teachings of the ancestors, the ceremonies, and the oral tradition through the Elders. It is within this context where perception arose that the ancestors understood the energy patterns to extend beyond modern scientific explanation. The teachings clearly demonstrate that patterns of energy contain an inherent consciousness that is made manifest by an act of will. This interconnection occurs within levels of creation as well as through an active participation in various forms of communication between the different worlds.

To demonstrate this point, allow me to share a story. When the Great Mystery was laying out the master plan for Creation, the Spirit forces came forth to request their positions. During this time a large boom rang out at four separate intervals. The Great Mystery, unable to find what was making the sound, requested that the stars shine bright so that the source might be made visible, but to no avail. It was then that the voice spoke out, stating that it was the Spirit of the Drum and that it had come forth to make a request that it be included in the master plan.

In this case, the pattern remained unseen until it chose to manifest itself within the master plan of Creation. Consequently, in my own pattern, each time I play my drum I am reminded of the sacredness of the initial manifestation. I am also connected to the process and the beings whose lives are presently extended as the wood and hide comes together to form the circle of Creation. It is this multi-layering of voice that gives deeper meaning to the feeling and emotions of my heart and its connection to my extended family and their universal heartbeat.

One can then say that this is understandable in the context of myth or the story, but what has it to do with an understanding of present-day reality? Allow me to layer one story over another to bring into focus another experience that occurred two weeks prior to the writing of this chapter.

I went with a colleague to a non-Native Christian preschool to present a cultural workshop to the children. We spent time explaining the concept of the circle, sweetgrass, the Eagle feather, and so on. After break we resumed and I began by showing the children my pipe and explaining the process and the meaning contained within its symbolism. At this point one of the teachers stated that the children had been to a museum and had seen a pipe. Therefore, never being one to miss an opportunity, I began to explain why it was very important for First Nations people to see the pipe displayed in the proper way when it is held by a museum. As I joined the bowl and the stem together to indicate the sacredness of the union, one of the small children sitting directly across from me in the circle immediately began to attempt to get my attention.

I noticed him looking up at the ceiling and then at the bowl of my pipe. He kept saying, "Miss, Miss, look in the pipe! Look in the pipe!" I looked into the bowl of the pipe, which was predictably blackened from use, and looked at him and said, "Ah, what is it that you see in there?" He immediately responded by saying, "There is a big (symbol) in your pipe!" I immediately responded by explaining to him that what he had seen was very important because it was connected to the Elder who had taught me all about the pipe. I then asked him how the (symbol) had gotten into the pipe. He responded by saying that it had come down through the ceiling and had gone into my pipe. I asked him how it had gone into the pipe. He said he wasn't sure, that it had just "gone into the bowl of the pipe."

In this case the Elder had taught me about the pipe, had commissioned the bowl, had participated in my sweats and fasting and the rituals around the earning of my pipe. This blond, blue-eyed child of four years intuitively entered into this process and recognized the connection between us, although there was no visible manifestation nor had anyone ever mentioned the symbol at any time. I do not claim to understand why this child experienced the visualization of the spirit unveiling, but I do understand that such things occur far more often than society will admit.

After the children had left, the teachers asked me how he knew about the symbol. The only explanation I could give was that he had seen it, and that it is quite natural for a child of that age to express what he sees. Young children will often speak of dreams as if they were reality and as if reality were dreams. Such children are open doorways to all levels of reality; in the final analysis, are we the dreamers or the dreamed? In this same interaction, the teachers started to share experiences they had never disclosed to their colleagues or others unless they were extremely close to them. This disclosure occurred as a result of a safe environment where they would not be ridiculed.

A couple of days later I went to Toronto to present a workshop at a university and stayed at a friend's place. I was relating the experience to her when she looked at me and stated that she felt much better. Responding to my puzzled expression, she explained that the previous evening she had taken her four-year-old upstairs to bed and was making little prayers with him. When they were finished, he looked around the room and smiled and whispered to her, "Mummy, look at all the little fairies that are here with us." Again, was this an intuitive response to the visible manifestation of the little people, as I know them to be called within the oral tradition? Or was it a materialization from his Celtic tradition? Would his mother be able to return to her university position the next day and discuss this openly and not be subject to ridicule?

The point I am making with these stories is that no one culture has ownership over intuition or over any spiritual process. It seems apparent that it is the cultural approach to the social, educational, and spiritual methods that makes the participants doubt their abilities and negate their process and understanding. They master denial, usually at a young age when they are not even aware that the spiritual process exists. This reminds me of a quotation from Gaston Bachelard:

> It might perhaps be simpler if we were to follow the tried and true methods of the psychologist who describes what he observes, measures levels, and classifies types—who sees imagination being born in children without ever really examining how it dies in ordinary men. (1971: 2)

We are all undeniably victims of such methodologies. At what level of awareness do some of us make a conscious choice to return to the womb in the metaphysical sense to restart the process and re-enchant our lives?

One of the questions that I have been asked by people of all cultures is, "Where do we start to find our path?" In many cases these people are standing in the shadow of colonial guilt, feeling disconnected from a land mass they feel has been taken from its rightful owners. They appear burdened with the shame of their ancestors' behavior patterns, which continue today both on this continent and in all of the Americas. They stand powerless against the multinational corporations that continue the destruction on a global scale. Many women feel that patriarchal organized religions offer little in the way of female-centered rituals that allow for strong self-recognition and actualization.

In most of the cases I am unable to find adequate answers, yet I can sympathize with the pain and confusion. The only comfort I can offer is that no one has ownership over Mother Earth. First Nations peoples have been given, through the inherent teachings, the position of stewardship for the land and will maintain that position for as long as it is physically possible. The effects of colonialism on First Nations people were devastating. However, because of our inherent teachings and our unshakable belief in the Creator, we know that we will succeed in fulfilling our roles. I also understand that perhaps few nations have had to scrutinize their societies in the way the First Nations have had to do. As a result, we are seeing a return to our spiritual beliefs and our own educational, medical, and legal systems. The

Elders and Clan Mothers are strengthening their roles and are being sought out for their counsel by all members of their society. The children are being educated at unprecedented rates. The universities are becoming aware of the difference in First Nations consciousness and are being challenged by the students to accommodate this difference. All levels of government are being held accountable to find solutions to the land and treaty rights disputes. Alcohol and substance abuse programs are becoming commonplace and healing circles are ever-expanding in First Nations communities and beyond. First Nations culture is now reflected in the mass media, mainstream art galleries, theaters, on the music charts, in literary circles, in university curriculums, and on international levels.

This is not to say that all is exemplary in First Nations culture. We still have many critical problems, but we are taking control and are finding solutions. We are walking our own paths to self-determination. I firmly believe that much of our success has been due to our strong spiritual beliefs. Therefore, if I were able to make a recommendation to anyone, it would be to center an inward gaze into his/her own being and culture. Ask for spiritual guidance in a way that is comfortable for you. Have an unfaltering belief that your answers will emerge. The test of intuition's experiential validity is at least the measure of allowing it to happen.

Some of our main resources are the spiritual Elders who so generously share their time with us as we look for particular and intuitive responses to the natural walk. They have a way of entering into our consciousness and opening pathways that are nonexistent prior to their generous giving. I spend my time with many people—Elders, colleagues, and friends—who have a deep understanding of the spiritual process. These insights, sites, and sights as well as hindsight about the spiritual paths are spoken of constantly, with respect and reverence for the Great Mystery.

The concept of the Story-teller and the stories is among the most valuable treasures First Nations have maintained; it is a vast source of intuitive tools. The stories are created by the People from the inner and actual landscapes. They are the resonance of ancient voices describing their world and how that world interacts with the present. The creation stories unfold in a tapestry of understanding of how "Otherness" is woven into the ever-emerging, shifting patterns of Creation. The words are chosen carefully because they are imbued with their own essence. They contain the sacred passage to the inexplicable, a bridge connecting the worlds, revealing how deeper levels of understanding equal their rate of emergence. They are the sacred word maps pulled from the sacredness of the land. They chart the course we walk and can be named the tracings of virtual geography. Through the stories, we are named. They reveal the ancestors' codes that guide our paths through unseen territory. They reveal the hidden landscape of the mind as we spiral in and out of uncharted memory. They perceive our essence by giving meaning to our personal mythologies and unveiling our signs and symbols. They are the essence of memory tracings guiding us to the initiation rites that position our relatives and ourselves on the web of life.

They are our guides in auditory and visual language, for some are literally written on the stones and the only way to perceive them is to make a pilgrimage to the sacred sites. It is difficult to understand the stories of other nations. They do not work for us, as they are born of their landscape and of their sacred truth. These stories may be enjoyed and used as examples but one must treat them as fragile—they are only shared for a brief moment. They can broaden our understanding of difference, and in doing so give us a deeper understanding of ourselves. Yet we must find and make our own stories as we journey across this sacred land.

Perhaps the most important element of a story is the discovery of a particular symbol and the enlightenment it brings to our lives. First Nations peoples are constantly aware of the symbols that surround them in actual and metaphysical landscapes. This awareness does not occur through classification or a physical description of the "object." One can say that this is a tree because it is round and hard with green things growing on it. The same applies to the eagle, the hawk, or the sparrow. Naming is only one form of recognition that helps us to learn their physicality and how to identify them. Then comes the desire to know who they are, what their purpose is, and what their teaching abilities are. These are their greatest gifts.

A friend of mine and I had a recent conversation with a First Nations man who explained to us that he was a truck driver who had recently decided not to drive anymore and had just resigned his position. My friend asked him if it was because he was away from home too much. He stated that a few days earlier he had been driving down the highway when an eagle smashed into the front window, almost causing him to lose control and roll his truck into a ravine. My friend immediately asked if everyone was OK. He then said, no, that he had broken his arm but it was fixed and he was going to be all right. The conversation ended and he went on his way. My friend commented on the fact that the driver did not mention who "he" was. I laughed and she seemed more confused than ever. I had to tell her that he was talking about the eagle!

This story helps one to comprehend how an understanding of the symbol goes beyond the subject/object relationship of most classifications. The us/it syndrome becomes a we/we relationship and a dialogue occurs at the level of the essence of the other being. This is an invaluable gift in our current position where most people are afraid or suspicious of Nature. If more people could understand the participating consciousness within our environment, there would be less abuse and domination over natural resources, capital, investment property, or whatever other terms the moneymakers care to call Nature. Our stories are born out of the sacredness of the land and they are our symbolic guides. Yet these symbols are being destroyed at an unprecedented rate. The rate of species extinction is frightening and incalculable as the chain reaction occurs through the food chain and across the ecological integrity of the land. An Elder once told me that the species are not being made extinct only through monetary abuse but also because we have abandoned them. We are not doing our physical and spiritual work by honoring and caring for them in the proper way. There is too little dialogue with the Sacred. A truck driver who knows what it means when the eagle comes to call also knows that this is not coincidence but guidance, and can be so understood with an open mind. Like Einstein, First Nations cultures know that the Great Spirit does not play dice with the universe.

First Nations people recognize that story-telling is the oldest form of education. It is also a venue that allows the sharing of the sacred knowledge and respect for the practices of the people. The stories grow, shift, and change with the teller and the life experiences of the people. Yet they always loop around and return to their source, the sacred Mother Earth. We women intuitively understand this knowledge when we give birth to our children. In that act of creating life, a paradox emerges, as we also understand that we will in turn return to our source, the giver of life, the Sacred Earth.

In this chapter, there are many words about the story and the story-teller and what it means to be a participant in the story. The most important realization we can come to is that we are the story—the text, the subtext, and the final epitaph. We will become the ancestors in the generations to come, and the extension of our wisdom will be the intuition of the future. Therefore let us envision future stories filled with wisdom and enlightenment and let them be guides for those waiting to enter the earth walk. Let them narrate a different measure, one of healing the Sacred Hoop for all nations. Let us not forget that we must ultimately end our earth walk and move into a different dimension. Therefore, I leave you with the words taught to me by an Ojibway Elder, Shkima, "And let my eyes ever behold the red and purple sunsets, so when my life fades like the setting sun, my Spirit can come to You without shame."

Stories, like the land, are places where intuition speaks, and where nature's self-organizing intelligence is demonstrated. Like land, which makes intelligence from its physical elements, story divines the meaning of that physicality by asserting Mother Earth's spiritual dimensions. We speak in story after land manifests meaning. Minds live somewhere, and intuition may be our best bet for knowing where and why.

Conclusion

Joe Sheridan

In conceiving of intuition as a place and a process, we can begin to think of its relations with other places and qualities. In so doing, we open the possibility of creating an environmental ethic that values a vision of mental health inseparable from the spiritual and ecological. A biophilia that seeks to love and think with things themselves is resonant with an imperative to *be somewhere*. As modest a proposal as this may be, it remains a contrarian's objection to a culture increasingly living both everywhere and nowhere at once. Everywhere is achieved by speed of light communication and nowhere, as Joshua Meyerowitz (1989) reminds us, is the home we make in everywhere. To this I would add that it is also the home nowhere and everywhere makes in us. The problem with disappearing into a nanosecond is that we never imagined it was so big in there. Believing *ourselves* to be the most important place in the world is a villainy revealed in even the most minor expedition into rotting infrastructures and landfills, or stockyards and stock markets. There lies, at its most venal and engorged, the tic that is the consequence of our denial. Ugly, murderous, leaking, and accusatory, there unfolds an affrontery to our instincts of unrivaled malignancy. There can be no denial of the urgency of the problem on the instinctive and intuitive level. Not only is this Cartesian separation claiming a desperate future, but it also is making much that is ugly both tolerable and commonplace. In generating inner landscapes that are aesthetically intolerable, we create inner landscapes that prefer the comfort of illusion and virtuosity. As the integrity of biological systems suffers under the relentless pounding they daily withstand, minds cannot be far behind.

The prickling of aversion to industrial deterioration and decrepitude is a hope and a signal reminder of our hunch that there are better places for a mind to mind. In the recovery of our belief, we may find that there are better ways, that we can restore to our lives and the places where we live a resonance as beautific as Linda Akan described. In giving back to ourselves that which is necessary to a profoundly ecological existence, we are as blueberries reclaiming land once sterilized by acid rain. In gaining such a foothold, we may expect to once again establish old growth (so too with mind and being). With intuition as the guide to a lost or marginalized biophilia, there remains the possibility of "old growth meaning" consistent with old growth places and old growth children. Calvin Luther Martin recently summed up the matter by saying, "Our best hope may be in the faith Loren Eisley had that there must be a small, simple, child-sized hole in the metaphysical hedge we all walk along in life —an entrance into the awesome mindscape of the Spirit of the Earth. He was convinced a child would spot it easily—and spend the rest of his life in search of it" (1994: 287).

Martin's faith is that Sean Kane (1994) discovered that hole in his recent book, *Wisdom of the Mythtellers*. Perhaps it will be the field of mythology that signals the future direction of the study of intuition. It is certain that the mythopoeic movement within environmental studies has found adherents. In claiming the naturalness of intuition, we may wish to look at the intuition of nature as a palpable manifestation of its self-organizing intelligence. Kane phrases it this way:

> Myths sing a map of the landscape of the hunter, but they are sung from the landscape's point of view. This otherness of myth ensures that the impulses of the hunter are tuned to overall balance of life in that region. In fact, myths

often tell of a loss of balance that is righted by the initiative of a supernatural being in his or her animal form. The sense of a mutual relationship as advantageous to both animal and man is then woven as story into tribal custom, with the supernatural patron serving as the ancient kinsperson of the clan, the one who gives it special favor. (1994: 77)

Kane's "oral mapping" is a concept that allows for understanding the multiple voices of the complexities of intuition. Yet it is indisputable, we believe, that story is not possible without intuition. Whether story is the expression of intuition or not is hardly an engaging subject, but the relatedness of the two seems vitally important. Kane's implication is that wilderness and story-telling are the same thing (Sheridan, Urion, and Mackinaw 1996). Thus, if story is what happens when we understand place, then it may be intuition that divines both the sacredness of place and the appropriateness of our stories to that spirit. Seen in this context, natural places are best for the discovery of the sensibilities of intuition, as are those built places that honor the spirit of place. Taken as the aesthetic and ecological standard of nature and culture, the experience of these places allows us a standpoint from which to judge the goodness and the badness of the environments we create and live in, giving equal credibility to the importance of mindscape and landscape alike.

References Cited

Akan, Linda
  1993 "Pimosatamowin Sikaw Kakeequaywin: Walking and Talking, A Salteux Elder's View of Native Education." *Canadian Journal of Native Education*, 19: 191–214
Bachelard, Gaston
  1971 *The Poetics of Reverie*. Boston: Beacon Press.
Benton-Banai, Edward
  1988 *The Mishomis Book:The Voice of the Ojibway*. Minneapolis, MN: Red School House. (A book that considers the importance of seven-year increments in the cycle of human development.)
Cobb, Edith
  1977 *The Ecology of Imagination in Childhood*. New York: Columbia University Press.
Devereux, Paul
  1982 *Earth Lights*. London: Turnstone Press, Book Club Associates.
  1989 *Earth Lights Revelation*. London: Blandford Press.
  1990 *Places of Power*. London: Blandford Press.
  1992a *Earth Memory*. St. Paul: Llewellyn. (Originally published by London: Foulsham/ Quantum, 1991.)
  1992b *Secrets of Ancient and Sacred Places*. New York: Sterling Publishing. (Originally published by London: Blandford Press, 1992.)
  1992c *Symbolic Landscapes*. Glastonbury, UK: Gothic Image.

1993 *Shamanism and the Mystery Lines.* St. Paul: Llewllyn. (Originally published by London: Foulsham/Quantum, 1992.)

1994 *The New Ley Hunter's Guide.* Glastonbury: Gothic Image.

1996 *ReVisioning the Earth.* New York: Simon and Schuster/Fireside.

Devereux, Paul, with Geoffrey Cornelius

1996 *The Secret Language of the Stars and Planets.* San Francisco: Chronicle.

Devereux, Paul, with Laurence Main

1992 *The Old Straight Tracks of Wessex.* Cheltenham, UK: Thornhill Press.

Devereux, Paul, with Nigel Pennick

1989 *Lines on the Landscape.* London: Robert Hale.

Devereux, Paul, with Ian Thompson

1979 *The Ley Hunter's Companion.* London: Thames and Hudson. (Reissued in digest form as *The Ley Guide,* London: Empress, 1987.)

Devereux, Paul, with Craig Weatherhill

1994 *Myths and Legends of Cornwall.* Cheshire, UK: Sigma Press.

Devereux, Paul, John Steel, and David Kubrin

1989 *Earthmind: Communicating with the Living World of Gaia.* New York: Harper and Row.

Dooling, D. M. and Paul Jordan-Smith

1989 *I Become Part of It: Sacred Dimensions in Native American Life.* San Francisco, CA: HarperSanFrancisco.

Egan, Kieran

1979 *Educational Development.* New York: Oxford University Press. (In addition to Benton-Banai, this book also discusses the importance of seven-year increments in the human development cycle.)

1988 *Primary Understanding.* New York: Routledge. (See especially chapter 2, "The Domestication of the *Sauvage* Mind.")

Evernden, Neil

1985 *The Natural Alien.* Toronto: The University of Toronto Press.

Kane, Sean

1994 *Wisdom of the Mythtellers.* Peterborough, Ontario: Broadview Press.

Leopold, Aldo

1952 *A Sand County Almanac.* New York: Oxford University Press.

Lovelock, James

1979 *Gaia: A New Look at Life on Earth.* New York: Oxford University Press.

1988 *The Age of Gaia.* New York: W. W. Norton.

Martin, Calvin Luther

1994 Review on back cover of Sean Kane's *Wisdom of the Mythtellers.* Peterborough, Ontario: Broadview Press.

Maturana, Humberto and Francisco Varela

1988 *The Tree of Knowledge.* Boston: Shambala Books.

Meyerowitz, Joshua

1989 *No Sense of Place.* New York. Oxford University Press.

Sheridan, Joe, Carl Urion, and Raven Mackinaw

1996 "Wilderness and Storytelling: The Same Thing." *Canadian Journal of Native Education,* Spring.

Shiva, Vendana

1993 *Monocultures of the Mind.* Halifax, Nova Scotia: Fernwood Press.

Swimme, Brian

1984 *The Universe is a Green Dragon.* Santa Fe, NM: Bear and Company.

Wilson, Stanley

1993 "An Indigenous American's Interpretation of the Relationship between Indigenous Peoples and People of European Descent." A presentation to the World Indigenous People's Conference on Education. Wollongong, NSW, Australia.

5

WHEELS WITHIN WHEELS, BUILDING THE EARTH

Guy Burneko

Intuition, Integral Consciousness, and the Pattern That Connects

From about fifth grade on, I became very interested in evolutionary cosmology and non-Western religious tradition. Later, doctoral work in literature, philosophy of science, the evolution of consciousness, analytic psychology, symbolic anthropology, comparative philosophy, and continental philosophy at Emory's Graduate Institute of the Liberal Arts in Atlanta indulged nearly to satiety the cultivation of those interests. And it allowed me to conceive the world as being built through our sharing of meaning and not exclusively in the zone of things and stuff. The rich delights of having lived, as well, in Dalian, in the People's Republic of China, on the tundra of the Yukon-Kuskokwim delta at Bethel, Alaska, and in patches of the United States as extraordinary as Asheville, North Carolina, Oneida, New York, and the city-state of San Francisco have also been knit into my experience and helped enliven my thinking.

On these and other bases, then, this transdisciplinary chapter considers intuition nonobjectivistically and nondualistically. I take this approach because of a long-standing intrigue with how nondualist, mystical, and mythopoeic traditions of our own and other cultures complement scientific views on contemporary issues and problems. As Albert Einstein once said,

> A human being is a part of the whole called by
> us "Universe," a part limited in time and space.

He experiences himself, his thoughts and feelings
as something separated from the rest—a kind of
optical delusion of his consciousness.

In *The Ever-Present Origin*, Jean Gebser identifies a handful of "consciousness structures" and elaborates on their respective constructions of spacetime, their essences, properties, efficient, and deficient forms of manifestation, and so on. No one would accept his pat taxonomy without question, but as an overarching "score" for consciousness studies, it will serve as well as anything from such other adepts as Vico, W. I. Thompson, Spengler, Gimbutas, or Teilhard—not to mention the wisdom traditions of other cultures, and thence the paleolithic understandings still being decoded by our epoch.

Use of Gebser allows some insights concerning the topic of intuition in connection with his discussion of the "integral consciousness structure" and the way in which this structure complements and supersedes the prevailing "rational/mental" structure familiar in the so-called developed world.

Gebser's story might be put briefly as follows. There are several consciousness structures: the archaic, the magical, the mythical, the mental, and the integral. They seem to succeed and to "improve upon" one another across time. But it just looks that way because the one that tends to have predominated the past few centuries— since around the time of Leonardo and the "invention" of perspective in painting—happens to be the linear, perspectival rational/mental mode on which we pride ourselves. "Rational" indicates the relative prominence of its "deficient"— quantitative, immoderately divisive—directive/discursive form of manifestation. What the deficient rational consciousness does is spatialize and dualize thought. For instance, it makes a conception of time as a linear current with upstream and downstream sectors such that the past or upstream end is construed to "come before" (in sequence) the ("new and improved") present. And it dualizes experience into the sectors of "subject" and "object." The way we read the "history of consciousness," then, is a function of the sort of consciousness we are using.

For Gebser, the master way of thinking for several generations has been sectorizing, perspectivizing, linear, and piecemeal—so effectively that this way of thinking has eclipsed the other structures that are also accessible to us. The end of the story is that the incipient consciousness "mutation" (evidenced in Western society from around the beginning of the twentieth century) called the *integral* structure "presentiates" simultaneously all consciousness structures and allows an "aperspectival" no-longer-just-rationally-piecemeal way of being. With Gebser, the "temporal concrescence" associated with integral consciousness also permits the realization that "origin is ever-present."

In his view, the advent of integral consciousness is not a product of an evolution. To speak of an evolution of consciousness would be simply to impose the sectorizing, perspectival grid of rational thought on the *integrum* and to take the part, the linear, for the whole. Gebser speaks of mutations of consciousness, not of its "progress."

The aperspectival supersession of our usual space and time perspectives makes possible a view of intuition as an efficient practice, a knack, of holistic and non-dual integrality, and aids in a discussion of intuition and integrality with respect to the work of Carl Jung, Gregory Bateson, and others. "What is necessary," writes Gebser (1986: 268), "is that this integrity and integrality be actualized."

As with Jung, Gebser's sense is that intuition is not "supersensible" but "points to the possibilities of the whence and whither that lie within the immediate facts" (Jung 1933:93). And integral/intuitive perception, in Gebser's words, "cannot be represented but only 'awared-in-truth' " (1986: 267).

Here is a nondual understanding—intuition is the enactment and presentation of the reality-process, of ever-present origin; it is not a re-presentation in concept or insight. It is not just thinking "of" the world but embodied doing "as" the world. In archetypal terms, it is the mode of cognition of the *unus mundus*, psyche and matter as one reality (cf. von Franz 1992: 39–62). Unfortunately, "mode of cognition of" phrasings lead us to think of cognizers and things cognized that are typical of the sectorizing rational/mental consciousness structure at issue. Intuition in this chapter is not "intuition about" the way an undivided world works, but "intuition as" the way it works. Intuition is worldmaking, *poiesis* rather than *mimesis*.

The premise is that consciousness and reality are not two and that meaning, not substance alone, eventuates (as) the reality process. We may speculate that reality has no particular "essence" or "nature" but that born of meaning. The pregnancy of this notion swells with both inquiry concerning psychokinesis in the "role of consciousness in the establishment of physical reality" on the one side, and the premise of a hermeneutic or interpretive ontology on another. We may speak of a cosmogonic aspect of consciousness.

THE BITS-AND-PIECES SCHOOL OF INTERHUMAN NOETICS

For Gebser, the principal characteristics of the perspectival world are: directedness and perspectivity, together with—unavoidably—sectorial partitioning. We are, however, dealing here with the deficient rational phase of the perspectival world (Gebser 1986: 74). The etymology of the efficient or *mental* mode of this conscious-ness is, nevertheless, hardly more promising. "The Greek word *menis*, meaning 'wrath,' and 'courage,' comes from the same stem as the word *menos*, which means 'resolve,' 'anger,' 'courage,' and 'power'; it is related to the Latin word *mens*, . . . [mean-ing] 'intent, anger, thinking, thought, understanding, deliberation, disposition, mentality, imagination' " (1986: 75). The notions of argumentativeness, controversy, polemics, "making a case" and "winning," or "proving a point" are present at the nativity of rational/mental consciousness by this assessment, and thus exacerbate, politically and discursively, its innate divisiveness. Rational/mental consciousness bespeaks, "the emergence of *directed or discursive thought*" (1986: 75).

In fact, argues Gebser (1986: 76), "[rational/mental consciousness] individualizes man from his previously valid world, emphasizing his singularity and making his ego possible." In provisional historical summary, he writes:

> Leonardo's development of perspective with its emphatic spatialization of man's image of the world marks the beginning of the deficient phase of the mental structure, . . . a phase characterized by *ratio*; and while . . . at the outset . . . the mental consciousness structure had a definitely qualitative accent, the word *ratio* is definitely quantitative. Whereas the Greek world of the classic period is a world of measure and moderation . . . the late European world and particularly its [American and Russian derivatives], are worlds of immoderation (93). . . . Perspective fixes the observer as well as the observed: it fixes man . . . and the world. . . . Compelled to emphasize his ego ever more strongly because of the isolating fixity, man faces the world in hostile confrontation (94). . . . In every extreme rationalization there is not just a violation of the psyche by the *ratio* . . . but also . . . : the violation of the *ratio* by the psyche, where both become deficient. (97)

Altogether, the rational/mental consciousness renders the world one of pieces whose "value" may thus be only objectivistically quantified. The mix-'n'-match epistemology hereby entailed, the comparison of pieces and the abstraction from them of general "ob-jective" laws, is inescapably re-presentational and mimetic. Since the pieces are sectorized into only external relations with one another, and since the abstract concepts are fixed in essence, the outcome can be nothing but a mechanistic and mimetic world-experience.

The outcome of this type of consciousness is mechanistic in the rule-bound application of the alleged "laws of thought" involved, i. e., the Aristotelian "excluded middle" to be treated later. And it is mechanistic in its metaphysic of only external/objectivistic interaction among persons and objects. Indeed, the perspectivized ego becomes an atom in a world of mutually externalized atomic egos. And the foundation of truth—there has to be a fixed, one-and-only, apodictic referent for all the mix-'n'-match—becomes a starry *noumenon* somewhere over the rainbow. It is the absolutist, fundamentalist, foundationalist point of re-ference for a mimetic or co-respondence idea of truth. Hereby, the issue becomes truth in re-plication, whether in science, ethics, religion, or in the re-production of dominant class, gender, and noetic values.

This correspondence theory of truth is so familiar that an alternative seems inconceivable. Yet the abiding complementarity of mentalities was presaged some time ago by Blake when he wrote:

> I turn my eyes to the Schools & Universities of Europe
> And there behold the Loom of Locke whose Woof rages dire

Washd by the Water-wheels of Newton. black the cloth
In heavy wreathes folds over every Nation; cruel Works
Of many Wheels I view, wheel without wheel, with cogs tyrannic
Moving by compulsion each other: not as those in Eden: which
Wheel within Wheel in freedom revolve in harmony & peace.
(*Jerusalem* plate 15: 14–20)

We may find in his poetic vision something of the integral consciousness whose minute articulations are the imaginally, intuitively, and synchronistically enacted ever-present origin, whose "message" of the "building of the earth" (cf. Teilhard de Chardin's book of this title) is this: *Do now what is only given to you; every meaning is unique.*

Unique meaning is new and singular meaning. It is not, at least in first instance, confirmable, replicable, or generalizable. It is far from being in equilibrium with already made systems of meaningfulness. In this context, the intentionality we associate with making or finding meaning will be that of non-imposition. Otherwise, we are merely imposing into the reality structure already accomplished meaning products that accord with previous familiar "intents and purposes" rather than eventuating fresh meaning in the universe. One way by which we will later come to speak of a non-impositional intention in reality-making/interpreting will invoke the Greek myth of Hermes and the Daoist consciousness/knack of *wu-wei* ("non-doing").

However, before moving to explore what Jung alluded to in this regard as the "cosmogonic meaning of human consciousness" (cf. von Franz 1992: 17), a consideration of some of the sociopolitical and ethical concomitants of our prevailing rational consciousness is in order.

Ethics, Politics, and Epistemology

The feedback relation between the dualistic ontology and epistemology of the rational/mental consciousness predisposes us to dual ethical and political views. From such foundational dualism, it can be but a step to authoritarianism and absolutism or the tyranny of expertise and objectivation.

This step is more or less straightforwardly expressed in an early rational/perspectival attempt to supersede mythic thought, despite its invocation of myth throughout. Plato sectorizes thought, perception, and the world (i.e., into ideally formed *noumena* and worldly *phenomena*) and then adds an ethical sectorization ranking one above the other in value, while also dividing knower from known and relegating to the "guardians" the authority to impose the proper view—from infancy on where possible. And the poet is to be banished from the city because s/he "destroys the *calculating part*" of the soul (Bloom, trans. 1991: 605b, emphasis added).

The poet is declaimed for singing "the irritable and various" (605a) rather than "hymns to gods or celebration of good men" (607a).

While at the foundation of Western rationalism, the priestly and regulative philosopher-king is exalted for keeping his eye on the immutable ideal in noetic meditation, the poet is repudiated for letting himself participate in world and noetic development as a unprogrammed shamanic and re-creational unitive experience. The irony is that each is liminal with respect to ordinary consciousness.

Plato's discussion of the *eidola*, or ideas, moreover, treats them as Cartesian in their distinctness, fixity, and univocity, altogether impeaching the interpretive pluralism inherent in images. Thus, Plato recruits univocal mimetic intuition as normative and legislative, partly by falsifying its polysemous character and uniqueness, in order to suppress poetic intuition and its seemingly chaotic motions of existential self-organization. It is no cause for surprise that over the entrance to Plato's Academy was said to be inscribed, "Let no one destitute of geometry enter my doors." This was, the *Republic* says, "for the sake of knowing what is always, and not at all for what is at any time coming into being and passing away" (527b; see also Gebser 1986: 84).

We may take this rationalizing step as an early theme in the politics of consciousness and in what Professor Timothy Leary (1968) aptly called "the politics of ecstasy." It adumbrates Platonic legitimations of later totalistic, authoritarian, and expertise-fetish rationalizations of political governance as well as dysfunctional and abusive absolutisms in family and intrapsychic life. The ways by which these hang together will become more evident when, in a discussion of emotional (child) abuse, we find repeated the ideology that obliges us to deny the testimony and intuition of our own experience in deference to an imposed *mimesis* and re-production of authorized/idealized values or feelings and generalized interpretations about "reality."

It is a conservative mentality voiced consistently in the Western litany from the sermonizing of William Bennett, Newt Gingrich, and Lynne Cheney on Capitol Hill all the way back to the *agora*: "Now to state it briefly, the overseers of the city must cleave to this, not letting it be corrupted unawares, but guarding against all comers; there must be no innovation . . . contrary to the established order; but they will guard against it as much as they can. . . . For they must beware of change . . . taking it to be a danger to the whole" (Bloom, trans. 1991: 424b–c).

We should comprehend clearly that a genuinely intuitive or poetic conception of mind is not simply an idle philosophers' debating point. It has political bearing on the very design of social organization, institutions, and policy. Authentic intuition, furthermore, is not solely the province of poets, as the history of science and maths attests eloquently. Nor is it entirely "undisciplined," as evidenced, for example, by the practice of the "active imagination" and "necessary statements" uncovered by Jung (von Franz 1992: 233, 267–68), the medieval doctrine of the *intellectus agens*, the classical and Christian understanding of *kairos*, the alchemists' distinction pointed out by von Franz between *imaginatio vera* and *imaginatio phantastica* (1992: 259), or the intuitive Kabbalistic interpretive strategies of *dillug* and *kefitsah* ("association," jumping and skipping among related ideas [see also Chinese *ko'i*]) described in Scholem's illuminating *Major Trends in Jewish Mysticism* (1954: 135).

In the intuitive "building of the earth," we might say, as does Thomas Berry in *The Dream of the Earth*:

> the human is less a being on the earth or in the universe than a dimension of
> the earth and indeed of the universe itself. . . . Nor is this source distant from
> us. . . . whatever authenticity exists in our cultural creations is derived from . . .
> spontaneities within us . . . that come from an abyss of energy and a capacity
> for intelligible order of which we have only the faintest glimmer in our con-
> scious awareness. (1988: 195)

This broadly nondual view in turn offers a context for a closer look at the microdesign of self in one-sidedly rationalized society. We may now turn from Plato's Athens to more recent commentary on this context and, foremost, on the interlinkage among ethics, politics, epistemology, and ontology in the potentially abusive "authoritative" dualist/essentialist and perspectivalist canon.

From the radical dualist Manichaeism of Augustine through the Lutheran and Protestant-Capitalist mindset and thence to authoritarian, totalist, and fascist regimes, social psychologist Erich Fromm traces a combination of heteronomous re-production, sense of lack, and feeling of alienation. These cumulatively signal the flight from spontaneously lived existential and noetic freedom into the total embrace of authoritatively determined and predictable objective certainty. As Fromm writes:

> Ours is only that to which we are genuinely related by our creative activity. . . .
> Only those qualities that result from our spontaneous activity give strength to
> the self and thereby form the basis of its integrity. The inability to act sponta-
> neously, to express what one genuinely feels and thinks, and the resulting
> necessity to present a pseudo self to others and oneself, are the root of the
> feeling of inferiority and weakness. Whether or not we are aware of it, there is
> nothing of which we are more ashamed than of not being ourselves, and there
> is nothing that gives us greater pride and happiness than to think, to feel and
> to say what is ours. . . . If the individual realizes his self by spontaneous activ-
> ity [in love and work] and thus relates himself to the world, he ceases to be an
> isolated atom; he and the world become part of one structuralized whole; he
> has his rightful place, and thereby his doubt concerning himself and the
> meaning of life disappears. This doubt sprang from his separateness and from
> the thwarting of life; when he can live neither compulsively nor automatically
> but spontaneously, the doubt disappears. He is aware of himself as an active
> and creative individual and recognizes that *there is only one meaning of life: the act of
> living itself.* (1969: 288–89)

Guy Burneko

By such a formulation as this, we can begin to see that arrayed against the intu-itive aptitude for existential spontaneity bred of wholeness and "poetic" connected-ness, and of living as a vital phase or node of a growing integral whole (and not merely as a mechanical piece of an objective co-location), is a bulwark of interact-ing philosophical and socioethical contraceptives.

Intuition as a mode of integral consciousness indifferent to dualistic and refer-ential criteria of meaningfulness and veracity has become internalized by us through our pedagogy, as well as other forms of social reinforcement, to seem untrustworthy, wrong, or worse. And the objectivist mindset that authorizes *ratio* (and vice versa) cannot allow arational and aperspectival intuitive consciousness a "legitimate" place in re-producing the world, for re-production is not its issue.

Any serious attempt in science, politics, art, philosophy, or religion to cultivate an intuitive/holistic consciousness is, given the preceding, contravening Mom and Dad as well, the *politique de baba*. For emotionally, epistemologically, and otherwise, we have come to take as veracious and real an external and *therefore* authoritative real-ity, or interpretation of reality, by which in comparison our uncarved intuition seems childlike, primitive, or defective. And each time we turn to dualist philoso-phy, political or scientific authority, or objective reality to confirm and legitimate our experience, we are, emotionally speaking, calling home first, because "father knows best." Because we do not trust ourselves and the place we occupy in and as the fabric of reality, we deny that we co-eventuate this reality; that we and the uni-verse are not two.

We slide away from intuition murmuring of "subjectivity" and "irrational-ism"—as if (by way of quick comparison) the natural numbers that found our prized objectivist *ratio* weren't themselves irrational from the get go. "The famous Poincaré said, 'the problem is, the natural integers are all exceptions. . . . ' "; "this was the rigorous proof by Kurt Gödel that the entire edifice of mathematics is built upon the given properties of natural numbers and the fact that the latter are irra-tional and remain so" (von Franz 1992: 163, 199).

It is now worthwhile to take a closer look at how from infancy and childhood we sometimes give support to the denial or trivialization of the intuitive, the holis-tic, and the integral or aperspectival, and thus repeat down through the generations the deficiencies of a particular consciousness that has become dominant in our cul-ture. We might also note that the very fact that we can critique this dominant mode of perception indicates that it has become relativized. In our lifetimes, we have begun to see evidences of a superseding integral awareness and, with it, a renais-sance in interhuman polity and noetics.

In Gebser's (1986: 85–95) view, the deficient magical and the deficient mental consciousness reinforce one another in that each is focused on manipulating the seemingly external world for control or gain. Though far less effectively than Morris Berman does by using the example of Newton in his *The Reenchantment of the World* or Alice Miller does with the examples she gives in *The Untouched Key*, the refrain I

sound here is that emotional child abuse as we have come to understand it is com-
pact with the excesses of anti-intuitive rational/mental deficiency coupled with
corresponding magical-might imperatives and a lost wholeness. The thesis would be
that if you develop a one-sidedly perspectival and dualist epistemology, a mechanistic cosmology and ontology, a mimetic ethics and a hugely materialist, manipulative, technocratic, rationalist world order, such abusiveness is the perfectly normal
concomitant and sequel—simultaneously an effect and a cause of the re-production of the entire problematic. This idea is not new, as Frances Vaughan (1979: 82),
following Lawrence LeShan, gently puts it in her *Awakening Intuition,* "the metaphysical system you are using is the metaphysical system that is operating." This indicates
the likelihood that fragmented, objectivistic, alienating systems in excess will establish a fragmented, alienating, and alienated species.

   Though in this situation we may not be prepared to resurrect hermetic anthropocosmologies to reunite microcosm and macrocosm, without our own postmodern complements to these, we will perish for want of an experience that can only be
intuitively eventuated from the very wholeness of our lived, felt, thought, and imaginally shaped cosmic experience. And such vision need not be standardized so that
we all agree the sun is a ball of hot gas. Indeed, the gift of intuition is that we find
and create unique meanings reducible neither to "our selves" nor to "the universe."

   Throughout Alice Miller's work on the emotional abuse of children, we find a
connection between the taught mistrust of intuition and the authoritative objec-
tivism of excessively ratiocinative consciousness. As found in Abrams, she lets us see
that the part of the object-rule is often played by the (as often as not unwittingly
abusive) parent:

> the child, who has been unable to build up his own structures, is . . . dependent
> on his parents. *He cannot rely on his own emotions, has not come to experience them through
> trial and error, has no sense of his real needs, and is alienated from himself in the highest degree.
> Under these circumstances he cannot separate from his parents.* . . . This is no obstacle to the
> development of intellectual [rational/mental] abilities, but it is one to the
> unfolding of an authentic emotional life. (1990: 132–133, emphasis added)

   I contend that we do not rely on our own intuitive (imaginal, synchronistic, etc.)
experiences. We have not come to experience them sufficiently through trial and
error, and deny the real needs they address in our individual, interpersonal, and cultural life. Thereby we are alienated from ourselves and our world. Under these circumstances, we do not separate ourselves from the objective/rational (version and
verification of) reality; it gives us the dependent sense of security and identity we
need. We are, in a curious way, dependent on a world from which we are exiled.

   In Morris Berman's (1984: 2) far-reaching analysis of the links between our
objectivist and one-sidedly rationalistic worldview and the atrophy of our intuitive
and authentic interpersonal experience, we learn that our "loss of meaning in an
ultimate philosophical or religious sense—the split between fact and value which

Guy Burneko

characterizes the modern age—is rooted in the Scientific Revolution of the six-teenth and seventeenth centuries." Until this time, he claims, the cosmos was a place of "participatory knowledge" and of "*belonging*. A member of this cosmos was not an alienated observer of it but a direct participant in its drama." And the attendant "participating consciousness" bespoke a "psychic wholeness" that we have since lost. His major thesis:

> we are *not* witnessing [in contemporary anomie and cultural disintegration] a peculiar twist in the fortunes of postwar Europe and America. . . . Rather, we are witnessing the inevitable outcome of a logic that is already centuries old. . . . What I am arguing is that the scientific world view is *integral* to modernity. . . . It is *our* consciousness. . . . Science, and our way of life, have been mutually rein-forcing, and it is for this reason that the scientific world view has come under serious scrutiny at the same time that the industrial nations are beginning to show signs of severe strain. (8)

The hyper-rational/mental consciousness of the modern world and the accompa-nying deference granted its interpretive authority have, in our social soul, truncated the integral, participatory, and intuitive aptitudes for world- and meaning-making.

INTUITION AND THE *UNUS MUNDUS IMAGINALIS*

A great virtue of the traditional intuitive systems like *Kabbalah, Tantra, Ars Chemica*, and so on, inheres less in their universal systematicity than in their *meaningfully nond-ual and processual integration* of the subjective with the objective, in lived symbolic/imaginal anthropocosmologies that, states Gilbert Durand, "have many more ways of establishing relationships than do concepts . . . [in] the modality of the *mundus imaginalis*" (Durand n.d.: 90−91). Their virtue, once more, is not that they weld together a shared mentality but that they spontaneously eventuate from and aid, in turn, the unique meaningfulness of transpersonal and interpersonal experi-ence. They are the psychocosm of undivided nature and thought in conscious *poiesis*. Only for us who study them objectivistically from afar in time and space are they examples of descriptive *mimesis*.

Of course, our usual perspectival, sectorial rationalism finds it hard to sustain a reality/experience irreducible entirely to the category/sector called "psyche," "mind," or "consciousness" on the "one side," or to that called "reality" or "cos-mos" on "the other." We insist that the world have a substantive bottom. We tend in logically exclusivistic either/or fashion to resist the experience that consciousness and reality co-eventuate, are re-ciprocal and co-constitutive to the degree that, "at bottom," we cannot really say they are two. Yet to say they are one would be yet another sort of categorical positivist assertion about the "essential nature" of the reality/mind event.

Imaginal and intuitive "mind" allows this nondual event to "speak" for itself. And since it speaks not "of" some kind of world but *as* that world, it speaks *as* and *from* a different logical type (cf. Wilden 1980). So any "articulation" of integral and intuitive consciousness in rational/mental terms must seem paradoxical, ambiguous, and even silly. That is because the rational mind can only objectivistically "talk about" by de-fining and thus dif-fracting in quantitatively useful ways. It renders opposed and contradictory in its sequential terms what in "its own" sphere is simultaneously co-constitutive and undivided.

Gödel's famous theorem understands that the rationalized system is a partial and special case of {(un)general(izable) _____}. The trick with the brackets, parentheses, and the blank space suggests that the very notion of ontological category, of what noun to put in the blank, is rationally problematic as is also the logical category of ungeneralizable/generalizable. There is a question here of what, finally, legitimizes total universalizing reason against what Clifford Geertz (1983) calls "local knowledge," others call regional or plural epistemologies (Feyerabend 1987, Serres 1982, Bachelard 1968), Blake calls, "minute particulars," Jung and von Franz call synchronicity, and I call intuition.

In the Hillman/Jung school of psychology represented by Roberts Avens's (1980: 8) *Imagination Is Reality*, the imaginal intuition or the *mundus imaginalis* (the domain of the phenomenology of psyche) "point[s] to an order [a *metaxy*] of reality that is ontologically no less real than physical reality on the one hand, and spiritual or intellectual reality on the other." Following Jung to argue that the realm of the imaginal is "the only reality we apprehend directly: everything we know is transmitted through psychic images," Avens (1980: 33–34) also affirms that:

> In the beginning is *poesis*—the making of soul through imagination and metaphor. . . . behind scientific empiricism (the "facts" of science, "pure" thought and "objective" observations) lies a world of . . . primordial reality— the imaginal world. Images are the basic givens of all psychic life and the privileged mode of access to the soul.

The apt "mode of cognition of" (and "as") the world in this circumstance would be reminiscent of an integral/intuitive, meditative,

> art of being fully attentive and at the same time fully relaxed—one of the hardest possible things for modern man. For in the end it involves relativization, decalcification of the Apollonian and the heroic ego or, more exactly, a separation of our awareness from the imperial ego by creating a vantage point from which the ego too can be seen as an image among other images. (Avens 1980: 39)

The nondual or aperspectival implications of this noetic strategy should be made explicit; and they can be highlighted in these ways. First, we may recall that for Jung the archetypes of the collective unconscious are not only irrepresentable in themselves; but also in their "psychoid" aspect, they merge indistinguishably with one another as nature itself (von Franz 1992: 4). Second, a point touched upon later, the unconscious/conscious enactment apparent as synchronistic, as well as other "natural" phenomena (see von Franz 1992: 36), evidences an "acausal connecting principle" common to mind and matter (see also von Franz 1980: 99–102). Third, if the ontological domain of real-ization is imaginal, if even the categories of ontology, reason, and reality are foremost imaginal, and if the imaginal psyche is not severable from nature—i.e., cosmogenesis—then imaginal psyche, the intuitive, may be taken as the "native" mode (organ?) of consciousness of/as *kosmos.* This is true both in the sense of the word "cosmos" as the universe in its greatest (now psycho-physical) extent, and in the sense of cosmos as order, organization, rhythm, differential pattern, and meaning. In other words, the implications bespeak a poetic dimension of nature both continued as and contextualized by mind and psyche. Nature or reality, and mind, consciousness, or intuition, may not be separate; and they may not be "things" in the usual substantive sense of the word.

In a nondual ontoepistemology, these insights point simultaneously to the acts of nature, and of mind/soul/heart/psyche, and to what Bateson (1979) calls "the pattern that connects." It suggests, once again, that meaning and stuff are complementary eventuations of a reality process irreducible to either (but one in which stuff is seemingly overdetermined by meaning, pattern, difference/*différance*, information, and existential hermeneutics). The "ontological" foundation of "all this" is not ascertainable by sectorial means; and "what we are looking for" may not be other than "we who are looking." Who[m] we think we are is inseverably a function of the way "we" look to such a degree that the objective case is provisionally *sous rature,* under erasure, deferred (cf. Culler 1982: 85–110).

Taking up Jung's discussion of the psychoid aspect of the archetype that patterns the "visible" image as being in itself "an empty, formal element, a *facultas praeformandi,*" Gebser states:

> the acategorical elements over-determine and transform the three-dimensional system into four-dimensionality and make possible the arational perception of what is no longer rationally representable. (Gebser 1986: 400-402)

The archetypes that pattern culturally and personally diverse imaginal consciousness are on the one hand phases of, not "outside," the natural and material cosmos that they in turn, on the other hand, spontaneously overdetermine and constellate in meaningfully creative *poiesis,* often mediated by states of alert relaxation or meditative awareness. Gebser (1986) reminds us here that this is not in the sense

> that [someone] can exercise, say, a new kind of magic power . . . or a new kind of mental superiority. . . . It is rather that his or her being present is in itself sufficient to effect new exfoliations and new crystallizations which could be nowhere manifest without his or her presence. . . . The new consciousness structure has nothing to do with might, rule and overpowering. Thus, it cannot be striven for, only elicited or awakened. Anyone who strives for it, intending to attain it

mentally, is condemned to failure at the outset. . . . There is a need for a certain detachment toward oneself and the world, a gradually maturing equilibrium of all the inherent components and consciousness structures predisposed in ourselves, in order that we may prepare the basis for the leap into the new mutation. . . . The new consciousness structure is not a "higher" structure. . . . [I]t is an integral structure where such valuations as three-, two-, or one-dimensional are irrelevant (300–301). . . . We should also avoid the error of placing the "effected" into a causal relationship with the "effecting" (285–86). . . .

[I]ntegration cannot be effected by mere thinking . . . but requires . . . the "sense" of *perceiving as well as imparting. . . . Only through this reciprocal perception and impartation of truth by man and the world can the world become transparent for us.* (261)

A way of tracing this theme may be to consider a little more closely Bateson's idea of the ecology of mind, and the archetypal psychologists' (Jung and von Franz) idea of the *unus mundus imaginalis* as metaphors for the consciousness/reality psychocosm. The operating reason-mode here would be much more the "fuzzy logic" of Bart Kosko's *Fuzzy Thinking* than, say, the exclusionary forced choice logic, A or not-A, dominant since Aristotle. In answer to rational-perspectival questions of the form, "Is it mind or matter, 'inside' or 'out'?", the aperspectival answers henceforth will be "more or less"; *"everything is a matter of degree"* (Kosko 1993: 18).

Consider reflections from Bateson's (1979) *Mind and Nature: A Necessary Unity*:

The pattern which connects is a *metapattern. . . .* It is that metapattern which defines the vast generalization that, indeed, *it is patterns which connect. . . .* Mind is empty; it is no-thing. It exists only in its ideas, and these again are no-things. (11) (Cf., Whorf's conclusion that "reference is the lesser part of meaning, patternment the greater" [Whorf 1956: 261].)

So, Bateson (1979: 92) also states:

The interaction between parts of mind is triggered by *difference,* and difference is a non-substantial phenomenon not located in space or time. . . . Mental process requires circular (or more complex) chains of determination. . . . In mental process, the effects of difference are to be regarded as transforms . . . of events which preceded them. . . .

The description and classification of these processes of transformation disclose a hierarchy of logical types immanent in the phenomena. I shall argue that the phenomena which we call *thought, evolution, ecology, life, learning,* and the like occur only in systems that satisfy these criteria.

Such systems occur wherever difference is in circulation; thought is not unique with human systems by this understanding. Bateson (1979) continues:

Information consists of differences that make a difference (99). . . . [T]hought and evolution are alike in a shared stochasticism. Both are mental processes in terms of the criteria offered [above]. (149)

This is to say, organization or pattern, not substantive stuff, is the mediator and "locus" of intuitive meaning. And pattern is differentially made. It does not reduce to localizable "items" be they material or ideal.

Keeping in mind the virtues of the inclusively fuzzy mode of logic noted above, as von Franz says late in *Psyche and Matter*, Jung's idea of a collective unconscious is, "by his definition, partly trans-spatial and trans-temporal" (1992: 286). The advantage in this formulation is not so much that it speaks out of both sides of its mouth as that it allows us to invoke fuzzy thinking to interpret our consciousness pattern/repertoire, and thus to de-perspectivate rational mental awareness somewhat, in a step "toward" integral or intuitive *both* A and not-A experience. And it also allows us to see that this very mode illustrates the multivocal and multivalent imaginal feature of an intuitive, integral, aperspectival awareness.

Another way of approaching this point is to note that an integral ecology of imaginal consciousness both receives and imparts meaning. The archetypes mutually contaminate one another, the units of mind are circularly and recursively co-involved, and "the difference that makes a difference" (which is a condition or concomitant of consciousness) reduces to no-thing, and is thereby free to circulate "in" but not necessarily "of" spacetime things. This is not unlike the god disclosed by the felicitously negative medieval theology of John Scotus Eriugena, of which we cannot say what it is because it is not "a what." In its corollary form, from Meister Eckhart, this is to say, "if the intellect therefore, in so far as it is intellect, is nothing, it follows that neither is understanding an existence" (Moran 1989: 211). Given the preceding argument, we could take "understanding" to overdetermine "existence" in a self-organizing hermeneutic ontology; existence then would become a subset of the {____} that connects. In any case, we learn that by virtue of their mutual "contamination" and their psychoid nature, the archetypes and, thus, the imaginal world, mediate, share in and imaginally articulate a meaningful pattern differential that is irreducible to any of the (logically or ontologically "existent") sets or elements thereby presented (von Franz 1992: 4–9).

From the idea of the archetypal *unus mundus imaginalis*, then, we have the image of a tendency-to-pattern in the psychocosm. The tendency can be construed as a pattern-potential of the basic form 0,1, x,y, or *yinyang*, form-and-void. But every one of these patterns or pattern dispositions is a function of the irreducible, nonlocalizable differential. It may be a bivalent differential (as Kosko notes of Aristotelian logic), and it may be a multivalent one. But the fact that it is differential implies that it is also circuitous in Bateson's sense. The difference is shared, participated, transmitted, distributed among, common to, irreducible to the items themselves. In the *unus mundus* as the ecology of mind/world, consciousness is irreducible pattern/process re-ferred not to an external "real" *noumenon/phenomenon* so much as implicated in a "holomovement" (to use Bohm's term), of no certain "nature." Kosko writes that black and white are special cases of gray; "multivalence reduces to bivalence [only] in extreme cases" (1993: 28).

An enactive theory of integral or intuitive consciousness allows us to develop this logic. In one phrasing, this development becomes the claim of Francisco Varela and colleagues (1991: 202) that:

> organism and environment are mutually enfolded in multiple ways. . . . The treatment of the world as pregiven and the organism as representing or adapting to it is a dualism. The extreme opposite of dualism is a monism. . . . enaction is specifically designed to be a middle way between dualism and monism.

Another way, that of von Franz, says that

> "meaning," . . . concerns a holon, or rather *the* holon . . . and simultaneously it concerns that *one* individual who realizes it [in] . . . "acts of creation in time." (von Franz 1992: 271)

Von Franz continues:

> The archetype above all represents psychic probability. . . . [I]t . . . underlies . . . psychophysical equivalences. . . . [Meaning] would have to be understood partly as a universal [pattern] existing from all eternity and partly as the sum of countless individual acts of creation occurring in time . . . a *creatio continua*. (1992: 305)

And what is probability? Answers Kosko (1993: 59), "*The whole in the part is probability. It is the probability of the part.*" In this regard, an integral, aperspectival, or intuitive consciousness is the enactment of a reality process of which it is a probabilistic mode and a cosmogonic agency/context. It appears to be this rather than the observation of such a process from a putative distance that allows the A or not-A reductions we take as rational mental perspectives, and whose dualistic epistemology (as Robert Jahn sagely pointed out in introductory remarks to the 1994 "Academy of Consciousness Studies") we confuse with "absolute ontology."

If Kosko (1993: 102) is (more-or-less) right, "paradoxes are the rule and not the exception. . . . A and not-A holds to some degree." And this is the office of the intuitive — to hold in meaningful simultaneous im-plication the irreducible and thus, per-force, aperspectivally presentiated integrality of the "infinitely-many" world-process.

In an older idiom, human intuition is the *officina omnium*. Long ago, arguments concerning this were made by Maximus the Confessor and John Scotus Eriugena:

> Maximus says that man, who forms a connecting link through all differences and all extremes . . . is said to contain the whole universe in himself: . . . Eriugena says that what Maximus calls "*extremitates*". . . including the most widely separated things in the universe . . . are united in man . . . : therefore, he is rightly described as the "*officina omnium*," the workshop of everything. (Stock 1967: 5)

Because pattern/consciousness "is" or mediates a differential nothing, it is everything. To the extent it is the epistemologically and ontologically A *and* not-A everything, it is nothing (self-subsistent in itself; cf. Buddhist *anatman, sunya*). And, it is by virtue of being "nothing" in itself in touch with everything, that it evokes, creates, and displays the pattern that connects.

In this case, the apposite "logic" for and of the world is less a bivalent logic of exclusion and suppression than an integral or imaginal intuition. Cross-cultural mythemes for this include the Greek Hermes-noetic. For Hermes, and the herme(neu)tic world, experience is "such-ness" and "cannot . . . be reduced to something else: neither to a concept, to a 'power', nor to a 'spirit' . . . not even to an idea" (Kerényi 1986: 45–46, cf. also Buddhist *tathagata*). Hermes, messenger (*angelos*) and god of crossroads and hermeneutic interpretation, "speech-gifted mediator and psychogogue" writes Kerényi (vi), is a "way of being" (4), a *dao*, whose path is adumbrated in one of his traditional epithets: Hermes *Stropheus*, "the socket" in which the pivot of the door moves (84).

With respect to preceding reflections about issues ranging from Kosko's fuzzy logic to the psychopolitical absolutism implicit in perspectival and dual rational consciousness to the imaginal marriage of self and cosmos, subject and object, we may find a superseding integral/intuitive "reason" in Hermes *Stropheus*:

> a middle realm [*metaxy*] between being and non-being. . . . The primordial mediator and messenger moves between the absolute "no" and the absolute "yes," or, more correctly, between two "nos" that are lined up against each other. . . . In this he stands on ground that is no ground, and there he creates the way. From out of a trackless world—unrestricted, flowing, ghostlike—he conjures up the new creation. (Kerényi 1986: 77)

Epistemologically and ontologically labile, the integral hermetic consciousness moves with and as the world in a seemingly divinatory "comprobability" whose whole subtends every part. And the "findings" of such an intuitively premised reason eventuate as

> the sum total of pathways [of] Hermes' playground: the accidental "falling into your lap" . . . and every sort of evasion from the restrictions and confinements imposed by laws, circumstances, destinies. . . . that world which Hermes opens to us. (Kerényi 1986: 54)

But what is the portion of accident in a reality inseverably mediated by participating consciousness and probabilistically "informed" in every part by a whole that is "itself" inexhaustively irreducible to A or to not-A? What falls into the lap of intuition is a display of psychocosm constellated from the broader metapattern that connects.

Jeremy Campbell's (1982) *Grammatical Man: Information, Entropy, Language, and Life* highlights grammar as a model of the stochastic self-organizing mix of accident and order in this connection and points (almost Kabbalistically) to that grammaticity as characteristic of mind and nature. Campbell (1982: 28) states that stochastic series "are not always totally unpredictable, but they do contain an element of the unknown." He then parlays this A and not-A into a claim about messages, saying that "messages display a certain pattern, and the patterns change in a manner determined partly, but only partly, by their past history. This [is] a clean break with determinism" (29).

And with messages, we are returned to the realm of Hermes, to irreducible difference that makes a difference, and to the fuzzy conjugation of structure and anti-structure (cf. Victor Turner's *The Ritual Process*) that, in the context of an imaginal psychocosm, elicits a cosmogonic reading of Campbell's (1982: 264) conclusion that "structure and freedom, like entropy and redundancy, are not warring opposites but complementary forces." This is the grammatical or hermeneutic view. It is a way of saying that as a handful of simple yet ever-dynamic rule/patterns "in" and "as" the psychocosm both eventuate and interpretively organize, impart and perceive, generate and select, the "minute particulars" through the complexity/consciousness that we (also) are in love and thought, and in the not-two of mind and nature, so, also, randomness and probability are conjugated in a speech of life "moving away from the simple, the uniform and the random, and toward the genuinely new, the endlessly complex products of nature and of mind" (Campbell 1982: 265) in the building of the earth.

"Human society," asserts Campbell (1982: 260-61) has "emergent" properties: "It evolves in unpredictable ways. Like a *kosmos*, its order is intrinsic, generated from within. . . . Cause and effect as a model of human activity will not suffice. . . . A healthy, evolving society needs as much variety of knowledge as possible, and this variety must be maintained constantly. Uniformity would be fatal, because it would lead to enormous redundancy," maximal forms of whose imposition we know as abusive, authoritarian, and dictatorial or as fundamentalist and literalist regimes.

The cosmogonic aspect of intuitive awareness is, it thus seems, abetted by liminal and "altered states of consciousness" that allow respite, release, and liberation from the usual impositions and routinizations of consciousness. The traditional strategies apposite to the holistic, imaginal, or intuitive/integral consciousness structures are often those associated with shamanic, initiatic, or mystical schooling (see such classic researches as Mircea Eliade's *Shamanism*, Victor Turner's *The Ritual Process*, and Gershom Scholem's *On the Kabbalah and Its Symbolism*). In the language of Gebser's (1986: 531–532) *The Ever-Present Origin*, this

> does not mean that it is the number of those who realize and live the new that is decisive; decisive is the intensity with which the individuals live the new. . . . Only as a whole man is man in a position to perceive the whole. . . . The new attitude will be consolidated only when the individual can gradually begin to disregard his ego. . . . [I]t is not a loss or denial of the "I," not an ego-cide but an overcoming of ego. Consciousness of self was the characteristic of the mental consciousness structure; freedom from the "I" is the characteristic of the integral consciousness structure.

This is another way of reiterating Gebser's (1986: 300) earlier point that just "being present is in itself sufficient to effect new exfoliations and new crystallizations which could be nowhere manifest without his or her presence."

PENULTIMACIES

I understand spacetimemeaning as a continuum. And I speculate that meaning/consciousness, as a dimensionality, is related to spacetime as and in pattern/rhythm/grammar. The metapattern that gives meaning to an assertion of this sort reduces to none of its parts. So this *kosmos* exists just as much between our ears as

Guy Burneko

we suppose it does in some equally hermeneutic "out there." In which case, knack and how we live life is of foreground importance; ontological reference is the lesser part of meaning and existential authenticity the greater (see Whorf 1956).

This knack also suggests letting language do the thinking for a change, letting languaging be free self-organizingly to empattern as it will, unencumbered by our usual utilitarian obsession that its only job is to communicate with as little slippage and static as possible—an anthropocentric view that tacitly presupposes that we already know all and everything worth saying. And as for and with Hermes this thinking-without-a-thinker, *so to speak*, "creates the way" by its own going; another cross-cultural analogue for this is that of the classical Chinese daoists who say, "the way comes about as we walk it" (Chuang-tzu 1981: 53). The way is traditionally marked by what the Chinese called *wu-wei*, or "non-doing," "non-striving," "action without effort," which like *tzu-jan* (more recently spelled *ziran*), "natural self-so-ness," finds its intuitive and epistemological/ontological counterpart in the "pivot of the *dao*" or *dao shu*—"the pivot of the way of things' mutualities". Like Hermes *Stropheus*, writes Wu Kuang-ming (1990: 175):

> the subject must fit himself in the Pivot, fit the Pivot "in the center of the circle". . . of the world, and thereby respond endlessly and freely to things by "following along" . . . and "walking both" . . . ways—the way of things and the way of the subject.

This deautomatization and dehabituation of our conventional mental and egological rigidities and bivalence (see Deikman in Ornstein 1973) finds expression in Chinese tradition in a form of sagely speech called "goblet words." I take this form of speech as the apposite metadiscursive mode of integral and intuitive consciousness, the silly poetic logic of lucky hits and of the self-eventuating world process/patternization un-referred to ex-clusively ob-jective canonization—neither a solipsistic soliloquy nor an encyclopedic re-production. This is the speech of the way or *dao*, of a nondual and aperspectival or intuitive orientation typified by Zhuangzi (Chuang-tzu) who, hums Wu:

> wants us to adopt a flexible "attitude" that best fits our disposition *and* the disposition of the situation in which we are at the moment. Since both subjective and objective dispositions are constantly changing, our positions should accordingly shift. This is what it means to be *alive*. It entails a vivacious playing with any position and a meandering among many situations. (1982: 19)

It is in this play of difference, wheel within wheel, that the ecology of meaning and nature, consciousness and reality, constitutes its poetic emergence. Attentive participation and resonance is all.

"The effect upon the soul of such a work is in the end not at all dependent upon its being understood" (Blumenthal 1978: 105).

{_____}

REFERENCES CITED

Abrams, Jeremiah (ed.)
   1990 *Reclaiming the Inner Child.* Los Angeles: Tarcher.
Avens, Roberts
   1980 *Imagination Is Reality: Western Nirvana in Jung, Hillman & Cassirer.* Dallas: Spring.
Bachelard, Gaston
   1968 *The Philosophy of No: A Philosophy of the New Scientific Mind.* Trans. G.C. Waterston. New York: Orion Press.
Bateson, Gregory
   1972 *Steps to an Ecology of Mind.* New York: Ballantine.
   1979 *Mind and Nature: A Necessary Unity.* New York: E. P. Dutton.
Berman, Morris
   1984 *The Reenchantment of the World.* New York: Bantam.
Berry, Thomas
   1988 *The Dream of the Earth.* San Francisco: Sierra Club.
Blake, William
   1965 *The Poetry and Prose of William Blake.* Ed. David V. Erdman. Garden City: Doubleday.
Blumenthal, David R.
   1978 *Understanding Jewish Mysticism.* New York: Ktav.
Campbell, Jeremy
   1982 *Grammatical Man: Information, Entropy, Language, and Life.* New York: Simon & Schuster.
Chuang-tzu
   1981 *The Inner Chapters.* Ed. A. C. Graham. London: George Allen & Unwin.
Culler, Jonathan
   1982 *On Deconstruction: Theory and Criticism after Structuralism.* Ithaca: Cornell University Press.
Durand, Gilbert
   n. d. "Exploration of the Imaginal." Trans. Ruth Horine. In *Circé: Cahiers de Centre de Recherche sur l'imaginaire.* Vol. 1. Paris: Lettres Modernes.
Eliade, Mircea
   1964 *Shamanism: Archaic Techniques of Ecstasy.* Trans. Willard R. Trask. Bollingen Series LXXVI. Princeton: Princeton University Press.
Feyerabend, Paul
   1987 *Farewell to Reason.* London: Verso.
Fromm, Erich
   1969 *Escape from Freedom.* New York: Avon.
Gebser, Jean
   1986 *The Ever-Present Origin.* Trans. Noel Barstad with Algis Mickunas. Athens: Ohio University Press.
Heidegger, Martin
   1968 *What Is Called Thinking?* Trans. J. Glenn Gray. New York: Harper & Row.
Jung, Carl G.
   1933 *Modern Man in Search of a Soul.* Trans. W. S. Dell and Carey F. Baynes. New York: Harcourt Brace & World.
   1969 *The Archetypes and the Collective Unconscious.* Trans. R. F. C. Hull. Bollingen Series XX. Princeton: Princeton University Press.

Kerényi, Karl

1986 *Hermes: Guide of Souls.* Dallas: Spring.

Kosko, Bart

1993 *Fuzzy Thinking: The New Science of Fuzzy Logic.* New York: Hyperion.

Leary, Timothy

1968 *The Politics of Ecstasy.* New York: College Notes and Texts.

Miller, Alice

1990 *The Untouched Key: Tracing Childhood Trauma in Creativity and Destructiveness.* Trans. Hildegarde and Hunter Hannum. New York: Doubleday.

Moran, Dermot

1989 *The Philosophy of John Scottus Eriugena: A Study of Idealism in the Middle Ages.* Cambridge: Cambridge University Press.

Ornstein, Robert E. (ed.)

1973 *The Nature of Human Consciousness.* San Francisco: W. H. Freeman.

Plato

1991 *The Republic of Plato,* 2nd ed. Trans. Allan Bloom. New York: Basic.

Scholem, Gershom G.

1965 *On the Kabbalah and Its Symbolism.* Trans. Ralph Manheim. New York: Schocken.

1954 *Major Trends in Jewish Mysticism.* New York: Schocken.

Serres, Michel

1982 *Hermes: Literature, Science, Philosophy.* Eds. Josué V. Harari and David Bell. Baltimore: Johns Hopkins University Press.

Stock, Brian

1967 "The Philosophical Anthropology of Johannes Scottus," *Studi Medievali* series 3A, 8 (1): 1–57.

Teilhard de Chardin, Pierre

1969 *Building the Earth.* New York: Avon.

Turner, Victor

1977 *The Ritual Process: Structure and Anti-Structure.* Symbol, Myth, and Ritual Series. Ithaca: Cornell University Press.

Varela, Francisco J., Evan Thompson, and Eleanor Rosch

1991 *The Embodied Mind: Cognitive Science and Human Experience.* Cambridge, MA: MIT Press.

Vaughan, Frances E.

1979 *Awakening Intuition.* New York: Doubleday.

von Franz, Marie-Louise

1980 *On Divination and Synchronicity: The Psychology of Meaningful Chance.* Toronto: Inner City.

1992 *Psyche and Matter.* Boston: Shambhala.

Whorf, Benjamin Lee

1956 *Language, Thought and Reality: Selected Writings of Benjamin Lee Whorf.* Ed. John B. Carroll. Cambridge, MA: MIT Press.

Wilden, Anthony

1980 *System and Structure: Essays in Communication and Exchange,* 2nd ed. London: Tavistock Publications.

Wu Kuang-ming

1982 *Chuang Tzu: World Philosopher at Play.* American Academy of Religion Studies in Religion 26. New York: Crossroad & Chico: Scholars Press.

1990 *The Butterfly as Companion: Meditations on the First Three Chapters of the Chuang Tzu.* Series in Religion and Philosophy. Albany: SUNY.

PART II

INTUITION, SCIENCE, AND PRAXIS

6

Intuition in the Development of Scientific Theory and Practice

Evelyn H. Monsay

Introduction

At various times in my life, I have worked as both a theoretical and experimental physicist, an engineer, and a manager of technical programs. I began my professional career in theoretical physics, in the area of relativistic quantum field theory and phenomenology. I studied the most abstract, and yet fundamental, issues in physics: the apparent nature of the universe as consisting of infinitesimal particles and the fields through which they interact. I moved into applied physics and engineering, working on the physics of thin films, underwater sound, and photonics— the interdisciplinary study of optics, quantum optics, and electronics. During my days in an industrial setting, I also earned an m.b.a. and worked as a technical project manager and as a program manager, with overall responsibility for engineering, finance, marketing, and contract issues. In all of my pursuits, the power of intuition has been quite obvious to me.

As an undergraduate, I discovered that the professors' reliance on what they called "physical intuition" gave them an advantage in problem solving over my own laborious, reasoned—and often incorrect—approach. I wanted this ability to look at a physical situation and "just know," instantly, what approach would work to solve it. It seemed to me that I would need a lot more knowledge before physical intuition would be available to me. Later I would find that not only more knowledge of

Evelyn H. Monsay

physics, but also more knowledge of every possible field—arts, sports, humanities, business, and so on—would enhance this ability. More than just the application of collected facts about physics seemed to be involved.

I recall one particularly clear example of intuition at work, later in my career in industry. I was working on a design for an underwater sound sensor, a hydrophone, based on the transmission of laser light via optical fibers. If sound were present, a moveable diaphragm would respond, alternately blocking and then clearing the path of the laser's beam emitted from the optical fiber within the "tin-can"-shaped hydrophone. I had not invented this hydrophone; in fact, I was new to this field of research. I was involved, along with another, more senior engineer because there was a problem in the actual operation of the hydrophone in an undersea environment. At the underwater depths typical for operation of a hydrophone, the air-filled, tin-can body of our hydrophone would be crushed. It is common practice, in such a situation, to fill the cavity with oil. The oil prevents crushing, but, in our case, it also would prevent the tiny movements of the diaphragm that would produce the signal from which we could detect underwater sound. While discussing this situation with two other engineers one afternoon, one of whom was the senior engineer I was assigned to work with, I suddenly knew I had the resolution to our problem. First came this "knowing," then an essentially kinesthetic feeling for what was involved, and finally, the words to describe the invention: a corrugated metal strip or tube that could produce the compliance of air by its compression and relaxation, even in an oil-filled can. I blurted this discovery out, worried that I knew very little about the hydrophone industry and was probably way off base—even though I had a sense that I had to be right. The senior engineer immediately understood. He said, "You mean a bellows. That ought to do it!" I had never seen a bellows of this sort before, but was glad to receive the confirmation first from my more knowledgeable colleague, and then, later, from experiment.

But is this sudden illumination called intuition always correct? In another incident, in a different research area, two of us had two different "intuitions," which opposed each other. One of us had to be wrong. The issue involved the transmission of a laser beam in seawater that would be heated by the sun at its surface, and so was hotter above than below. My colleague's intuitive, meaning "un-reasoned, un-calculated, immediate," conclusion was that the laser beam would be bent so as to completely miss our receiver after its trip through a certain water path. However, my intuitive feeling was that the deviation of the laser beam would be very minor, and would not interfere with reception of the laser beam at all. My colleague cited the way that air above a hot tar surface distorts the light transmitted across it, creating wavy versions of objects beyond. But, I "just knew" he was wrong! The resolution came with a calculation that ended the argument in my favor. Why was intuition right in my case, and yet wrong for my colleague?

Many questions are raised by my personal experience with intuition. Is a great deal of specific knowledge required to receive intuitions, as I deduced from my college professors? Or not, as I myself found with the hydrophone invention? What kinds of knowledge help intuition? Can some types of learning hurt the intuitive process? Intuition for me has always seemed to come from somewhere else, from "the blue," and I usually perceive it as a "knowing," or feeling, or image, before words or equations can be employed. Do all intuitions share this mystical quality? Finally, can intuition be wrong, as it was for my second colleague mentioned above? These questions, and more, motivated my research into the nature of intuition in science. What I have found from others and discovered myself now follows.

Evelyn H. Monsay

WHAT IS INTUITION?

Intuition has been defined by the dictionary (Neufeldt and Guralnik 1994: 709) as "the direct knowing or learning of something without conscious use of reasoning; immediate understanding." Several words with related meanings are entangled with the notion of intuition. Insight, "the ability to see and understand clearly the inner nature of things, especially by intuition" (Neufeldt and Guralnik 1994: 699), is the result of validation of intuitive knowing. Inspiration, a "breath from within," and a "stimulus to creative thought or action" (Neufeldt and Guralnik 1994: 699) is essentially a synonym for intuition, with an emphasis on action.

Imagination is a form of thought associated with mental images. Imagination typically refers to the appearance of images in the mind, sometimes intuitively received, which can be manipulated and require translation into words. Ferguson (1992) asserts that the inventor and the engineer work predominately with images. In fact, many scientists and technologists attach a great deal of importance to mental images. The theoretical physicist Richard Feynman, an inventor of quantum field theory, thought that Einstein failed to develop a unified field theory because he "stopped thinking in concrete physical images and became a manipulator of equations" (Dyson 1979: 62). Einstein himself had said that imagination is more important than knowledge. Imagination shares the global, nonrational nature of intuition, and is a close cousin to it.

Creativity is a process in which intuition plays a major role. The creative process usually involves immersion in a particular problem, followed by a period of incubation in which the problem is *not* consciously considered, and then the arrival of an intuitive notion as the solution to the problem. Intuitive ideas, at this point, typically arrive "lightning quick." Since active concentration on the problem under consideration has often ended long before the intuition arrives, it apparently comes "out-of-the-blue." Intuition is very closely connected with the creative process.

Bastick (1982), a psychologist, adds to the dictionary definition qualities such as emotional involvement, empathy, a feeling of correctness, a global view, and an emphasis on the preconscious, preverbal nature of intuition. Bastick notes that "intuition need not be correct," and that it is "influenced by experience."

It is apparent from my personal experiences that I would agree with Bastick on these points. I should mention that in all cases where intuition has helped me I have wanted to solve a particular problem very, very much; hence, the emotional component has always been present. Also note that the reason why my second colleague's intuition was not correct could easily have been his particular previous experience with physical systems.

However, there has been a great deal of disagreement on the nature and role of intuition in science among psychologists, philosophers, and physicists. Intuition has been praised as the most certain route to perfect knowledge, and yet damned as a dangerous predecessor of authoritarianism (Bunge 1962) by philosophers. Psychologists have battled over whether intuition is a unique way of knowing, or just "one trial learning" (Bastick 1982: 5). Jung's treatment of intuition is unique in psychological theories since he postulates that intuition is one of the four universal, fundamental mental functions: thinking, feeling, sensation, and intuition. In Jung's approach, intuition is available as a way of knowing for everyone at all times, to different degrees. Typically, scientists acknowledge the essential role of intuition in scientific discovery, but downplay that role so as to honor the "scientific method" as the manner in which science gets done. As Cohen (1977: 366) stated,

> I am sorry that it is necessary to shudder at the introduction of terms like "intuition" or "creative imagination," but shudder we must. . . . As to intuition, many philosophers do not like to use the term, although many scientists do use it. And yet how else can one explain the process whereby certain rather incredible scientific men have been able to see results long before they could prove them, and in some cases even when they could not ever find such a proof.

In the sections that follow, I will briefly relate the role intuition has been assigned in doing science over time. The trend in recent years has been away from a philosophized methodology, toward an awareness of the major role of discovery, and so, intuition, in science as it actually gets done. I will then present anecdotal evidence from scientists, mathematicians, and engineers of the role intuition and its cousin, imagination, play in scientific discovery. I will also look at the various types of intuition referred to by scientists and philosophers. A large number of variants, such as the "physical intuition" of my college professors, have been defined at various times by various people, creating confusion and, in some writings, allowing the concept of intuition to be dismissed completely as *not* a useful way of knowing for the scientist. I will consider means I have identified for doing science and determine where intuition enters in these practices. I will also discuss the question of whether intuitive abilities can be enhanced. Finally, I will examine whether intuition in science can be wrong, and if so, why.

The Role of Intuition in Philosophies of Science

Evelyn H. Monsay

Philosophers have long been interested in science as a particularly objective and dependable way of knowing. This has led to attempts to define a method by which science should be carried out and which will ensure the validity of scientific knowledge. At times, it seems, the methods abstracted by the philosophers have not been the same as those employed by the scientists!

For Aristotle, true knowledge would follow from logical deduction based on axiomatic first principles. Of course, the required first principles had to be givens, i.e., self-evident; in fact, they were often the result of naive physical intuition, a variant of intuition that will be discussed later. The commonly held notion of how science gets done is called the "scientific method," and originated with Francis Bacon (Bauer 1992). Bacon said that true knowledge would follow as generalizations based on observations of nature.

Bacon's concept of the scientific method is the predecessor of the dominant philosophy of scientific thinking in this century, Logical Positivism. The term "positivism" originated with Auguste Comte in the early nineteenth century (Bechtel 1988), and requires that true knowledge be empirical, that is, based on experience. The use of the term "logical" emphasized the view that clarity, precision, and rationality of thought and language are required in science. Although widely critiqued and disputed by philosophers and scientists themselves, Logical Positivism resulted in the still widespread, popular view of the scientist, even espoused by scientists themselves—especially in public—as "empirical, pragmatic, open-minded, skeptical, sensitive to the possibilities of falsifying; thereby establishing objective facts leading to hypotheses, to laws, to theories" (Bauer 1992: 20).

However, Logical Positivism has many problems. One problem with this inductive approach is that one never knows when the very next observation might completely contradict the current empirical generalizations—theories or laws. Karl Popper (1959) addressed this issue with his notion of falsifiability. Popper recommended that, instead of seeking confirmation for successful hypotheses, scientists should focus on demonstrating that some hypotheses can be proven false; this would be the route to true knowledge. Another problem, or at least a major gap, involved the lack of any attention to the source of the scientists' generalizations, the hypotheses. It was well known by the originators of Logical Positivism, and by scientists, that discovery often occurs in nonrational, nonlogical ways. The creation of scientific hypotheses, theories, and laws is often due to imagination and intuition. For the Logical Positivist, nothing can be said about the discovery process itself, and the resulting hypotheses would need to be backfitted with a thoroughly logical structure. A third major issue, called the "theory-ladenness of facts" by Bauer and others, involves the increasing evidence that empirical observation is not an objective basis for evaluating scientific hypotheses. To a certain extent, what we think we observe is colored by what we expect to observe, or what we choose to look at.

Evelyn H. Monsay

Finally, Logical Positivism implies a continuous, bit-by-bit accretion of scientific knowledge. However, historical analysis, as carried out by Thomas Kuhn in particular, shows that instead, scientific progress follows a cycle of revolution and cleanup. According to Kuhn (1970), scientists work within a general dominant framework for thinking—a *paradigm*—making predictions, observations, and minor adjustments to theory in the paradigm, until so many unresolved problems are accumulated that a crisis is reached. At this stage, a new paradigm is devised that, in a revolutionary move, displaces the old way of thinking. Due to the theory-ladenness of facts as mentioned above, there may not even be a compatibility of observations, of data, between the old and the new paradigms.

If philosophers cannot agree that Logical Positivism describes how science gets done, then what method do philosophers of science suggest? One interesting suggestion has come from Paul Feyerabend, who espouses a principle of methodological anarchism. "The only principle that does not inhibit progress is: *anything goes*," writes Feyerabend (1978: 23). Feyerabend believes that any and all methods should be used by the scientist, and ideas should not be tossed out even if apparently falsified, since they may yet provide insights into true knowledge.

In the following sections, I provide anecdotes of what scientists including myself report as their "methods"; the role that intuition and its adjunct, imagination, play will become clear. For now, however, the question remains as to what makes scientific knowledge so dependable and science so greatly successful. Bauer suggests that the reliability of scientific knowledge comes from the social structure of science (Bauer 1992). The frontiers of scientific research are not disciplined, rational, logical enterprises. Instead, scientists use whatever techniques they can to gain new understandings. It is the institutions established by scientists that take the raw material of scientific research and "filter" it through many stages of scrutiny—peer refereeing of papers, conferences, corroboration, or correction—before it becomes scientific, "textbook," knowledge. It is only at this stage, when cleaned up and rewritten, that it *looks like* the scientific method may have been used to gain true knowledge. Likewise, Popper (1994: 69) states "that the objectivity of natural and social science is not based on an impartial state of mind in the scientists, but merely on the fact of the public and competitive character of the scientific enterprise and thus on certain social aspects of it."

The Role of Intuition According to the Scientists

What role do scientists themselves give to intuition? In my introduction, I included several occasions in my life in which intuition played a role. In fact, I find that most of my inventive ideas arise with the characteristic suddenness after a prolonged "stewing," and with the initially ineffable character assigned to intuitive thought. Other scientists have also written that intuition plays a role in their work of discovery.

Einstein has been quoted as saying, "The supreme task of the physicist is to arrive at those universal elementary laws from which the cosmos can be built up by pure deduction. There is no logical path to these laws; only intuition, resting on sympathetic understanding can lead to them . . . " (Hoffmann and Dukas 1972: 222).

The astrophysicist Nicolò Dallaporta stated (Dallaporta 1993: 331),

> If one insists that "true science" is rooted only in experiment—and this in some sense constitutes the basis of the positivistic philosophical attitude— one must then admit that, in respect to the totality of knowledge required for the understanding of the whole cosmos, its capacity of grasping "reality" is clearly limited to portions of the universe not too dissimilar from our own surroundings, and that any attempt of speculation overpassing these limits is not truly "scientific," but only 'metaphysical.'
>
> If however one is reluctant to limit to such an extent the concept of "science," one must then admit that a wider range attributed to "science" cannot be associated to positivistic philosophy; so that, if one wishes to include the domain of "physico-metaphysics" as belonging to "true science," then "science" is only partly based on observation or experiment; as much, let us say as are poems, sagas, or epics, while it includes vast portions of imagination, fantasy, and intelligence, which make it akin with art and poetry in the largest sense. This is by no means a criticism, as art, as well known, includes sometimes much more truth than anything else. Reality, then, becomes unfathomable, and science acquires, besides its objective aspects which of course it maintains, a subjective character, which makes it more akin with human nature in its more general aspects than pure rationality.

Dallaporta, as an astrophysicist whose observations involve objects removed from our direct physical senses by huge distances and times stretching back billions of years, suggests that if we are to allow the study of such objects, then we must consider the whole of science to admit some "metaphysical" aspect, opening the door to intuition, imagination, and even fantasy.

But what about modern physics' reliance on the extremely logical, rational, and abstract field of mathematics? Hideki Yukawa, Nobel Prize winner for his theory of the pion, writes, "Nevertheless, I feel very uneasy about the fact that this one-sided trend to abstraction lacks something which is very important to creative thinking. However far we go away from the world of daily life, abstraction cannot work by itself, but has to be accompanied by intuition or imagination" (Yukawa 1973: 107). The process by which abstractions can become part of our intuition about the physical universe will be examined later in this chapter.

Mathematician Henri Poincaré was an astute observer of his own creative process. He reported how he worked intensively on a certain mathematical problem, right after which he left on a "geological excursion." Poincaré (Harman and Rheingold 1984: 28–29) continued:

Evelyn H. Monsay

Evelyn H. Monsay

The changes of travel made me forget my mathematical work. Having reached Coutances, we entered an omnibus to go some place or other. At that moment when I put my foot on the step the idea [a resolution to his mathematical problem] came to me, without anything in my former thoughts seeming to have paved the way for it . . . but I felt a perfect certainty. . . . Then I turned my attention to the study of some arithmetical questions apparently without much success and without a suspicion of any connection with my preceding researches. Disgusted with my failure, I went to spend a few days at the seaside, and thought of something else. One morning, walking on the bluff, the idea came to me, with just the same characteristics of brevity, suddenness and immediate certainty.

The modern notions of magnetic and electric fields largely originated with Michael Faraday. In his memorial lecture on Faraday, the mathematical physicist Hermann von Helmholtz remarked (Shepard 1976: 137):

It is in the highest degree astonishing to see what a large number of general theorems, the methodological deduction of which requires the highest powers of mathematical analysis, he found by a kind of intuition, with the security of instinct, without the help of a single mathematical formula.

Koestler noted (Shepard 1976: 137) that Faraday not only had an aversion to writing, but even to "language itself," and also "lacked any mathematical education or gift [beyond] the merest elements of arithmetic." But his invisible "lines of force . . . rose up before him like things."

Helmholtz himself reported that his own best ideas came to him suddenly, upon waking, or when hiking near Heidelberg and no longer actively thinking about his problem. The solutions sometimes came to him essentially complete (Shepard 1976).

Many famous scientists have had vivid mental images of the concepts they have worked with, instead of verbal, logical understandings. One of the most impressive examples is provided by Nikola Tesla, the eccentric inventor of fluorescent lighting, the three-phase electrical distribution system, and the self-starting induction motor. According to Tesla, his mental images of inventions he pursued were vivid enough for him to be able to run his mental models for weeks and then examine them for wear, all in his mind's eye (Shepard 1976).

Describing his research style, mathematician Harald Cramér (1970: 29) reports that

In some cases, this strenuous [mental] work, pursued during days and nights, may be enough. . . . [W]hen no further progress is within sight, a strangely interesting phenomenon will often appear. The concentrated efforts of the conscious part of the mind will seem to have set some wheels going on a deeper level, and the subconscious mind takes over the work. . . . And then there is so to speak a "knock at the door" of the conscious mind, the intuitively attained result is presented, and left over to be verified and rigorously proved by conscious work.

In fact, researcher N. Rashevsky proves that the life of a scientist may be very dangerous if the "'knock at the door' of the conscious mind" comes at the wrong moment. He states, "I personally was twice in danger of my life when the solution of a problem suddenly occurred to me while I was crossing a busy intersection" (Rashevsky 1970: 195).

Types of Intuition

One of the problems of studying the role of intuition in science is to be able to know which variety of intuition one is dealing with. Although some subtle differences should be illuminated, the "variety" to which I refer here is to a large extent, I believe, spurious. But since other authors have defined a multitude of different types of intuition, especially Bunge (1962), these categories must be addressed. I have already mentioned the "physical intuition" often referred to by physicists. Other varieties include visual intuition, spatial or geometric intuition, sensible intuition, kinematic intuition, intellectual intuition, which lies between sensible intuition and pure reason, and the strangely oxymoronic logical intuition of mathematicians and logicians.

Spatial/geometric intuition, founded on visual intuition, involves the realm of images and the imagination. This is the conceptual arena in which the link between imagination and intuition can be made clear. Visual intuition underlies the creation of mental images. Spatial/geometrical intuition is the ability to abstract a geometrical concept such as a curve or graph, and its associated arithmetical, algebraic, or analytical function from the mental image. This is a very tame sort of imagining based closely on the senses, or sensible intuition. Abstract creative imagination must be based on a metaphysical or even mystical intuition.

Sensible intuition is linked to the senses and common sense, or to what physicists would call "naive ideas." Sensible intuition should *not* be confused with physical intuition. In fact, references to "intuitively based errors" made by some educators who wish to make the teaching of physics easier (Fischbein 1987) should be careful to distinguish between the kind of intuition that causes errors (sensible intuition), and the kind of intuition that makes progress in physics much easier (true physical intuition). Sensible intuition can be wrong because it is based on the naive experiences we all have with very complicated physical systems. A block given an initial push along a table does not continue at a constant speed, as Newton said it would; it soon comes to a stop. The naive idea, or sensible intuition, built from this experience is that constant motion of an object requires a constant force. This is Aristotle's idea of the impetus. Why is this sensible intuition wrong? It is because the physical system under consideration is complex. We do not have just a block, a table, and an initial force; we also have friction between the block and the table. *Physical intuition* in this case would be based on experiences of isolated, simple systems, such as a block on

Evelyn H. Monsay

Evelyn H. Monsay

an icy surface, which, given a push, does continue in constant motion quite a distance, and additional experiences with surfaces of increasingly higher friction. The physical intuition described here could be said to relate to kinematical intuition, that is, a gut feeling for how objects really move.

Is physical intuition the same intuition that is described by Einstein, or Poincaré? I think we are dealing with two different phenomena, even though the difference may be one of degree, not type. I would associate physical intuition with the everyday, "normal" science described by Kuhn (1970) between revolutions and within a given paradigm, whereas the intuition associated with the great innovations of the revolutions I would call metaphysical intuition. Scientists' everyday work is that of solving puzzles. In everyday science, intuition and insight are required to solve the numerous puzzles that arise when a dominant scientific theory is manipulated so as to apply to as many experimental results and observations of nature as can be conceived. The experience needed to support this work and its associated intuition need only come from the one framework of the current paradigm. The gut-feeling, short-circuiting of reason experienced in solving these puzzles is physical intuition. However, for the creative theories that characterize a shift in paradigm, intuition must reach beyond what is understood, and beyond the current framework; hence, this intuition must be meta (i.e., beyond)—physical. Experience from fields other than physics may be critically important to the production of intuitive solutions in this case. Support for this notion comes from research in psychology. "In difficult problems, the critical associations may come from nonscientific areas, such as hobbies. In such cases, chance favors the scientist with a distinctive life-style and highly personalized nonscientific activities" (Mansfield and Busse 1981: 97–98).

So, physical intuition would be that type associated with everyday scientific research within a given paradigm. With Aristotle, we might conclude that physical intuition would be interchangeable with sensible intuition: the physical world was whatever presented itself directly to the senses. But certainly in the modern physics of atoms and elementary particles, of general relativity and its black holes, physical intuition cannot be identified with sensible intuition. In fact, Dallaporta essentially argued for the liberation of physical intuition from the senses in his quote given previously in this chapter. So, what is the basis for physical intuition these days, and why is it not also considered metaphysical intuition given its separation from sense data? Basically, the reason it is still different from metaphysical intuition is because the foundation of physical intuition is made to expand as each new paradigm is developed and assimilated. The senses provided the foundation for physical intuition initially. But when Newton created a paradigm shift with his theories of motion, the foundation for physical intuition changed so as to reflect the new understanding of kinematics and dynamics. Everyday puzzle solvers could make leaps of logic due to gut feelings (physical intuition) based on a more sophisticated experience of reality. As a graduate student and practitioner of quantum field theory, I can see, in retrospect, how the development of my physical intuition progressed through stages in this manner. For example, when I was first introduced to Feynman diagrams and the associated quantum field theoretic concepts and equations, I did not have any experience with this level of reality (more correctly, *abstraction* of reality) and I could only do the calculations out completely, logically, and often more times than I should have, lacking the intuition as to what aspect of a problem would be more or less important to the solution. Of course, I could have no sensory experience with electrons, photons, quarks, or gluons, but I would be able, through more experience with these concepts, to make them part of my reality and available for intuitive leaps of logic. This process of conversion of abstract concepts into my experience of reality did happen, and I became more intuitive in my approach to quantum field theories. However, the way in which this intuition worked, always staying within the thinking of the paradigm, would classify it as *physical* intuition rather than metaphysical intuition.

Yukawa (1973: 120) describes this process the following way:

> Not only is something essential to be abstracted from our rich but somewhat obscure intuitive picture, but it is also true that a certain concept, which was constructed as the fruit of man's ability to abstract, changes very often in the course of time into a part of our intuitive picture. From this newly constructed intuition, one can go on toward further abstraction.

Einstein (1960) also described a stratification of science, with each new "layer" being further abstracted from the physical senses, but bringing a higher logical unity to the science. Interestingly, Einstein sees this layering of concepts as fluid, it not being absolutely clear in which layer—more or less connected to the senses— a concept lies. Perhaps this is the physicist's understanding of the theory-ladenness of data described earlier.

How Science Gets Done

So how does science get done? From my point of view as a working scientist, several techniques of scientific discovery can be described and related to intuition.

Induction

This technique is the staple of the Logical Positivist, except that, as noted previously, the Positivist does not want to deal with the admittedly nonrational process of actual formation of the hypothesis based on collected observations. It is in the making of a hypothesis that intuition, dreams, fantasies, and techniques such as those that follow, enter. The formation of a hypothesis is really a form of pattern recognition, which is intimately related to the global nature of intuitive thought identified by Bastick (1982) and Fischbein (1987).

Evelyn H. Monsay

Deduction

In the Aristotelian mode, begin with a hypothesis believed to be true. Then make systematic observations to validate or refute the hypothesis. Again, intuition enters here in the production of the original hypothesis. (For Aristotle, the hypothesis would be self-evident and axiomatic—intuitive in the sense of logical intuition.) Both deduction and induction are involved in the fundamental selection of what problem to attempt to solve in doing research. Selection of the right problem— one that is doable and yet significant—is one of the most important distinguishing characteristics of great scientists, and is greatly influenced by the intuition of the selector (Mansfield and Busse 1981).

Analysis

This technique involves breaking down a problem or data set into parts or segments. Intuition is involved here in the selecting of the most *appropriate* breakdown of the original problem. Any of the elements of research—data, equations, or equipment—can be analyzed so as to suggest solutions to the overall problem.

Synthesis

The opposite process to analysis, synthesis involves grouping concepts, components (for carrying out experiments), or data in useful ways. Since intuition is basically a synthesizing process due to its global nature (Fischbein 1987), we expect it to come into play. It is also useful to note that the choice of which elements to synthesize and which to leave out is also dependent on intuition.

Playing Around

In this technique, the uses of analysis and synthesis of the elements of research— e.g., equations, data, and equipment—are alternated so as to hit on the best hypotheses, theories, or experimental approaches. Since intuition is important in the component activities—analysis and synthesis—it is also a factor here, as both a sensitivity to what to exclude or include and as a method to determine when a correct formulation has actually been reached.

Serendipity

This is "luck" in the sense of first playing around, and in the process, making "mistakes," and then recognizing the problem to which a solution has just been found! Pasteur made such a mistake and identified penicillin. Intuition is involved in realizing that a mistake according to logic and reason is, in fact, just a solution to another problem, in these cases.

Analogy

Considered a manner of pattern recognition by Yukawa (1973), when thinking in analogies, treat one problem, step-by-step or as a whole, in the same way in which another, similar problem was once treated. This requires knowing when one problem is sufficiently similar to another, and that is one point at which intuition enters. As a form of pattern recognition, it is again the global nature of intuition that comes into play.

Simplification

This technique involves reducing, in a reasonable manner, a complex situation to one that can actually be understood and in which problems can be solved. While reason can often provide the necessary simplification for a well-understood, yet complicated system, intuition is most useful in seeking the initial simplifying principles for systems that are not yet understood. This technique is related to analysis and analogy in its breaking apart of the elements of a problem, and its search for an appropriate "handle" on the situation through its similar behavior to some other, already understood system. The issue of problem selection is often dependent on the simplification technique.

Expansion

Here, we ask "What if?" and follow the implications of an initial idea through to various new resolutions. Intuition often will be the guide to the appropriate questions to ask.

Simulation

Give a computer the rules of the game (usually, a set of equations) and initial conditions, and using trustworthy numerical techniques, let the computer evolve a system in time. Then the system evolved by the computer can be examined and compared to real data. It seems that this technique would answer the philosophers' requirement for a foolproof way to obtain true knowledge that wouldn't even require a degree in science; however, such is not the case. No matter how mechanical the process of simulation seems once the computer starts rolling, intuition plays a significant role in setting up the scenario on which the computer crunches. Inappropriate choices of inputs in the set-up, made without the correct physical intuition, may provide wrong answers, or even misleading "right" answers, to the questions studied.

Thought Experiment

Create a mental picture of the conditions to be investigated and record the "data." Einstein (Polanyi 1958: 10) provides us with an example of this technique in his autobiography, in which he discusses his discovery of relativity

> after ten years' reflection . . . from a paradox upon which I had already hit at the age of sixteen: If I pursue a beam of light with the velocity c (velocity of light in a vacuum), I should observe such a beam of light as a spatially oscillatory

electromagnetic field at rest. However, there seems to be no such thing, whether on the basis of experience or according to Maxwell's equations. From the very beginning it appeared to me intuitively clear that, judged from the standpoint of such an observer, everything would have to happen according to the same laws as for an observer who, relative to the earth, was at rest.

Identification

Become one with the object under consideration and follow "your" behavior. In my own experience, I have used this technique to aid in my understanding of a complicated system's behavior in a turbulent underwater environment. I mentally traveled along with a small parcel of ocean water experiencing both the effects of the turbulence and of the physical behavior I wished to model, and arrived at a better intuitive understanding of how the phenomena interact.

Animation

Give an object a life of its own, in your mind, and follow its behavior. Physicists often talk about the objects of their study, such as electrons, in an anthropomorphic way. While the staunchest of the objective scientists will dismiss this as mere words, I believe it is a creative technique in which the scientist really does benefit from the intuition gained as the animated object does whatever "he" or "she" wants.

CAN INTUITIVE ABILITIES BE ENHANCED?

Many researchers believe that the conditions conducive to creative and imaginative thought, and therefore related to intuition, can be defined. Carl Rogers (Harman and Rheingold 1984) suggests three "inner" conditions and two "outer" conditions for creativity to flourish. The inner conditions include: (1) openness to experience, including a tolerance for ambiguity; (2) an internal locus of evaluation; and (3) the ability to toy with elements and concepts, much like the technique called "playing around" presented previously. The outer conditions for creative expression are psychological safety and psychological freedom. External evaluation and restrictions on responsible expression are antithetical to creative development. Westcott (1968: 187) sees "logical constraints placed upon thinking for the purpose of ordering communication and justifying conclusions . . . as the archenemies of intuition."

Given the conditions cited above, we can next turn to analyses of the creative process itself (LeBoeuf 1980). An intuitive notion is received most readily by a well-prepared mind. In a preliminary sense, the preparation involves developing knowledge in a particular field, and for even greater creative power and more metaphysical intuition (in the sense described previously), knowledge and experience in a broad range of endeavors. In terms of the particular creative process, immersion in the problem to be solved or total involvement with the factors of a situation is required. The better the definition of the problem or the nature of the solution required, the more likely an intuition will arrive. Emotional involvement, as well as mental preparation, is a predisposing factor.

Preparation must be followed by an incubation period, in which conscious consideration of the problem is suspended, for intuition to appear. The importance of this fallow time is well documented by scientists themselves, as well as by psychologists studying creativity. In practice, the need for an incubation period would translate into planned periods during which work is temporarily suspended—either by recreation, or by shifting to a different problem or interest.

The arrival of the intuition itself, if it is to come, will then appear with characteristic suddenness, as if "out of the blue." At this point, the remaining step in the creative process is verification. Whether or not intuition is to be trusted will be discussed in the following section. In any case, scientific intuitions must be elaborated and verified (at which point they may be called "insights"), and even backfitted with a logical derivation before they are published.

Finally, Jonas Salk (1983: 79) sees the development of increased intuitive powers as a necessity of human evolution. Salk writes:

> A new way of thinking is now needed to deal with our present reality, which is sensed more sensitively through intuition than by our capacity to observe and to reason objectively. Our subjective responses (intuitional) are more sensitive and more rapid than our objective responses (reasoned). This is in the nature of the way the mind works. We first sense and then we reason why. Intuition is an innate quality, but it can be developed and cultivated. . . . Reason may be seen as that which man adds to explain his intuitive sense. . . . Intuition must be allowed free rein and be allowed to play. Only then do we select, from among the patterns that emerge, the intuitively arising basis on which to contribute to metabiological and metabiospheric evolution. The intuitive mind establishes the parameters, the premises on the basis of which reason is formulated to correspond to intuitively perceived patterns.

ARE INTUITIONS ALWAYS CORRECT?

One of the distinguishing features of intuition identified by psychologists and scientists themselves is a feeling of certainty—the intuited idea is self-evident and correct. As humorously stated by British professor and engineer Eric Laithwaite (1985: 11), "A scientist is often wrong but never in doubt." But scientists are also familiar with how their beginning students' naive intuition, the sensible intuition of unstructured experience in the physical world, leads them astray in physics class. Some philosophers, including Bergson, Spinoza, and Croce, have considered intuition the way to true and perfect knowledge (Westcott 1968). However, as already mentioned, Bunge sees intuition as mere rapid inference and very open to fallibility.

Evelyn H. Monsay

Psychologists have sought for ways to define intuition so as to test for it and determine its validity in the laboratory. In particular, Westcott (1968) has studied "perceptual inference" as a behavior based on intuitive ability. Westcott has presented incomplete images, with varying degrees of incompleteness, to subjects and recorded the detail required for a correct first guess of what the image represents.

My conclusion is that intuition will be correct based upon the type of intuition with which we are dealing, and the quality of the circumstances (as described in the previous section, under which it arrives). Sensible intuition will not provide correct insights even in the realm of everyday experience. An intuition based on the experience of a block pushed on a table will not provide the correct insight for the behavior of that same block pushed on an icy pond. Physical intuition, used by the working physicist, must be built up stage by stage, away from immediate sensory experience into layers of abstraction. Intuition of the highest quality—metaphysical intuition that produces ideas beyond the realm of what can be known in the current framework of knowledge—must be built on a much broader foundation of knowledge than physical intuition. Metaphysical intuitions in science must be built on a foundation that comes from complete understanding of the scientific paradigm already in place, as well as including activities and knowledge from the whole panoply of human interests. The degree to which the foundation of knowledge has been built up will determine the quality of the intuition received, or perhaps more correctly, the trueness to its original, ineffable form with which it can be expressed in the conscious mind.

Given the preparation of a broad background of knowledge, the additional requirements for high-quality intuition are both the conditions and allowance for the steps of the creative process as described previously. Correct intuition will be more likely if there is an emotional need for a solution to a certain problem. The quality of the intuition will be enhanced if, after intense involvement with the problem, conscious attention is turned away from it for a while. True intuitions will only be expressed if an individual is open to new ideas and not subject to constraints of censorship, no matter how incidental the constraints seem. In particular, intuitions must be recognized and recorded *before* the censorship of one's own reason takes over. Only after the intuition as received is safely written down should the verification stage start.

In conclusion, we see that the common public picture, often promoted by scientists themselves, of the unemotional, rational scientist who mechanically pursues the Scientific Method as a sure highway to true knowledge is wrong. Instead, we see the emotionally involved thinker whose imagination is fueled with intuitive notions of realities yet to be developed into the reason of tomorrow.

REFERENCES CITED

Bastick, Tony
    1982 *Intuition: How We Think and Act.* New York: John Wiley & Sons.

Bauer, Henry H.
  1992 *Scientific Literacy and the Myth of the Scientific Method.* Illinois: University Press.
Bechtel, William
  1988 *Philosophy of Science: An Overview for Cognitive Science.* New Jersey: Lawrence Erlbaum Associates, Inc.
Bunge, Mario
  1962 *Intuition and Science.* New Jersey: Prentice-Hall, Inc.
Cohen, I. Bernard
  1977 "History and the Philosopher of Science." In *The Structure of Scientific Theories*, 2e, ed. Frederick Suppe. Illinois University Press.
Cramér, Harald
  1970 "Notes on Research Work in Mathematics." In *Scientists at Work*, eds. Tore Dalenius, Georg Karlsson, and Sten Malmquist. Stockholm: Almqvist and Wiksell.
Dallaporta, Nicolò
  1993 "The Different Levels of Connections Between Science and Objective Reality." In *The Renaissance of General Relativity and Cosmology*, eds. George Ellis, Antonio Lanza, and John Miller. Cambridge, Great Britain: University Press.
Dyson, Freeman
  1979 *Disturbing the Universe.* New York: Harper & Row.
Einstein, Albert
  1960 "The Method of Science." In *The Structure of Scientific Thought: An Introduction to Philosophy of Science*, ed. Edward H. Madden. Boston: Houghton Mifflin Company.
Ferguson, Eugene S.
  1992 *Engineering and the Mind's Eye.* Cambridge, MA: The MIT Press.
Feyerabend, Paul
  1978 *Against Method: An Outline of an Anarchistic Theory of Knowledge.* London: Redwood Burn Limited, Trowbridge & Esher.
Fischbein, Efraim
  1987 *Intuition in Science and Mathematics: An Educational Approach.* Dordrecht, Holland: D. Reidel.
Harman, Willis and Rheingold, Howard
  1984 *Higher Creativity: Liberating the Unconscious for Breakthrough Insights.* Los Angeles, CA: Jeremy P. Tarcher, Inc.
Hoffman, Banesh and Dukas, Helen
  1972 *Albert Einstein: Creator and Rebel.* New York: Viking.
Kuhn, Thomas S.
  1970 *The Structure of Scientific Revolutions*, 2e. Chicago: The University of Chicago Press.
Laithwaite, Eric R.
  1985 "A Scientist is Often Wrong but Never in Doubt." In *Science and Uncertainty*, ed. Sarah Nash. Middlesex, England: Science Reviews, Ltd.
LeBoeuf, Michael
  1980 *Imagineering: How to Profit from Your Creative Powers.* New York: McGraw-Hill.
Mansfield, Richard S. and Busse, Thomas V.
  1981 *The Psychology of Creativity and Discovery: Scientists and their Work.* Chicago: Nelson-Hall.
Neufeldt, Victoria and Guralnik, David B.
  1994 *Webster's New World Dictionary of American English*, 3e. New York: Simon & Schuster.

Evelyn H. Monsay

Polanyi, Michael

　1958 *Personal Knowledge: Towards a Post-Critical Philosophy.* Chicago: The University of Chicago Press.

Popper, Karl R.

　1959 *The Logic Of Scientific Discovery.* New York: Basic Books.

　1994 *The Myth of the Framework: In Defense of Science and Rationality.* London: Routledge.

Rashevsky, N.

　1970 "Some Ideas on the Nature of Research." In *Scientists at Work*, eds. Tore Dalenius, Georg Karlsson, and Sten Malmquist. Stockholm: Almqvist and Wiksell.

Salk, Jonas

　1983 *Anatomy of Reality: Merging of Intuition and Reason.* New York: Columbia University Press.

Shepard, Roger N.

　1976 "Externalization of Mental Images and the Act of Creation." In *Visual Learning, Thinking, and Communication*, eds. Bikkar S. Randhawa, and William E. Coffman. New York: Academic Press.

Westcott, Malcolm R.

　1968 *Toward a Contemporary Psychology of Intuition: A Historical, Theoretical, and Empirical Inquiry.* New York: Holt, Rinehart and Winston.

Yukawa, Hideki

　1973 *Creativity and Intuition: A Physicist Looks at East and West.* Tokyo: Kodansha International Ltd.

7

Subjectivity and Intuition in the Scientific Method

Brenda J. Dunne

Since 1979, the Princeton Engineering Anomalies Research (PEAR) Laboratory has been studying the role of human consciousness in the establishment of reality through interdisciplinary scientific investigation of anomalies arising in the course of human and machine interactions. In the course of designing and carrying out numerous controlled experiments addressing this theme, and attempting to develop theoretical models to enable better understanding of the observed consciousness-related anomalies, the role of intuition has proven to be a salient factor in the scientific process, and a critical complement to rigorous analytical methodology.

On the one hand, the generation of anomalies under controlled laboratory conditions demands acknowledgment of, respect for, and incorporation of such inherently subjective qualities of experience as aesthetics and intuition. On the other hand, the controversial nature of the very premise that human intention or desire can have an influence on the physical world requires impeccable adherence to the tenets of the scientific method in order to withstand the critical scrutiny of the scientific mainstream. The philosophy of the PEAR program represents an attempt to integrate these two dimensions, without sacrificing the integrity of either, in what we have come to regard as a "marriage of the white coat and the white turban."

As in any marriage, demands for compromise on both sides have generated a certain dynamic tension that, when constructively deployed, has proven to be an

Brenda J. Dunne

immense creative resource in these studies. It has stimulated critical examination of many of the conventional presumptions typifying contemporary science to determine which axioms are truly essential to its practice and which may be merely self-justifying conventions. Of equal importance has been the need to ponder the reliability of personal beliefs and proclivities, to ascertain to what degree they are truly intuitive as opposed to being convenient defenses against the often painful processes of self-scrutiny and reassessment of entrenched habits. Over the years, these considerations have led us to realize that although the exclusion of intuition and subjectivity in scientific practice can often result in pointless and unproductive lines of investigation, intuition untempered by critical analysis can just as easily lead to unsubstantiated conclusions, misinterpretatation of data, or self-delusion. The search for an optimal balance reflecting the best of both worlds has been an evolving process, resulting in an experimental program that not only deploys the most sophisticated technology and rigorous analytical methods, but also maintains a sincere concern and respect for the well-being and insights of its human participants and encourages their deep personal involvement.

Before beginning to assess scientific presumptions, however, one must decide what one means by the word "science." Simply raising this question confronts one almost immediately with a conceptual bifurcation that might be described as the distinction between a "thing" and a "process." To the majority of nonscientists, the word "science" invokes an image of a body of esoteric knowledge, represented in abstract mathematical symbolism, propagated by an intellectual elite who, having passed through a rigorous process of increasingly challenging planes of academic qualification, have ultimately achieved initiation into the secrets of nature. To many laypersons, the scientist's survival of this arduous process confirms him or her as a high priest of established knowledge, endowed with the implicit authority to define for those less qualified what is real and how it works. Questioning the authenticity of this revealed wisdom is risky, entailing the potential humiliation of being labeled "unscientific": a perjorative term suggestive of irrationality, illiteracy, or in extreme cases, heresy.

Unfortunately, this rather limited view of science as an ordained body of knowledge closely guarded by a fraternity of specially trained experts extends even to many scientific practitioners themselves. Those who maintain this posture tend toward a rather dogmatic conservatism wherein "truth" resides in an absolute, inviolable, and impersonal physical reality definable solely in reductionistic and mechanistic terms. They deny the relevance, or even the existence, of any form of intangible subjective reality, and exclude such "metaphysical" concepts as intuition, imagination, or creativity from consideration as legitimate topics for scientific study. Although most of the members of the scientific community who take satisfaction in propagating this public image speak for only that minority of scientists who are more concerned with flaunting their own authority than with advancing new knowledge, they unfortunately tend to be among the more vocal and visible representatives of the profession. In actual practice, this limited conception of science as a circumscribed body of knowledge encourages increased hyperspecialization in already well-established areas of investigation and inhibits the exploration of novel ideas and innovative forms of scholarly inquiry.

A more positive, and certainly more productive, way to define science is in terms of a process of acquiring knowledge. As we discussed in our book, *Margins of Reality* (Jahn and Dunne 1987), science ideally is a journey of discovery that moves forward on two feet. One of these is termed "experiment"—an observation or measurement performed under controlled conditions to acquire information about a specified topic or process. The other is called "theory"—a stated model, principle, or formalism to explain, correlate, or predict observational experience. When these two feet are well balanced and working in concert, science moves forward, shifting its weight successively from empirical experiment to explicating theory, or from predictive theory to confirmatory experiment, to advance understanding in a given arena of inquiry. But if either foot is lame, or clad in technical or logical gear unsuited to the prevailing territory, or if the path extends through a particularly obscure or hostile environment, progress is slower and more tentative. Then each step must be cautious, first testing its ability to support the next advance of its counterpart and, when insecure, retreating to a firmer position. Under such hazardous conditions, experiments that yield unreliable or inadequate data can cause the theoretical foot to lurch off balance, and ill-posed theories that improperly acknowledge the empirical evidence, or are inherently inadequate to deal with the phenomenological ground, may impel subsequent experimental steps into unproductive directions. Avoidance of such digressions, or survival of them when unavoidably encountered, requires technical skill and experience that must be balanced by intuition, imagination, and creativity. The difference between a sterile experiment and an effective one of equal rigor may lie as much in the impressionistic aspects of its interpersonal and environmental ambience and user-friendly protocols and feedback as in the elegance of its instrumentation and data processing. Similarly, the effectiveness of a theoretical framework may depend as much on its metaphorical potential to encompass the broadest possible range of applications as in its analytical precision or quantitative formalisms.

In a sense, one might view this scientific two-step as a very specialized case of the 125 common, and ordinarily unconscious, process employed by any living organism whose survival depends on establishing and maintaining a balanced relationship with its environment. The scientific method might thus be regarded as a particularly deliberate and disciplined attempt on the part of human consciousness to observe and formalize the mechanisms by which it acquires, interprets, stores, and utilizes the information it obtains from its environment. Ultimately, all human knowledge, whether individual or collective, devolves from this dynamic interplay of experience and conceptualization. Throughout life we accumulate information from the world around us, either incidentally or by design, which we then endeavor to assimilate, categorize, interpret, and apply to the prediction of, or accommodation to, future

Brenda J. Dunne

events. Two principal modes of operation, which might be termed discrimination and association, complement one another in the course of this activity. The former is more linear and focuses on distinctions—what makes one thing different from another—while the latter is more integrative and searches for similarities among apparently disparate concepts or experiences. It is in the course of establishing such associations that human consciousness proves itself to be particularly adept at creating models useful for guiding future decisions and avoiding past mistakes, and modifying them as needed on the basis of their empirical effectiveness.

Formal specification of the scientific method is usually attributed to Sir Francis Bacon, the renowned seventeenth-century philosopher, scientist, and statesman. As one of the principal architects of the Scientific Revolution, Bacon's articulation of the need for balance between empirical observation and deductive logic has influenced all subsequent scientific endeavors. Although his descriptive metaphoric prose would probably not pass muster among most contemporary journal editors, his representation of this essential dialogue spoke eloquently of the importance of defining science in methodological terms:

> those who have treated the sciences were either empirics or rationalists. The empirics, like ants, only lay up stores, and use them; the rationalists, like spiders, spin webs out of themselves; but the bee takes a middle course, gathering her matter from the flowers of the field and garden, and digesting and preparing it by her native powers. In a like manner, that is the true office and work of philosophy, which, not trusting too much to the faculties of the mind, does not lay up the matter, afforded by natural history and mechanical experience, entire or unfashioned, in the memory, but treasures it, after being first elaborated and digested in the understanding; and, therefore, we have a good ground of hope, from the close and strict union of the experimental and rational faculty, which have not hitherto been united (Bacon, *Novum Organum*, Part I, quoted in Taylor 1945: 86)

Virtually all of the prominent scientists of Bacon's era who were instrumental in bringing about this Scientific Revolution were themselves "heretics," rebelling against the intellectual suppression of a dogmatic religious authority. Many of them were practicing alchemists, others were theologians, but all regarded themselves as philosophers who sought a rational, analytical basis for their metaphysical beliefs. Over the better part of the seventeenth and eighteenth centuries, the practice of science not only explicitly acknowledged the centrality of subjective experience, but also regarded it as inseparable from, indeed as the very source of, its analytical activities. Even René Descartes, the renowned mathematician whose philosophy of mind/matter dualism is regarded as the source of contemporary materialistic reductionism, was himself a scholar in the long tradition of the early Greek philosophers, and regarded mathematics primarily as a metaphysical tool. Descartes' stated goal was the integration of all knowledge, both scientific and metaphysical, with philosophy ultimately serving as the basis for this unification. He believed that all the sciences taken together "are identical with human wisdom, which remains one and the same, however applied to different subjects" (quoted in Cohen 1985: 153), and described his rationalization for a mathematical methodology by observing that:

> The long concatentations of simple and easy reasoning which geometricians use in achieving their most difficult demonstrations gave me occasion to imagine that all matters which may enter the human mind were interrelated in the same fashion. (quoted in Davis and Hersch 1986: ix)

In one venue or another, this relationship between the subjective and objective facets of reality has been incessantly debated throughout the subsequent three centuries of scientific endeavor. However, as science began to acquire a powerful intellectual authority in its own right, the relationship became increasingly estranged and the balance gradually shifted toward a greater emphasis on the objective and more easily quantifiable characterisitcs of the observable world. For the better part of the last two centuries, this posture has proven highly effective for measuring and predicting the behavior of relatively large-scale physical phenomena, and has provided a firm base for the establishment of a socially, politically, and economically influential scientific infrastructure as well. But it has also made it easy to dismiss the metaphysical concerns that prompted the establishment of modern science in the first place, and has diverted attention from the scientific method itself toward topical reinforcements of established points of view.

By the early part of the present century, the emergence of increasingly sophisticated technology made it possible to extend scientific exploration into the previously inaccessible domains of subatomic and cosmological phenomena, and this in turn began to raise new questions about the objective nature of observation and the subjective participation of the observer. The advent of quantum theory, with its treatment of observation as a probabilistic and participatory process, raised subtle hints that there might be more to reality than purely objective, physically observable deterministic phenomena. While most of the pioneers of this theoretical initiative acknowledged the broad implications of such possibilities in their less technical writings, these were generally dismissed by subsequent generations of physicists as irrelevent speculation (Jahn and Dunne 1987). More recently, however, as the concept of information has come to dominate virtually all scientific domains, it has become increasingly difficult to ignore the implications of some active participation of consciousness, with all its troublesome subjective nuances, in the establishment of reality.

The entry of science and technology into the world of information brings with it two intriguing problems, neither of which have been adequately acknowledged, let alone addressed. First, there is the self-evident distinction between *objective* and *subjective* information. The former, the hard currency of information processing devices of all kinds, is thoroughly and uniquely quantifiable, and ultimately reducible to binary digits. For example, the objective information contained in any given book could in principle be quantified by digitizing each of its letters and every aspect of its syntactical structure. But the magnitude of subjective information the book presents clearly depends on the native language, previous knowledge, cultural heritage, degree of interest, and prevailing mood of its reader, and thus would seem to defy quantification. Nonetheless, we seem innately driven to attempt some quantitative specification; e.g., we might say "This book is more interesting, or more informative, than that one." Likewise, we might attempt to digitize the information displayed by a brilliant sunset or a magnificent waterfall in terms of the prevailing distributions of optical frequencies and amplitudes, but in so doing we would largely fail to convey the subjective beauty of the scene. The second complication arises from the proactive capacities of human consciousness to *create* information, as demonstrated quantitatively in our own laboratory experiments. When we shift from being "observers" to being "participants" in the world of information, we change the name of the game immensely. Instead of simply acquiring and utilizing information, we are now generating it, and with that capability comes all manner of opportunity, along with a deeper level of responsibility. Thus the quantification of subjective information stands as a major challenge to the science of information.

The true practice of science, like that of any spiritual discipline, requires a profound sense of humility and dedication, balanced by a mastery of technique. In the case of science, such technique includes strict requirements for objective assessment of evidence obtained under the most rigorous of experimental conditions, independent of any overlay of personal assumptions, desires, or expectations. But denial of such assumptions, desires, or expectations cannot achieve this end. To the contrary, such denial can actually prove counterproductive, since it essentially relegates the biases to the realms of the subconscious where they impede the processes of intuition and creativity with little resistance. Subjective bias can only be effectively set aside if it is first consciously acknowledged, a process requiring discipline of a different kind—one not usually encountered in the course of a standard scientific education.

The great intuitive leaps of insight, wherein inputs of apparently disparate bits of information randomly percolate below the surface of awareness, constantly rearranging themselves and eventually surfacing in a new meaningful pattern, require the spiritual detachment that only comes from self-examination. They express themselves through the sudden emergence of coherent information from a background of random noise, through the convergence of isolated threads of experience into an integrated and meaningful pattern of meaning, or through the recognition of an alternative interpretation of experience from an unfamiliar perspective. Although a number of prominent scientists have testified to the role of intuition in stimulating new insights and prompting creative approaches to challenging problems, they have seldom explicitly acknowledged this as a part of the scientific process, and intuition itself has certainly been given little place within established scientific epistemology or methodology (see Monsay, this volume). It is, in a very real sense, a mystical experience, but not one that is beyond the realm of science. On the contrary, as Albert Einstein (quoted in Barnett 1979: 108) observed, "it is the sower of all true science."

Superficially, application of the scientific method, with its insistence on strict objectivity, to this mystical domain of ultimate subjectivity—self-examination—may appear to present a formidable challenge. Notwithstanding, real scientific objectivity demands that the scientist's own subjective processes be raised to conscious awareness and taken fully into consideration. Only then can they be distinguished in some deliberate fashion from the empirical evidence under observation. To achieve this, the scientists must immerse themselves completely in the process they are studying, while maintaining the same detached awareness of their own subjective reactions as of the events transpiring under the microscope. Every scientific experiment, every theoretical model reflects to some degree the scientist's preconceptions, expectations, and desires; these are expressed in the choice of a problem, in the identification of a hypothesis, in the design of protocols and measuring equipment, in the determination of relevant variables to be examined, in the selection of the appropriate analytical tools for reducing and quantifying the data, and in the interpretation of the results and their synthesis within a preconceived model. Scientists who cannot admit a lack of knowledge, acknowledge a mistake or failure, or recognize the subjective factors that may have influenced their interpretation of experimental results are not only unlikely to contribute much in the way of creative new insights, but also do the scientific method a great disservice.

In our own laboratory program, for example, we confront this challenge by encouraging each member of the staff to participate in the generation of experimental data as well as in the design, analysis, or interpretion of the experiments. This firsthand experience of the processes under study not only helps us to be more sensitive to the needs of our outside operators, but also affords us the opportunity to observe our own subjective reactions to the phenomena. Similarly, we regard all the participants in our program as professional colleagues whose suggestions, insights, and criticisms are actively encouraged and solicited; these represent an important contribution to the research process. Over the years this policy has proven to be an invaluable resource in guiding the design of experiments and developing a better understanding of the results, as well as in creating an auspicious environment for the generation of subtle anomalies.

Consistent with the tradition of their alchemical ancestors, successful scientists achieve their most valuable advances in knowledge through the refinement and alteration of their own consciousness over the course of their manipulations of the physical world. Assiduous application of the scientific method is tantamount to a deliberate and systematic process of objectifying the activity of consciousness through a ritual of disciplined self-observation, wherein consciousness functions as the filter through which physical reality attains order and structure. As Werner Heisenberg put it:

> Natural science does not simply describe and explain nature; it is part of the interplay between nature and ourselves; it describes nature as exposed to our method of questioning. This was a possibility Descartes could not have thought, but it makes the sharp separation between the world and the I impossible. (1958: 81)

The method of questioning—the filters of consciousness, and the filtering process itself—are thus not only legitimate, but also critical topics for scientific study, and the process of acquiring knowledge is therefore of comparable significance to the knowledge thus acquired. Development of new modes of conceptualization that will permit accommodation of the intuitive, creative, and mystical dimensions of consciousness within the purview of science would not only retain for science the resilience and adaptivity necessary for its continued relevance and utility in the burgeoning age of information, but would raise the scientific method to its rightful place as one of the triumphs of transcendent human achievement.

REFERENCES CITED

Barnett, L.
  1979 *The Universe and Dr. Einstein*, 2nd ed. New York: William Morrow Bantam Books.
Cohen, J. Bernard
  1985 *Revolution in Science*. Cambridge, MA: The Belknap Press of Harvard University Press.
Davis, Philip J. and Reuben Hersch
  1986 *Descartes' Dream: The World According to Mathematics*. San Diego: Harcourt, Brace, Jovanovich.
Heisenberg, Werner
  1958 *Physics and Philosophy*. New York: Harper Torchbooks.
Jahn, Robert G. and Brenda J. Dunne
  1987 *Margins of Reality: The Role of Consciousness in the Physical World*. San Diego: Harcourt, Brace, Jovanovich.
Taylor, F. S.
  1945 *Science Past and Present*. London and Toronto: William Heinemann.

8

THOUGHT, ACTION, AND INTUITION IN PRACTICE-ORIENTED DISCIPLINES

Bob Harbort

INTRODUCTION

"How do you stand it then? How do you live at all if this wisdom of yours is not only the truth but also the price?" (Barnes 1961: 90). I have been interested in that question in one form or another for some years. It seems to me to be at the heart of the intellectual conundrum of the ethical role of the agent in knowledge: What is the relationship between what we each know as individuals and the common experience of humanity? How do we manage to bridge that gap? In fact, we *do* bridge it, every day. The path from thought to action goes across that bridge. In the quote above, the questions are being asked of a doctor. The wisdom referred to is the wisdom to progress from understanding to appropriate action. The price of such wisdom is realization of the wider ethical consequences of every act.

Rebecca Goldstein (1991: 242) contrasts "the reality of dreams" and "relative knowledge." She makes the point that there are different ways of knowing things—the personal, subjective understandings we each have, and the generalized knowledge of society as a whole. A facility for intuition in some sense relates to one's ability to slip the bounds of personal identity and become the representative agent of the common experience of humanity, but in a mode of action and intention that is still clearly personal. Angst, intuition, and insight are different places along the same spectrum of human experience.

This chapter is about the relationship of thought and action in practice-oriented disciplines such as medicine. Intuition fits into this research as a means of relating intentional behavior to global issues. My interest in intuition is a part of my research in artificial intelligence. I am interested in epistemological issues of problem-solving behavior in natural and computer-based agents. I began by using theories of interpretation as models of structured problem-solving. More recently I have begun to look at the relationships among personal identity, consciousness, and intentional behavior, with a goal of modeling the minimal amount of self-awareness necessary to achieve useful intentional behavior in a problem-solving agent. This will prove useful in designing artificial intelligence systems intended to work in restricted problem domains.

One of the difficult aspects of understanding problem-solving behavior is dealing with the generation of an intention to solve the problem on the part of the agent. While this is somewhat inherent in natural agents, it is hard to achieve in artificial systems. I think part of the problem is the lack of a way to relate locally understood contextual information to the more global context in which a problem to solve may be situated.

It is interesting to note that Aristotle closely linked thought and action, where the thought is always directed at some result of action (Aristotle 1982: 206). This linking is one of Aristotle's five modes of thought; it is called *phronesis* and it, of course, has two parts. The first is *sunesis*, or understanding, and the second is *praxis*, or action. Since the time of Aristotle, explaining how action arises from thought has been a thorny philosophical issue.

A major focus of Aristotle's philosophy is "prudence," the practical application of general moral principles to specific situations. In the twentieth century, people's ability to act prudently (in the sense Aristotle meant) has been constrained by the ascendancy of analysis—in its most general and Cartesian sense—as a primary mechanism of generating meaning. Analytic knowledge is decontextualized and fragmented. Epistemological models based solely in the analytic tradition are incapable of capturing many of the features of intentional behavior. A modern outgrowth of Aristotle's approach is philosophical hermeneutics, a collection of epistemological methods that model understanding as a contextualized and historically situated mediation between the universal and the particular.

Philosophical hermeneutics is aimed at explaining processes of interpretation as they apply to the broad social context of modern life. The mechanism is equally well suited to the study of thoughts and actions of individuals, so long as it is restricted to areas where there is a principle underlying the premises and a stated goal of action (Gadamer 1975: 278). Philosophical hermeneutics may be used to describe the change in frame of reference of a practical art from an objective, data-gathering one to an ethical, active one. It is this descriptive ability that makes it useful in studying the practice of medicine (Harbort 1977: 24–30). The problem is that philosophical hermeneutics addresses the relationship of thought to action at a philosophical level, without providing insight into the psychological processes that mediate the relationship. The purpose of this work is to extend the hermeneutic model through an examination of psychological and philosophical perspectives on intuition, motivation, and the role of experience in belief formation. In the following sections, I will examine the skill-oriented aspects of medical practice, discuss several aspects of intuition, and relate some ideas about intuition to epistemological questions about theory and practice, intentionality, and human culture.

Bob Harbort

MODELING MEDICAL PRACTICE: PATTERN RECOGNITION AND INTERPRETATION[1]

I have chosen to look at problem-solving in medicine because it is a good starting point for attempting to understand problem-solving in more general contexts. It provides a domain of knowledge that is restricted in scope, but not so restricted as to be artificial. It has aspects of learned behavior that follow to some extent the patterns of learned behavior in everyday life. Finally, it is practiced by real people and is thus observable in action in a natural setting.

I worked in clinical settings as a computer scientist and biomedical engineer for over fifteen years. When I decided to go back to graduate school to study theories of interpretation, it was because I felt that the state of medical informatics was not adequately supporting the problem-solving methods of the clinicians I saw every day at work. During my dissertation research, I took a year-long sophomore-level medical school course in clinical methods, during which I studied not only the course content, but also the training methods applied to the medical students.

Medicine, as practiced today, is both an art and a science. One way of resolving this seeming paradox is to examine medical practice through a hermeneutic approach. (Readers should note that this discussion deals with the clinical practice of medicine and not with individual, well-formulated medical sciences such as anatomy and biochemistry.)

One of the primary models of medical practice when it is considered to be a science is "differential diagnosis." This is often a good method for algorithmically performing diagnostic tasks, but it seldom matches the reality of human experience. The problem with differential diagnosis is that from any systematic starting point the aim of interpretation of medical facts is to arrive at the truth rather than at the probability of a hypothesis (Weed 1971: 47). It is precisely this orientation toward action that makes the practice of medicine of interest to those studying human problem-solving behavior. In its restricted domain, it gives us examples of two essential processes of human thought: the interaction of data and theory, and the merger of explanations into understanding. By studying how physicians practice, we can gain insight into more generalized mechanisms of arriving at truth-value, such as intuition.

There are three identifiable levels of the practice of medicine. At the technical level there are those items of practice that are so clear in meaning or effect they are considered unambiguous. These include such things as immunizations, antibiotic treatments, and well-defined laboratory tests for the identification of certain diseases. This level represents the application of principles of science to medical practice. Still at a technical level, but less objective in their applications, are those areas of medical practice that deal with problems we have not learned how to prevent, diagnose, or treat, such as heart disease and cancer. At a less technical level are the caring, understanding, supportive functions of medicine. Though medical information is provided at a technical and objective level, medical decisions are made on ethical grounds. The role of interpretation in medicine is in part to be found in the process of comparing irreconcilable sets of facts from these different objective systems in an ethical way.

A key feature of the hermeneutic model I am proposing here is the recognition that therapy is not a rule-based activity that commences upon completion of the diagnostic process. In the case of medicine, it is a necessary outgrowth of a more complete understanding of the patient, which started with a naive recognition of some provisional state and continued to evolve through diagnostic interpretation (Daniel 1983). Thus the act of caring for the needs of the patient is itself a part of the interpretive process.

At the early stages of interaction between physician and patient, conversation is used simply to define for the physician the perspective of the patient. This is necessary to contextualize the patient's medical problems in terms of his or her life. The process moves on to the interpretation of the patient's perspectives in terms of the specialized language of medicine. Finally, the application of skill and science is made in this new frame of reference. Thus understanding, in the hermeneutic sense, is a necessary part of therapy.

Most medical strategy depends on following a limited set of physiologic variables. These are monitored through a proto-diagnostic process that resembles quality-control checking. As variable values change, the guidelines for normality change, thus redefining the quality control limits and the process itself. Eventually this leads to a clear enough picture to allow the initiation of therapeutic action, in some cases even before any true understanding of the disease state has been attained.

The acquisition of a medical history relates those things that happen to all of us—having the flu, being in an accident—to the life of an individual. It is the task of the physician to interpret the aggregate of presented symptoms as a comprehensive diagnosis. He does this by seeking recognizable patterns among the presented symptoms. This is an area where explanation and understanding overlap. One might argue that in the case of something as seemingly objective as medicine, this is simply the perception of extant patterns (Ben-Bassat et al. 1977: 148; Galen and Gambino 1975: 42). But this is not the case, for the observer here is a skilled interpreter of facts. His interpretation is not controlled by his skill; rather the skill gives him something to interpret, and the facts he elicits arise from his skill (Watanabe 1977: 162). This embodiment of the skill in the practitioner rather than in the sciences that he utilizes is what elevates diagnostic medicine from a taxonomic science to an interpretive art. It leaves the practitioner neither totally free to carry out investigations of his choosing nor entirely at the mercy of his environment.

There are no solutions in medicine. The provisional nature of dealing with problems that cannot be completely defined is described by Polya (1957: 19): "We shall attain complete certainty when we shall have obtained the complete solution, but before obtaining certainty we must often be satisfied with a more or less plausible guess." Certainly one of the primary parts of the art of medicine is making the initial guess at a starting point for understanding of a patient's complex, dynamic set of interrelated problems.

Choice of a starting point for interpretation, however, is not methodologically part of the process, and it certainly is not objective. The skill orientation of the physician often determines his or her starting point, and the process of interpretation begins thereafter. "The act of understanding is at first a genial (or a mistaken) guess and there are no methods for making guesses, no rules for generating insights. The methodological activity of interpretation commences when we begin to test and criticize our guesses" (Ricoeur 1976: 81). The initial guess is most often the product of the interpreter's training and outlook. For the purposes of problem-solving, the "stem" of analogical reasoning used as an entry point into methodology cannot be restricted too much or the human problem-solver will be unable to realize his full potential.

The difference is apparent between the power to verify embodied in a scientific discipline and the power to convince embodied in a skilled interpreter. Clinical decision-making is based to a great extent on being convinced, and it is not clear how this relates to the power to evaluate probabilities, which is the operating principle of the sciences. Validating guesses, as opposed to weighing probabilities, is a process of mediating between the interpreter and the interpreted. The move is from understanding in a naive sense, to explaining (i.e., mediatively projecting reasons), to comprehension at a higher level. This has close corollaries in patient care activities, where one begins by treating the symptoms, gains an understanding of the processes that have brought the symptoms about, and then begins to treat the diseases that have become apparent through the mediative force of explanation (Watanabe 1977: 162). It is critical in this process that the manipulation and presentation of objective data be attuned to the interpretive skills of the clinician. A hermeneutic approach to modeling medical diagnosis and therapy offers advantages because it includes this process of dynamic changing among the multiple contexts of medicine as science and the specific context of the patient as person.

It has been demonstrated that it is possible to model the interpretive portion of medical diagnostics in several ways (Biss et al. 1976: 361). A hermeneutic model has advantages in adequate coverage of the importance of context, the mediation

Bob Harbort

between medical science and a particular case, and the relationship of understanding to intentionality. It is useful to discuss such a model because the discussion can be related to the evaluative portion of diagnostics. The hermeneutic model is also useful in relating the characteristics of information structures to the contextualization process necessary to start diagnosis and the recontextualization process that mediates the results of diagnosis and therapy into a new basis for understanding.

Objective data can contribute to interpretation in specifiable ways. The reality to be interpreted is important, but according to the hermeneutic model it is necessary to have a theory of reality that encompasses the scientific methods employed as if they were data. Habermas (1971: 308) points out:

> In the empirical-analytic sciences the frame of reference that prejudges the meaning of possible statements establishes rules both for the construction of theories and for their critical testing. Theories comprise hypothetico-deductive connections of propositions, which permit the deduction of lawlike hypotheses with empirical content. The latter can be interpreted as statements about the covariance of observable events; given a set of initial conditions, they make predictions possible. Empirical-analytic knowledge is thus possible predictive knowledge. However, the *meaning* of such predictions, that is their technical exploitability, is established only by the rules according to which we apply theories to reality.

To understand how this theory of interpretation applies to medical diagnosis, we must examine the functioning of thought processes at a level different from that of philosophical hermeneutics.

INTUITION

The rules by which we apply theory to reality capture only our surface behavior, and do not address motives or reasons for our actions. It is reasons for action we are after, and the concept of intuition is an important one in getting at them.

Some writers dismiss intuition as without merit. Minsky (1986: 329) describes it as "[t]he myth that the mind possesses some immediate (and hence inexplicable) abilities to solve problems or perceive truths." Quine (1978: 92–94) is somewhat more charitable, attributing intuition to unconscious perceptions. Because something is hard to get at, we often characterize it as irrelevant. Intuition is *not* irrelevant to the study of motives and beliefs; it should be studied for at least two reasons.

First, intuition is *there*. It exists as an operational construct in social phenomena, and has for thousands of years (see Laughlin, this volume). We must either come to understand what we mean by intuition or replace it with something else as heuristically useful. Second, intuition offers relief for the uncertainty in practical application of empirical models of explanation such as the one based on hypothetico-deductive inference (above).

On a broader level we must come to grips with the explanatory power of intuition. A world of explanations based only on science would be extremely limited because of the limited applicability of pure scientific inference. Scientific inference follows the rules of logic in its most fundamental and idealized sense. The data of scientific inference, and the sphere of its results, are firmly in the real world, which is not without error and uncertainty. Reconciling these two is difficult at a philosophical level (Haack 1974: 109–125). Some of these problems can be attacked through the use of statistical inference, but much of the world in which we like to think science reigns supreme is so uncertain and chaotic that we must look elsewhere for mechanisms to deal with our approximate knowledge (Haack 1974: 124). A way around this problem is to allow for the existence of a human agent in carrying out hypothetico-deductive inference. We can then make use of psychological constructs to provide for the approximateness of our science.[2] One of these constructs is intuition.

This chapter is about the role of conscious intuition in structured problem-solving activities where the problem-solver's eventual goal is some intentional activity. Operationally, in this context, intuition is the process of imagining something that turns out to be true. By "true" I do not mean to imply correctness in the logical sense but only in the sense that the thinker is willing to act upon his or her conclusions. The major implication of this is that no new perceptual or conceptual constructs are necessary to explain intuition. It is a mix of constructs, such as imagery and narrative formation, with an underlying basis of experience. Bergson (1946: 130) notes that familiarity is an important characteristic of when intuition works — it is more successful when the thinker is familiar with the question at hand, familiar with the language in which it is phrased, and so on.

Bergson defines intuition (1946: 306) as "the metaphysical function of thought: principally the intimate knowledge of the mind by the mind, secondarily the knowledge by the mind of what there is essential in matter. . . . " He relates this clearly to interpretation, and in a long section on Berkeley's psychological theories (1946: 136–42) illustrates that he is taking a hermeneutic definition of interpretation. Bergson characterizes the approach of modern scientific inquiry (and its philosophical underpinnings) as having a notion of the location of truth in "things":

> Modern philosophers have brought truth from heaven down to earth; but they still see in it something which is pre-existent to our affirmations. According to them, truth is lodged in things and facts. . . . Even a philosophy like that of Kant, which insists that all scientific truth is relative to the human mind, considers true affirmations as given in advance in human experience. (1946: 254)

Bergson (1946: 254) recognizes that this stems from our desire for an orderly universe: "This conception of truth is natural to our mind and natural also to philosophy, because it is natural to picture reality as a perfectly coherent and systematized

Bob Harbort

whole sustained by a logical armature"(1946: 254). Then, invoking his operational definition of intuition, he (1946: 148) reminds us that "[s]cience is the auxiliary of action." Consider these remarks by Bergson:

> But experience pure and simple tells us nothing of the kind. . . . Experience presents us a flow of phenomena: if a certain affirmation relating to one of them enables us to master those which follow, or even simply to foresee them, we say of this affirmation that it is true. . . . Reality flows; we flow with it; and we call true any affirmation which, in guiding us through moving reality, gives us a grip upon it and places us under more favorable conditions for acting. (1946: 255)

Finally, Bergson contextualizes truth-value, emphasizing its forward-looking nature yet noting the strong influence of reality:

> While for other doctrines a new truth is a discovery, for pragmatism it is an invention (1946: 256). . . . Every truth is a path traced through reality: but among these paths there are some to which we could have given an entirely different turn if our attention had been orientated in a different direction, or if we had aimed at another kind of utility; there are some, on the contrary, whose direction is marked out by reality itself: there are some, one might say, which correspond to currents of reality. (1946: 258)

In summary, intuition as a psychological construct allows an individual to use creative faculties to deal with real-world problems. As a philosophical construct, it allows an individual to apply personal knowledge in negotiating the uncertainties of reality. These represent the self-reflective and worldview components of Bergson's metaphysical definition of intuition. How an individual acquires the ability to use intuition is a question that must be answered by looking at processes of learning and thought.

Thought, Experience, and Action

The history of Western thought on thinking has been one of increasing reliance on the computational metaphor. Recent examples include Fodor (1968: 145–52; 1975: 28–29), Pylyshyn (1984: 196–97), Scholz (1987: 144–84), and to a lesser extent Rock (1985: 207–8). Also, recently, there has been a move toward other approaches, notably ones based on pattern recognition (Watanabe 1977: 161; Margolis 1987: 25–41). What follows is based on the pattern recognition approach, and specifically on Margolis's ideas on patterns of thought. I have taken this approach because it ties in theoretically with the pattern recognition approach to interpretation.

Margolis (1987: 78–80) defines two types of intuitive thought: checking a process or action and narrowing one's focus of attention. (These correspond roughly to the internal and external parts of Bergson's definition.) Margolis uses

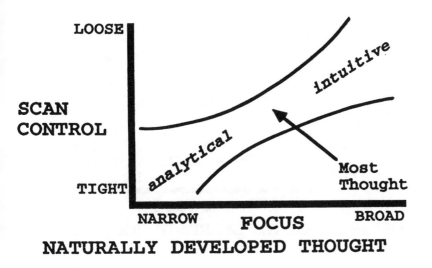

Bob Harbort

Figure 1

these two constructs to define a spectrum of modes of thought, ranging from analytical (intensive checking and narrow focus) to intuitive (minimal checking and broad focus). He develops the thesis that any instance of thought falls somewhere in this spectrum, but that we naturally think more at the ends than in the middle. (See Figure 1.)

This appears to me to be an adequate model of the thought processes humans develop naturally as they mature. It describes much of our everyday experience, and one can see its genesis in studies of childhood thought processes during development. It is not, however, sufficient to explain intentionally learned thought processes such as those that occur in the practice of medicine, law, and many other disciplines.

The two major drawbacks to Margolis's model as applied to practice-oriented thought are (1) that it does not model accurately the change in thought processes that occurs with increasing experience, and (2) that it offers no explanation for motivation to action.

I propose that intentionally learned thought processes can be modeled using Margolis's two constructs of intuition by combining them in opposite ways from his model. At one end of the spectrum of learned thought processes is the area of problem definition—it has a broad focus of attention coupled with intensive checking of processes and relationships. At the other end of the spectrum is the area of *praxis* (action)—it has a narrow, focused intent coupled with minimal checking of one's actions (see Figure 2). An example from everyday life might be the checking for causes you go through when your car's engine stops; you think of a variety of problems and evaluate them. When you realize you've run out of gas you set about getting more fuel with a good deal of focus but not much worrying that you can't figure out how to do it.

Bob Harbort

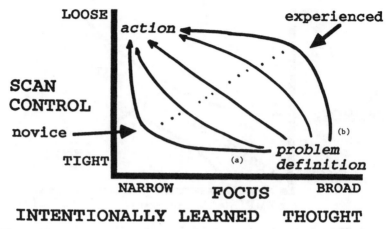

Figure 2

The previously defined interpretive combination of diagnosis and therapy can be modeled in terms of cognitive processes moving back and forth along the spectrum of learned modes of thought. It provides a basis for understanding the role of experience in forming thought patterns—the more experienced someone is in a discipline the more monotonic the progression of thought processes will be from problem definition to action. Less experienced individuals will proceed in a more cyclic fashion, placing more emphasis on external, objective reality and less on previous experience. (Compare this with Bergson's description of the flow of reality.)

Not only will the small steps toward problem-solving be different in skilled and unskilled cases, the overall trajectories will be different as well. In moving toward the narrow focus of the problem (see Figure 2, line 'a'), the novice will be slow to give up tight scan control, which provides continual feedback about the appropriateness of decisions. The expert (Figure 2, line 'b'), on the other hand, will rely more on experience and stop the extensive rehearsing of activity earlier in the process. Figure 2 illustrates the trajectories in terms of cognitive activities; what it cannot show is the dynamics of the situation. The expert's path to taking action (line 'b') will generally take significantly less time than that of the novice (line 'a'), even though the endpoints of the paths are the same.

Motivation to action in this model is related to reduction of uncertainty. Both of Margolis's intuitive constructs contribute to the reduction of uncertainty. As one's focus becomes narrowed, the global uncertainty of extraneous stimuli is reduced. As one's experience is reinforced, the uncertainty that is the result of having a worldview at variance with the facts is reduced. Action becomes possible when these two factors, narrowing of focus and reinforcing of experience, reduce uncertainty below some threshold.

Reality impinges on this process primarily by having differing amounts of connectedness for different episodes of thought and practice, depending on the area of one's focus. For example, the possible unintended side effects of setting a simple fracture of an arm are much less far-reaching than the possible unintended side effects of a lung transplant. Thus a physician with even minimal experience at setting broken bones would move more monotonically from problem definition to action in the case of a broken arm than in the case of a lung transplant.

A Bayesian Model of Intuition

A major feature of the above model of thought is that it explicitly incorporates the thinker's experience into the process. Since the beginnings of modern science in the late Middle Ages, practice-oriented disciplines have moved steadily away from Aristotle's framework of linking thought and action toward an ever-increasing dependence on scientific explanation. This has minimized the role of the agent in modeling processes. As mentioned above, differential diagnosis is a widely proposed but not very successful model of the human diagnostic process.

One moderately successful model of diagnostic reasoning is based on the work of Thomas Bayes (1702–1761), who defined a method for describing the probability of an event in terms of the probabilities of associated events; this has come to be known as Bayes' Theorem. Real diagnoses of problems in real people are often too complex to be accurately explained by Bayes' Theorem, however, as most realistic situations do not meet the necessary criteria of applicability.

Perhaps we have been applying Bayes' Theorem to the wrong set of probabilities. Based on my model of the thought processes relating problem definition to action, a more useful application of Bayes' Theorem is to include the agent's experience in the calculation of some of the conditional probabilities used in the theorem. It may be possible to extend the idea of a probabilistic accounting of a thinker's experience to produce a more quantitative, experimentally verifiable model of the role of intuition in problem-solving processes. This will require separate measurement of sign recognition (corresponding to Margolis' checking function) and event recognition (corresponding to breadth of focus).

The Problem of Belief

Heidegger (1971: 6) observed, "We never come to thoughts, they come to us." The previous sections have provided a model at several levels of how thoughts come to a thinker and become incorporated in thought processes. The role of more deep-seated beliefs in motivating action is much less clear. The direction of the idiomatic

Bob Harbort

expression "come to believe" is significant in its oppositeness to Heidegger's observation on thoughts. While holding a belief is not an active process (Quine and Ullian 1978: 9–10), coming to believe something *is* a process. It must be built up out of other, lesser levels of acceptance of truth-value.

Operationally, we do not use beliefs the way we do other evidence. To a degree, beliefs are what we use to check more mundane evidence against. What we believe and how we believe it is therefore very important to an understanding of problem-solving behavior. It is particularly important because doubt, the opposite of belief, is psychologically a very powerful block to action.

In examining the philosophical and psychological aspects of the practice-oriented disciplines, we need to be able to characterize the effects of an agent's belief structures on the move from thought to action. Some questions for further study in this area are: How does one tell a "true" belief from a delusion? Does it matter? How do the specifics of an agent's beliefs about underlying reality affect the use of the intuition constructs postulated above? How are an agent's beliefs affected by experience?

Intuition, Intentionality, and Human Interests

Massimo Piattelli-Palmarini discusses several shortcomings of intuition in his book *Inevitable Illusions*. One problem is that of mental shortcuts. He correctly points out that they make our thought *processes* inaccessible to correction, thus causing us ". . . to insist on the accuracy of our intuitions and conclusions" (1994: 6–7). He also discusses the serious problems of probabilistic intuition based on personal experience (1994: 194), and the human tendency to intuitively feel more comfortable when interpreting a sequence of events (or script) than a single event (1994: 132–33). All of these are valid criticisms, but they apply *only* to the "local," individually based form of intuition.

Intuition is a central part of humans' ways of thinking in a number of contexts (Heschel 1955: 14). A key to furthering our understanding of how we use intuition is to distinguish between "local" and "global" intuitive contexts. Local intuition may be thought of as generalization based on individuality. Global intuition, on the other hand, is based on the assertion that ". . . there is a transcendent meaning to the universe independent of our comprehension . . . " (Heschel 1955: 106). It is this global intuition that finally allows us to transcend our individuality and relate our values and our concerns to the human community in which we exist (see Burneko, this volume). Its tentative and accepting nature is open to nuance and correction, not resistant to it. It is not based on statistical interpretation of personal experience but on a *nonstatistical* relating of our experience to that of others. Finally, because its focus is global, its mechanism is one of distillation from general to particular rather than one of falsely constructing generalities out of randomly concatenated particulars.

One aspect of how intuition relates intentional behavior to more global contexts is its role as a bridging mechanism between theory and practice. Stanley Fish (1989:

581), who in his dual careers as a literary theorist and a lawyer is certainly well versed in such mechanisms, suggests that there must be something more subtle than didactics in the process of becoming a practitioner: ". . . articulation of the theory refers to knowledge acquired independently of it, and serves as a mnemonic and exhortative device." In a semiotic sense, theories represent templates or patterns for practical action to follow. It is our intuitive thought processes that allow us to fill in the action patterns with specifics that may not be of immediate concern but are a necessary part of the overall problem-solving process. Theory represents commonly held values and concerns; the global form of intuition allows us as individuals to apply these truths to specific instances of practical action. Thus skill-based practice like medicine is informed by both individual experience (knowledge and ability) and global concerns (relation to the common good).

Action based solely on experience is shallow and rule-driven, with (at best) periodic reevaluations of the agent's experiences to define a new basis for further static instances of action. Action based on an intuition for our "experience in common" has depth; it is a self-defining act, in addition to being an action for some purpose (Scruton 1980: 522). Action based on intuition is what relates the individual to the community. "To participate in a common culture is . . . to be gifted with a certainty in one's feelings. . . " (Scruton 1980: 530). It is global intuition that creates this certainty, ". . . when the matter is, in the last analysis, settled for the agent, when he sees his situation in terms of objective imperatives rather than subjective choices, imperatives that record for him the fact of his shared humanity, even in the midst of a predicament that is uniquely his" (Scruton 1980: 530).

To adequately understand practical knowledge and its application, we must have some form of assessment. The physician aims for the *right* diagnosis, not the most probable one. It is the achievement of the desired end that is the measure of success, not the application of the correct skills.[3] "[T]he practical equivalent of truth must be . . . finding satisfaction in what is achieved" (Scruton 1980: 531). Practical action is, necessarily, appropriate action. Part of its value lies in contextualizing the unique circumstances of the act in terms of intuitively understood common culture. "If I see a special significance in common culture, it is precisely because it provides concepts that classify the world in terms of the appropriate action and the appropriate response" (Scruton 1980: 535). It is this use of intuition that ties our isolated activities to the common good, and allows us ". . . to achieve order where there might have been chaos" (Scruton 1980: 536).

SUMMARY AND CONCLUSIONS

Starting from a model of medical practice based on philosophical hermeneutics, I have examined several philosophical and psychological perspectives on the concept of intuition. I have used an extension of Margolis's work on problem-solving to differentiate between naturally developed and intentionally learned modes of thought, and I have used this difference to characterize the role of experience in motivating action. I have also proposed a Bayesian model of accounting for experience in thought processes and discussed some of the problems of relating belief structures to problem-solving behavior.

The use of a pattern recognition approach to modeling problem-solving has extended previously developed interpretive models of medical practice in both depth and detail. As was the case with generalization from earlier results (Harbort 1987: 128–201), these techniques offer the promise of applicability to a wider field of study than medicine.

By looking at the role of intuition in the restricted setting of a practice-oriented discipline, we have gained a clearer understanding of its nature. We have seen how intuition operates to mediate between the particulars of a given situation and the generalities of common experience, facilitating the formation of intention and will to action. We have also seen how an understanding of the role of intuition helps practitioners to resolve some of the ethical dilemmas arising from the dual allegiances they owe to their clients as individuals and to society as a whole.

Extension of intuition as a concept into wider areas of cognitive science is underway. It is being applied not only to more everyday types of cognition but also to finer-grained modeling of cognitive processes associated with the kinds of technical tasks done by, for example, assembly-line workers. Mahan (1994: 113) summarizes the future direction of some research on cognition in manufacturing processes by emphasizing "... the importance of gaining a full understanding of intuitive cognition, [and] differentiating between intuitive cognition and its analytical counterpart." Fruitful areas for future work exist in relating intuitive cognitive processes to problem-solving and task-oriented activities. Some of these include further investigation of how intuition relates theory to practice, and more study of the use of intuition in situating an individual agent's acts within a framework defined by common culture.[4]

Notes to Chapter 8

1. Adapted from portions of chapter 3 of Harbort (1987).
2. This approach raises interesting philosophical questions for those who would construct "expert systems" to deal with problem-solving in domains where action is the intended result. Swartout and Smoliar (1987) and Miller and Fisher (1987) explore some of these problems.
3. Scruton (1980: 531) points out that the modern problem of dealing with the ends of actions arises from Kant, who was so convinced of the autonomy of practical reason that he could not acknowledge any basis for assigning it external validity.
4. Conversations with Deborah Finn, Sheila Langenhennig, Nancy-Laurel Pettersen, and Elbert Tuttle were instrumental in formulating the ideas presented here.

References Cited

Aristotle
  1982 *Ethics*. New York: Penguin Books. (This is J. A. K. Thomson's translation of *The Nicomachean Ethics*; the section referred to is Book 6, chapters 3–7, pp 1139b–1141b of Bekker's Greek text.)
Barnes, D.
  1961 *Nightwood*. New York: New Directions.
Ben-Bassat, M. et al.
  1977 "Pattern-Based Interactive Diagnosis of Medical Disorders," *IEEE Transactions on Pattern Analysis and Machine Intelligence* 2: 148–55.
Bergson, H.
  1946 *The Creative Mind*. New York: The Philosophical Library.
Biss, K. et al.
  1976 "Semantic Modeling for Deductive Question Answering," *IEEE Transactions on Computers* 24: 358–65.
Daniel, S. L.
  1983 "Humanities and Medicine: A Question of Relevance." In *The Crisis in the Humanities*, eds. S. Putzell-Korab and R. Detweiler. Potomac, MD: Studia Humanitatis.
Fish, S.
  1989 *Doing What Comes Naturally*. Durham, NC: Duke University Press.
Fodor, J. A.
  1968 *Psychological Explanation*. New York: Random House.
  1975 *The Language of Thought*. New York: Crowell.
Gadamer, H. G.
  1975 *Truth and Method*. New York: Seabury Press.
Galen, R. S. and S. R. Gambino.
  1975 *Beyond Normality: The Predictive Value and Efficiency of Medical Diagnoses*. New York: Wiley.
Goldstein, R.
  1991 *The Dark Sister*. New York: Viking.
Haack, S.
  1974 *Deviant Logic*. London: Cambridge University Press.
Habermas, J.
  1971 *Knowledge and Human Interests*. Boston: Beacon Press.
Harbort, B.
  1977 Unpublished manuscript.
  1987 Applications of Hermeneutics to Models of Medical Information (unpublished doctoral dissertation). Ann Arbor, MI: Dissertation Abstracts International.
Heidegger, M.
  1971 *Poetry, Language, and Thought*. New York: Harper and Row.
Heschel, A.
  1955 *God in Search of Man*. New York: Farrar, Straus and Giroux.
Mahan, R.
  1994 "Stress-Induced Strategy Shifts Toward Intuitive Cognition: A Cognitive Continuum Framework Approach," *Human Performance* 7: 85–118.

Margolis, H.
  1987 *Patterns, Thinking, and Cognition.* Chicago: University of Chicago Press.
Miller, P. and P. Fisher.
  1987 "Causal Models in Medical Intelligence," IEEE *Proceedings of the Symposium on Computer Applications in Medical Care* 11: 17–22.
Minsky, M.
  1986 *The Society of Mind.* New York: Simon and Schuster.
Piattelli-Palmarini, M.
  1994 *Inevitable Illusions.* New York: John Wiley & Sons.
Polya, G.
  1957 *How to Solve It.* Garden City, NJ: Doubleday.
Pylyshyn, Z.
  1984 *The Computational Theory of Mind.* Cambridge, MA: MIT Press.
Quine, W. V. and J. S. Ullian.
  1978 *The Web of Belief.* New York: Random House.
Ricoeur, P.
  1976 *Interpretation Theory: Discourse and the Surplus of Meaning.* Fort Worth: Texas Christian University Press.
Rock, I.
  1985 *The Logic of Perception.* Cambridge, MA: MIT Press.
Scholz, R.
  1987 *Cognitive Strategies in Stochastic Thinking.* Dordrecht: D. Reidel.
Scruton, R.
  1980 "Emotion, Practical Knowledge and Common Culture." In *Explaining Emotions,* ed. A. Rorty. Berkeley: University of California Press.
Swartout, W. and S. Smoliar.
  1987 "Explaining the Link between Causal Reasoning and Expert Behavior," IEEE *Proceedings of the Symposium on Computer Applications in Medical Care* 11: 37–42.
Watanabe, S.
  1977 "Pattern Recognition as Conceptual Morphogenesis," IEEE *Transactions on Pattern Analysis and Machine Intelligence* 2: 161–163.
Weed, L. L.
  1971 *Medical Records, Medical Education, and Patient Care.* Chicago: Year Book Medical Publishers.

9

Intuition as Authoritative Knowledge in Midwifery and Homebirth

Robbie Davis–Floyd with Elizabeth Davis

> The ways we attend to and with our bodies, and even the possibility of attending, are neither arbitrary nor biologically determined, but are culturally constituted.
>
> —*Thomas Csordas,*
> "Somatic Modes of Attention" (1993: 135)

I am a cultural anthropologist—one who studies human behavior. I bring to the investigation of intuition the "anthropological perspective," a critical gaze at the diversity of human cultures that sees them relative to each other. No one culture defines "reality"; rather, each human group, in constant interaction with its environment and with other groups, evolves a set of adaptations that include unique ways of being, of doing, and of knowing. Out of the diversity of "ways of knowing" in the Western world has emerged, in the past four centuries, a hegemonic emphasis on knowledge that is externally obtained—"facts" that are discovered through scientific research, information compiled with graphs, statistics, and machines. We in the West receive this knowledge from others: it is taught to us in classrooms, written down in books, downloaded into our computers. Storing up large amounts of this externally obtained knowledge in our brains is essential for success in Western technocratic society; we are graded on it, judged by it, succeed or fail on the basis of how much of this knowledge we have. And so we often forget, or tend to discount, internally obtained knowledge—the knowing that comes to us from the inside of our bodies, arising as a "gut feeling," an intuition.

Part of the anthropological enterprise is to go away from one's familiar environment for a year or so to do "fieldwork" in other cultures—to attempt, however slowly and clumsily at first, to both observe and participate in another culture and

Robbie Davis-Floyd with Elizabeth Davis

to come to know that culture "from the inside," through lived experience. When you have experienced and begun to understand another culture, you can know profoundly that your own culture is not the "real world," but just one way of interpreting that world, one system out of many. And so, in the course of this endeavor, many anthropologists have lived in and have come to understand cultures that value internal knowing just as much as Westerners value knowledge that is externally obtained. Such cultures often are geographically remote, in the Amazonian wilderness or the mountain fastnesses of Nepal. And some exist right in the middle of the technocracy. This chapter will investigate one such group—the subculture of American homebirth midwifery.

Less than two percent of American women give birth at home, so the midwives who attend them cannot fail to be aware of their marginal relationship to (some would say deviance from) the norms and values of the wider society. The vast majority of the women in that wider society give birth in hospitals, and accept, as part of that process, the authority of knowledge obtained from physicians and from machines. This acceptance has consequences that were eloquently articulated by sociologist Barbara Katz Rothman in an address to the 1992 Midwives' Alliance of North America Conference in New York City:

> Diagnostic technologies, from the most mundane and routine ultrasound to the most exotic embryo transplant, have in common that they work toward the construction of the fetus as a separate being—they reify, they make real, the fetus. They make the fetus a visible, audible presence among us, and they do that by doing two other things. They medicalize pregnancy, and they render invisible and inaudible, women.
>
> The history of Western obstetrics is the history of technologies of separation. We've separated milk from breasts, mothers from babies, fetuses from pregnancies, sexuality from procreation, pregnancy from motherhood. And finally we're left with the image of the fetus as a free-floating being alone, analogous to man in space, with the umbilical cord tethering the placental ship, and the mother reduced to the empty space that surrounds it.
>
> It is very very hard to conceptually put back together that which medicine has rendered asunder. . . . As I speak to different groups, from social scientists to birth practitioners, what I find is that I have a harder and harder time trying to make the meaning of connection, let alone the value of connection, understood.

As I sat in the audience listening to Rothman's speech, I understood that her words, spoken to a gathering of midwives who have no trouble at all understanding the value of connection, crystallized for these midwives their aloneness in the world of medicine, a world in which the subtle rewards of connection are often lost as the value of those technologies of separation is increasingly taken for granted. The hot exchange of breath and sweat, of touch and gaze, of body oils and emotions, that characterizes births in which there is an intimate connection between the mother and her caretaker, has given way in the United States to the cold penetration of needles, the distant interpretation of lines on a graph. Building on Rothman's earlier work (1982, 1989), I identify, in *Birth as an American Rite of Passage* (1992), the "technocratic model" of birth as the core paradigm underlying contemporary obstetric practices, including diagnostic technologies. As Rothman points out, separation is a fundamental tenet of this paradigm.

Under this model, authoritative knowledge—the knowledge on the basis of which decisions are made and actions taken (Jordan 1993)—is vested in machines and in those who know how to manipulate and interpret them. Fascinatingly, this is so despite the fact that the near-universal use of such machines on laboring women in the United States has not resulted in improved birth outcomes, as has been convincingly demonstrated by numerous large-scale studies[1] (Leveno et al. 1986; Prentice and Lind 1987; Sandmire 1990; Shy et al. 1990). These studies have shown that hooking women up to electronic fetal monitors results only in a higher Cesarean rate, not in better outcomes. In earlier works (1992, 1994), I discuss these machines as symbols of our culture's "supervaluation" of machines over bodies, technology over nature. I analyze obstetrical procedures, diagnostic and otherwise, as rituals that not only convey cultural core values to birthing women, but also enhance the courage of birth practitioners by deconstructing birth into identifiable and (seemingly) controllable segments, then reconstructing it as a mechanistic process. I found that these ritual procedures enhance courage not only for obstetricians and nurses, but also for the women themselves—being hooked up to some of the highest technologies society has invented gives many American women the feeling that they are being well taken care of, that they are safe. A reassuring cultural order is imposed on the otherwise frightening and potentially out-of-control chaos of nature.

But not all women are reassured by the technocratization of birth. There are some women in the United States who supervalue nature and their natural bodies over science and technology, who regard the technological deconstruction of birth as harmful and dangerous, who desire to experience the whole of birth—its rhythms, its juiciness, its intense sexuality, fluidity, ecstasy, and pain. Those women who most deeply trust birth place themselves quite consciously as far out of the reach of the technocratic model as they can get, choosing to give birth in the sanctity and safety of their own homes, and grounding themselves philosophically in a holistic model of birth (Davis-Floyd 1992: 154–59). Like the midwives who attend them, these homebirth women have no trouble understanding the value of connection; indeed, connection is the most fundamental value undergirding their holistic belief system.

There is increasing evidence that midwife-assisted homebirth is as safe as, and often safer than, hospital birth (see Davis-Floyd 1992: 177–84; Wagner 1994; Goer 1995), but this evidence is little known and not at all acknowledged in the wider culture, which still assumes the authority of the technomedical tenet that hospital birth is far superior to birth at home. Thus, as health care practitioners, all mid-

Robbie Davis-Floyd with Elizabeth Davis

wives, even those who attend women in their homes, are under tremendous cultural pressure to "do birth according to medical standards," as one midwife put it. But "doing birth according to medical standards" will in many cases mean using interventions and/or transporting the woman to the hospital, despite the midwife's alternative judgment. Midwives must attempt to meet these cultural imperatives. Such attempts place many midwives in conflict with their own holistic paradigm and the patience and trust in birth and the female body that it charters. Contemporary midwives cannot fail to be aware of this dilemma; it is a central defining theme of their practices and their lives, ensuring that for them, every homebirth that is not textbook-perfect will pose ethical, moral, and legal dilemmas that might end them up in a courtroom in danger of losing the right to practice. The level of tension between the technocratic and holistic paradigms with which homebirth midwives must constantly cope makes their occasional willingness to rely solely on intuition—sanctioned by the holistic model and condemned by the technocratic model—a strong marker of their commitment to holism and its underlying principle of connection.

The purpose of this chapter is to call attention to midwives' use of intuition as a salient source of authoritative knowledge. My intention is not to refine the concept of intuition, but simply to utilize Jordan's (1993) formulation of the notion of authoritative knowledge as a theoretical tool to help in understanding the role that intuition plays for contemporary midwives. To begin, I will briefly explore some recent theoretical perspectives on the nature of intuition.

On the Nature of Intuition: Theoretical Perspectives

> I think, because we're in a culture that doesn't respect intuition, and has a very narrow definition of knowledge, we can get caught into the trap of that narrowness. Intuition is another kind of knowledge—deeply embodied. It's not up there in the stars. It *is* knowing, just as much as intellectual knowing. It's not fluff, which is what the culture tries to do to it.
>
> —Judy Luce, homebirth midwife

Intuition is defined by the *American Heritage Dictionary* (1993) as "the act or faculty of knowing or sensing without the use of rational processes; immediate cognition." Salient characteristics of intuition as identified by Bastick (1982) include sudden and immediate awareness of knowing, the association of emotional affect with insight, the nonanalytic (nonrational, nonlogical) and gestalt nature of the experience, the empathic aspect of intuition, the "preverbal" and frequently ineffable nature of the knowledge, the ineluctable relationship between intuition and creativity, and the possibility that an insight may prove to be factually incorrect.

In *Women's Intuition* (1989), midwife Elizabeth Davis (who collaborated with me in the data collection for this study) points out that, regarding the acquisition of information, Western society gives authoritative status only to the highly linear modes of inductive and deductive reasoning. Yet as Laughlin (this volume) notes, it is well established that there is no creativity in science, indeed, in any domain of creative activity, that does not entail intuition. Why then is intuition so devalued in the West?

As a number of social scientists (Martin 1987; Merchant 1983; Rothman 1982) have pointed out, mechanistic metaphors for the earth, the universe, and the body have been gaining increasing cultural prominence since the time of Descartes. Conscious deductive reasoning, which can be logically explained and replicated, is the most machine-like form of human thought. Thus, ratiocinative processes — that is, processes in which one reasons methodically and logically — are reified in the West, while nonlogical, nonmethodical cognition is devalued. Intuition refers to our experience of the results of deep cognitive processes that occur without conscious awareness and cannot be logically explained or reproduced. Laughlin (1992, 1993a) postulates that intuition is *neurognostic*—inherent in the basic structure of the human central nervous system—which would account for the pan-human attributes of the experience of intuitive insight. He suggests that language and its concomitant ratiocinative conceptual structures did not evolve to express the *entire* human cognitive system and its operations, but only those relevant to social adaptation, noting that the kind of knowledge that can be expressed by the human brain's linguistic and conceptual structures is superficial in relation to the deeper neurocognitive processes, such as intuition, "upon which knowledge in its broader creative sense depends" (Laughlin 1993a: 70).

Summarizing the differences between left and right hemisphere functioning, Laughlin (this volume) notes that various anthropological theorists have taken these differences to the extreme of suggesting two types of culture defined by "rational" and "intuitive" ways of knowing. This suggestion is paralleled in contemporary popular writings by Rianne Eisler's (1988) distinction between "dominator" and "partnership" cultures, and Daniel Quinn's (1991) distinction between "Takers" and "Leavers." These distinctions are also paralleled by the differences between contemporary American homebirth midwifery and the technocratic society in whose midst midwifery exists and struggles to flourish. The technocracy is largely hierarchical, male-dominated, machine-oriented, and oriented towards left-brained principles of separation and discrimination, while homebirth midwifery is primarily egalitarian, nature- and female-oriented, and aligned with right-brained principles of holism and connection.

Of course, such apparently clear-cut dichotomies often mislead. It is important to remember that, in spite of hemispheric dominances, the whole brain is involved in all brain functions. Sharp functional division between the hemispheres occurs only in subjects whose brains were actually split or damaged, either by injury or by surgery (Sprenger and Deutsch 1981). In the normal, healthy brain, similarity and replication of function are much more common. Noting that biofeedback findings

Robbie Davis-Floyd with Elizabeth Davis

Robbie Davis-Floyd with Elizabeth Davis

on those in deeply meditative states confirm that interhemispheric coherence is highest in such states, Eugene d'Aquili (1978) has speculated that the highly aroused limbic system may have the ability to unify both hemispheres, flushing the brain free of dichotomy. Laughlin (this volume) suggests that intuition is "mediated by neural networks in both lobes, not merely in the right lobe," calling neurocognitive processes that produce intuition "transcendental" in part to stress their cross-hemi-sphere, whole brain functioning.

Science, for all its supervaluation of left brained deductive reasoning, could never have proceeded without the creativity of intuition (Bastick 1982; Hayward 1984; Jung 1971; Vaughan 1979), and no intuition-oriented culture could survive without heavy reliance on ratiocination. Likewise, even the most technocratic of physicians often find themselves following their intuition instead of their reason (Fox 1975, 1980), and even the most holistic of midwives, in this postmodern era, are likely to have attained a high level of competence in using the technocratic tools of birth, and are able to explain and defend their actions in scientific, linear, and logical terms. The praxis of postmodern midwifery entails, in many ways, the careful exercise of inductive and deductive reasoning even as it continues to rely for its pri-mary ethos on the enactment of bodily and psychic connection.

BACKGROUND AND CONTEXT: INTRODUCING THE POSTMODERN MIDWIFE

In the postmodern era in the Western world, we have gone beyond the anesthetized births of the 1940s and 1950s, the near-total demise of lay midwifery by the 1960s, and even the "natural childbirth" movement of the 1970s to a hegemonic focus on technology-assisted reproduction and technobirth, the basic principles and tenets of which have become formally encoded as the "standards of practice" regarded as authoritative in courts of law. Resistance to this technocratic hegemony in birth is strong and has spawned multiple movements and options that offer true alterna-tives, including the Bradley method of childbirth education (McCutcheon-Rosegg 1987); freestanding birth centers (Rooks et al. 1989); the homebirth movement (Kitzinger 1979; Sullivan and Weitz 1988); and the midwifery renaissance (Davis 1987; Gaskin 1990; Schlinger 1992). The fact that the legal system so completely supports the praxis of technobirth has forced those midwifery practitioners who take the risk of opposing it to become almost hyper-educated in the science of obstetrics so that they can both defend themselves against legal persecution by the medical establishment and work to change the laws that keep them legally marginal.

In response to such pressures, and in service to the increasing numbers of urban middle- and working-class women who request their services, "lay"[2] midwives in the United States have expanded from their original base of traditional practition-ers serving specific ethnic groups in bounded communities (see, for example, Susie

1988) to full participation in the postmodern world. In the Third World, as the viability of indigenous systems of birth knowledge is everywhere challenged by imported biomedical systems (Jordan 1993; Sargent 1989; Davis-Floyd and Sargent 1996, 1997), midwives are emerging as articulate defenders of traditional ways, as well as creative inventors of systems of mutual accommodation (MacCormack 1996). This phenomenon that I have labeled *postmodern midwifery*—midwives who are educated, articulate, organized, political, and highly conscious of both their cultural uniqueness and their global importance—is not limited to the United States but is increasingly emergent all over the world (see, for examples, Kitzinger 1990).[3]

My juxtaposition of "postmodern" (a charged word in the anthropological lexicon) with "midwifery" is far from casual. With that juxtaposition, I am trying to make salient the qualities emergent in the praxis, the discourse, and the political engagement of a certain kind of contemporary midwife. George Marcus has stressed that the power of the postmodern intervention in anthropology has inhered in its "radical critique" (1993: 6) of unexamined conventions and monological assumptions, both ethnographic and cultural. As Linda Singer points out in "Feminism and Postmodernism," in feminist writings this radical critique "recurs with variations" as:

> an explicit discursive strategy of challenging the terms, conventions, and symbols of hegemonic authority in ways that foreground the explicitly transgressive character of this enterprise . . . postmodern discourse disrupt[s] the project of closure by consensus, by insisting on exposing how differences inscribe themselves, even when they are explicitly refused or denied. The voice of rationality is shown to be riddled with contradictions it cannot exclude. (1992: 469–70)

This surely is an apt and accurate description of midwifery practice as described here. We will see how midwives, in their intentionally transgressive reliance on intuition, quite regularly expose the contradictions that the voice of rationality proves, in the domain of birth, to be unable to exclude. The transgressive nature of postmodern midwifery is further displayed in the fluidity with which the midwives interviewed for this study move between the biomedical and midwifery domains, appropriating the authoritative lexicon and the whiz-bang technologies of biomedicine to the holistic philosophy and "of service to women" ethos of homebirth midwifery. These same midwives, and others like them, have become adept at challenging the terms, conventions, and symbols of hegemonic authority in the courts, the press, state legislatures, and through the politics generated by the actions and interactions of their national organizations. Through such ongoing activities, as well as in countless aspects of the daily discourse and praxis of midwifery, these midwives self-consciously engage in the most radical of cultural critiques.

In the United States, the two organizations most instrumental in facilitating the advent and transgressive activities of the postmodern midwife have been the Midwives' Alliance of North America (MANA[4]), to which all of the midwives interviewed for this study belong, and the American College of Nurse-Midwives

Robbie Davis-Floyd with Elizabeth Davis

(ACNM). Although MANA was conceived and created (in 1982) as an umbrella organization that would unite all North American midwives, to date it has primarily
served as a vehicle for the collective voice of homebirth midwives; most members of
MANA actively attend births at home or in freestanding birth centers. The ACNM
(founded in 1955) limits its membership to certified nurse-midwives (CNMs). CNMs
must first become registered nurses, after which they undertake an additional year
or more of intensive academic and technomedical midwifery training. Most of the
6000 CNMs currently practicing in the United States work in hospitals; some work
in freestanding birth centers; and a few attend births at home.

In spite of the polarization between these two organizations, MANA members
have not lost sight of their original charter; in keeping with that vision, from its
inception MANA has insisted on inclusivity. It welcomes all midwives as members—
including CNMs (who constitute one-third of its membership) and *direct-entry midwives*, who are trained in midwifery schools, college midwifery programs, or through
hands-on apprenticeship training. The apprenticeship route to midwifery, not considered legitimate by the ACNM, is highly valued by the members of MANA for the
connective and embodied experiential learning it provides.

MANA as an organization operates by consensus, a process that requires a high
degree of agreement on basic issues and values. MANA's explicitly stated philosophy
of birth, arrived at through the consensus process, is holistic, and its 1400 members
have made it clear that they generally share in that holistic philosophy and
approach, as expressed in the following excerpts from the 1992 final draft of MANA's
Statement of Values and Ethics:

> We value:
> The oneness of the pregnant mother and her unborn child; an inseparable and
> interdependent whole.
> The essential mystery of birth.
> A mother's intuitive knowledge of herself and her baby before, during, and
> after birth.
> A woman's innate ability to nurture her pregnancy and birth her baby; the
> power and beauty of her body as it grows and the awesome strength sum-
> moned in labor.
> Our relationship to a process larger than ourselves, recognizing that birth is
> something we can seek to learn from and know, but never control.
> Expertise which incorporates academic knowledge, clinical skill, intuitive
> judgment, and spiritual awareness.
> Relationship. The quality, integrity, equality, and uniqueness of our interac-
> tions inform and critique our choices and decisions.

Various versions of the Statement of Values and Ethics were developed,
reviewed by the membership, revised, and revised again over the last four years until
full consensus was reached on the final draft, from which the above excerpts are
taken.[5] This set of values constitutes a direct challenge to the technomedical

approach to birth; its high degree of reflexivity is thoroughly postmodern. The enormous value that MANA midwives place on relationship and connection is evident throughout. I present these excerpts as a clear illustration of MANA's working philosophy—the context within which the high regard that the midwife-interviewees in this study have for intuition must be understood. The full conceptual and practical ramifications of this philosophy are complex and far-reaching, and will be addressed in future works. Here I will only point out the conflicts that will inevitably arise between this holistic (inclusive, egalitarian) philosophy and the exclusive, hierarchical demands of the technocracy, which until now has consistently devalued "lay" midwifery, and has given status and credibility only to CNMs, who took pains many years ago to constitute themselves as a profession associated with—and structurally subordinate to—the medical establishment.[6]

One of the most pressing issues facing independent postmodern midwives in the United States and Canada is this question of professionalization, which has been a divisive issue within MANA for some years, as professionalization involves more organization, regulation, bureaucracy, and limits on practice than some independent midwives have been willing to accept (see Schlinger 1992). Part of the fear has been that with the encoding of independent midwifery into a profession with specific certification and practice requirements will come—as has happened in so many other professions, including nurse-midwifery—a decrease in respect for "softer," situationally responsive elements of practice such as reliance on intuition. In this light, the interest of my collaborator Elizabeth Davis and some of her midwifery colleagues in writing, speaking, and offering workshops about the use of intuition at birth can be seen as an attempt to formalize midwives' understanding of intuition in order to heighten its status as a viable and valid source of authoritative knowledge—an endeavor in which this present study may also play a role.

METHODS

This chapter is based on interview data obtained from twenty-two white, middle-class American midwives about the role that intuition plays in their behavior at births. Seventeen of these midwives are empirically trained and primarily attend homebirths. Five are certified nurse-midwives (CNMs). Most interviewees are experienced midwives with three to sixteen years in practice; three have been in practice less than a year. Three of the CNMs attend births both at home and in the hospital; the other two are hospital based. Most of the midwives were attendees at the 1992 MANA conference in New York or the 1993 MANA conference in San Francisco; almost all of the interviews were conducted at these two conferences. While I can make no definitive claims as to the representative nature of my interview sample, I can affirm from many years of interaction with midwives that the attitudes, beliefs, and experiences of our interviewees are typical for MANA members.

Robbie Davis-Floyd with Elizabeth Davis

The interviews, which were tape-recorded, were generally from one-half to one hour in length. I began by interviewing midwives who were recommended to me as having "good stories" to tell. Some of the interviews ended up taking the form of story-telling sessions, as midwives walking by felt moved to join the session and recount their own experiences. Each one was asked to tell as much as they wished about incidents surrounding birth in which intuition had played a role. My goal was to elicit as many "intuition stories" from the midwives as I could, so that I could begin to gain a sense of if and how much these midwives relied on intuition, of the results in actual births of their acceptance or rejection of intuitive messages, and of their feelings about the value and usefulness of intuition as a diagnostic tool and guide to action—in other words, as a form of authoritative knowledge.

An additional twenty stories were gathered at a tape-recorded workshop on intuition called "Spinning Tales, Weaving Hope" by my collaborator, Elizabeth Davis, at the 1993 MANA conference in San Francisco, during which all the midwives present were asked to share any experiences with intuition that they felt were important. While Elizabeth Davis and I cannot be sure what role this workshop and the interviews I conducted played in these midwives' opinions and ideas about intuition, the mere fact that we, as authoritative figures, were particularly focused on intuition no doubt helped to validate or to enhance the idea of intuition as a legitimate source of authoritative knowledge in the minds of our interviewees. This was explicitly intended by Elizabeth Davis, who designed her workshop for just that purpose; in my case, it was an inevitable by-product of the interview process—yet another illustration of the essential connectedness of the anthropologist to her subjects of "study," and of the intense subjectivity of the anthropological endeavor (Clifford and Marcus 1986, Marcus and Fisher 1986).

That subjectivity was also much in evidence during the process of data analysis. As anyone who works with interview data knows, the process by which one arrives at an interpretation of that data is difficult to describe. When one interviews, as I often have in the past, from a pre-designed list of questions, one can compare the answers to a certain question or set of questions across the database. In this case, however, I was not working from such a list, but rather asking for stories and listening to them as they unfolded. I transcribed the tapes, read the transcriptions over and over, and discussed them at length with Elizabeth,[7] until salient themes and patterns began to emerge that shed light on our central organizing question: To what extent and under what circumstances do midwives utilize intuition as a source of authoritative knowledge for decision-making during birth?

Midwives and Intuition

Connection As a Prerequisite

The first fact that jumped out at us from our interview and workshop data was the enormous value midwives place on "connection." Connection, as these midwives experience it in homebirth, means not only physical, but also emotional, intellectual, and psychic links. It is not merely two-way, as with the connectedness of midwife to mother, or mother to child.[8] If we were to diagram it, we might draw something like a web, with strands connecting mother, child, father, and midwives, each to the other.[9] If, further, we were to look inside each individual, we might see other strands of the web connecting each individual to the deepest essence of herself. Our interviewees insisted that the degree of connection they are able to maintain with mother and child depends on the degree of connection they maintain to the flow of their own thoughts and feelings. So basic is the importance of this internal connectedness that many of them actively seek it during and even before birth. As Elizabeth Davis explained to me:

> Sometimes, especially when I've been doing a lot, it's really hard for me to clear myself and arrive at the birth open. So before I leave, I lie down and just try to unwind and unfold my concerns of the day and open to myself, so that I can also be open to the woman and her birth.

This effort to "be open" to oneself and to the woman and her birth is a common theme among homebirth midwives. The connectedness it facilitates extends not only to the psyche and emotions, but also to physical sensation and experience. Consider the following quote from a Canadian midwife:

> In our collective practice, one of the things that we became really aware of over time was that if one of the midwives at a birth had diarrhea [it was a message that we should] look at things a lot closer. Inevitably in those births something came up. . . .
> Q. How would you explain that? Why would a midwife get diarrhea if something's wrong with the birth—what's the connection?
> I think you're intuitively picking up that something isn't quite right here. It's coming out in the body—it hasn't gone into the head yet.

The physicality of this knowing of which she speaks is reinforced in this description by a California midwife:

> My scientific self believes that everything happens inside my skull, in my brain. [And I have intellectually learned many skills, many techniques.] But my physical experience is that [in dangerous situations in which my mind isn't sure what to do, which technique would be the very best]—say, the baby's head comes out, but it won't rotate, and the shoulders are stuck—a cone of power comes straight down the width of my head, through my body, and out through my hands. And my hands begin to do a maneuver, and my mouth begins to speak and I tell the woman to turn over [on her hands and knees], or I reach up and grab hold of the baby's butt and draw the baby down, or I do whatever I do—but I didn't know what I was going to do before that moment—and that's midwife intuition. [Maggie Bennett[10]]

From whence does this "cone of power" originate? While both Maggie and the Canadian midwife quoted above describe intuition as intensely physical, Maggie's "cone of power" adds a spiritual dimension as well. Asking many of our intervie-wees where intuition is located, we received the following responses: "All through the body"; "It's cellular"; "It's in my stomach"; "It's inner knowledge—you don't know where it comes from"; "Your heart, your dreams"; "Your connection to the universe"; "My higher self"; "My heart, my chest, my throat"; "I'm very audi-tory—I hear it as a voice coming from deep inside." We can conclude that for our interviewees, intuition seems to involve the body, psyche, and spirit, but not the rational mind.

The midwives say that they experience the kind of openness described by Maggie Bennett and Elizabeth Davis, and the connectedness it facilitates, as essen-tial to receiving intuitive messages. If they are closed—"shut down," "discon-nected"—they cannot hear that inner voice, and must rely on their extensive intellectual knowledge and accumulated expertise. While they see nothing wrong with this, they do seem to regard it as a qualitatively different type of care, as will be evidenced in the following section.

Learning to Trust

In both formal interviews and casual conversations with midwives, we heard them express strong familiarity with biomedical diagnostic technologies. Their in-group jargon is filled with technomedical terms, their midwifery bags bulge with technolo-gies,[11] and their homebirth charts look quite hospital-like, with maternal tempera-ture, blood pressure, and fetal heart tones duly recorded at proper intervals. Yet, these same midwives who are so competent at using the jargon and the diagnostic tools of technocratic medicine often perceive the information thus obtained as a highly adulterated blessing, perhaps a source of as many problems as it solves. As Elizabeth Davis explained this issue:

> What I see going on in a lot of midwifery training programs is the idea that here's this body of knowledge, and one needs to be schooled, and one needs to be tested—the idea that the student is empty and waiting to be filled, and the knowledge is there, and after you stuff it in, then the student is "qualified." But in midwifery, no amount of that is ever going to compensate for a lack of self-confidence or an ability to blend critical thinking with personal responsibility. What makes a really good midwife, I think, are those inner-based qualities of analysis and discernment, the emotions that she stays in touch with because she does not divorce her *self* from the process of learning, so that the feelings of self-respect, and self-love, and self-trust blend to make her humane and to keep her connected. I think in birth, if you're not part of the process, you're a threat to the process.

The other midwives we interviewed were in complete agreement with her. For all of them, being part of the process of birth, being connected, constituted the pri-mary ingredient of their success—an ingredient far and away more significant than their albeit considerable technical diagnostic skills. One of them even went so far as to say that:

> Assisting women at birth—that's all it is, is intuition. I listen to the baby's heartbeat, because, you know, I listen to the baby's heartbeat, but I don't really care about it, because I have this inner knowing that everything's fine.
> Q. Do you also know when everything isn't fine?
> Sure you know, there's an energy there.
> Q. Has there ever been a time when the stethoscope told you one thing but your intuition another?
> No. If I detect a problem with the baby's heartbeat, there have already been signs that I'm suspecting there may be a problem. The heartbeat almost never tells me anything, except it looks nice on a piece of paper to document it. I do that for the lawyers. [Jeannette Breen]

It is a working hypothesis of ours that the more intensely midwives are trained in didactic models of medical care based on ratiocinative processes, the less they will trust in and rely on their intuition. Since our interviews to date have focused on midwives who demonstrate their commitment to holism by attending MANA conferences, we have been unable to investigate the truth of this hypothesis. To do so, we would have to interview equal numbers of more medically oriented CNMs. All our interviewees report that learning to trust their intuition is an ongoing process. Our data do indicate some differences, however, between the way that process is experienced by medically trained CNMs and empirically trained midwives, who learn their skills through the one-on-one interaction of apprenticeship. The CNMs seem to begin by regarding intuition with mistrust, then move into trust through lived experience, while the empirically trained midwives seem to begin by trusting intuition, and move into confirmation of that trust through lived experience. Consider the following story told to me by a hospital-based CNM from the Midwest about her first salient experience with intuition at birth:

> Last year I [was] seeing a Laotian Hmong woman. She came when she was about four months' pregnant from a refugee camp. The very first time I met her I felt like there was something that was not right, but, although I kept looking, I couldn't find anything, ever. . . . Well I happened to be on call the night she was in labor, and her interpreter called me and told me she was going into the hospital and I asked the interpreter if she was coming and the interpreter said no, and—I had had this feeling all along, this voice that was telling me something bad was going to happen, and I thought, it's a mistake for the interpreter not to come, but I didn't say anything—I respected their plan.
> And the woman got to the hospital and she was complete with a bag of water that was bulging and a high presenting part. And the nurse said to me, "I think she should go to the high-risk birth center," and I knew that this woman would not be protected—I knew there'd be residents—and so I pushed aside the part that had been telling me something was wrong, and

Robbie Davis-Floyd with Elizabeth Davis

admitted her to the alternative birth center. And when I got there, about five minutes after she arrived up there, she was pushing already, and I [started to check her] and the bag of water broke with her next contraction, and my whole hand filled with umbilical cord.

She'd been in labor all day at home, and I don't know how long the cord was prolapsed, but as soon as I found it we tried to get her to push through, but she wouldn't push, so I pushed the baby's head up and we did a Cesarean section, and we got the baby out pretty fast but the baby has only lower brain stem function. Even though we did things right, we did things fast, it was a terrible outcome. And I think, had I listened to that voice, [the translator would have been there and could have convinced her to push] or she would at least have been admitted to a unit where things could have been done faster, and I don't know if there would have been a better outcome or not, but it's the strongest message of intuition I've ever had and from it I learned a lot about listening. I had never been raised to believe in the inner voice, but now I listen, when I slow down enough to hear those things. [Donna Hartmann]

Recounting her early years of homebirth midwifery practice, Elizabeth Davis, who is empirically trained, introduced the following story by saying, "This is the experience that first got me interested in the role of intuition in birth." In contrast to the two CNMs quoted above, her first reaction to a strong intuitive experience was not to resist or ignore, but to act upon it:

I had received a call that someone was in labor and [I laid down to unwind and open myself], and I heard this voice—I'm pretty auditory, and that's one of the ways my intuition shows up—and the voice said, "She's going to have a partial separation." I immediately fought back the voice—I think a lot of us, when we get intuitive messages, will argue back with our rational minds and refute them—we're schizo enough to do that . . . and that's what I did. I went over her history in my mind, and there was nothing that would indicate any risk for postpartum bleeding. And the voice said "No, sorry, this is going to happen." Then I responded with great confidence and said, "Well that's okay, because I've handled this before—I've done manual removals." But after that it came back, "No, you've never done this. You've never had to go this far up and you've never had this much bleeding." I was really scared, but I thought, "Well, this is my fear, and I'm just projecting, God only knows why."

But, I told my partner about it, and at the birth I drew up a syringe of pitocin in advance, and pushed fluids by mouth, and the kinds of things that I would do if I anticipated a potential problem with bleeding.

So she gives birth to this gorgeous little girl, the labor was uneventful, nothing strange, and she's holding her baby, and this bleeding starts. I follow up the cord to see where the placenta is and suddenly there's so much blood, and my hand is continuing from that point of exploration on up inside the uterus— I'm on automatic pilot, doing this manual removal as it was foreshown. And my partner is injecting the syringe of pitocin, and everything worked out great, I think because of the immediacy of the response and the complete lack of double guessing myself. Just going ahead and doing what was necessary without wasting time really kept her blood loss to minimum, even though it was considerable. We didn't have to transport, she didn't have to be transfused, she didn't go into shock, and that was amazing to me.

Reason vs. Intuition: Accuracy and Source

Bastick's (1982) comprehensive list of the qualities of intuition (see above) includes the possiblity that an intuition may be incorrect. With this most of the midwives in our study would disagree, as they tend to define intuition *per se* as inherently accurate (see also Vaughan 1979). Many of them told us that the trick, each time the inner voice speaks, is how to know whether or not it is a "real" intuition, and the struggle is to learn the difference between the inner doubt and debate that accompanies ratiocinative thinking, and the true voice of intuition. Their unwillingness to assume that an intuition can be wrong, we find, comes from their consensual belief that intuition finds its source in the spiritual realm or their own "higher selves," which by definition cannot be wrong, or from the deepest recesses of their bodies, which, according to the holistic model, are essentially energy fields operating in connection with all other energy fields, and therefore cannot be wrong either.

In contrast, reason/ratiocination, which is site-specific to the neocortex, *can* be wrong, according to these midwives, and often is so. Thus, if a midwife has what she thinks may be an intuition, but it turns out to be wrong, she is likely to conclude that it must not have been an intuition in the first place, but a product of her "rational mind." This is not to say that midwives devalue reason and ratiocination. They tend to be comfortable with their ratiocinative abilities, and keenly aware that these are culturally supervalued. The voice of reason is loud and aggressive; the harder task, as the midwives see it, is to identify and heed the truths spoken by the still, small, and culturally devalued inner voice. The worth of this enterprise is attested to by the outstanding safety record that contemporary homebirth midwives are achieving—a record that compares most favorably with the interventionist, expensive, and often iatrogenic "active management" of labor and birth in many hospitals. The midwives we interviewed for this study reported that they averaged a 90 percent or higher success rate for the birth-center or homebirths they have attended, the vast majority of which took place without drugs or other technological interventions. They transferred 8–10 percent of their clients to the hospital during labor; fewer than 4 percent ended up with Cesareans; and their perinatal mortality rates average 2–4/1000. These statistics contrast with the extremely high percentage of women in the hospital who receive drugs during labor (over 90 percent), the near-universal technological interventions in hospital birth, the national Cesarean rate of close to 21 percent, and compare favorably with hospital perinatal mortality rates for low-risk women of 2–4/1000. (For excellent reviews of all

Robbie Davis-Floyd with Elizabeth Davis

available recent studies on midwifery birth outcomes, see Goer 1995: 297–347 and Rooks 1997, Chapter 9.)

Maggie's Story: A Case Study in Reliance on Intuition

Although all these midwives know "the rules," the protocols of standard midwifery practice, they often circumvent or ignore them completely in the actual doing of birth. Clearly they do not consider such protocols authoritative *per se*. Brigitte Jordan (1993) has said that authoritative knowledge is interactionally displayed knowledge on the basis of which decisions are made and actions taken. How far into actions and interaction can intuition take a midwife? Given the external diagnostic technologies at her command, including those of the hospital to which she can transport her client, how authoritative can she consider that inner voice to be? What happens when what that voice tells her conflicts with more culturally accepted external parameters of normal, with standard protocol? We will take as a case study here a birth attended by midwife Maggie Bennett, president of the California Midwives' Association, which took her far beyond medically accepted standards, right out onto the ragged edge of intuition and trust:

> [Once I had a client named Jane]—it was her third pregnancy, she was 39. Her first pregnancy . . . was complicated and that child had some physiological problems. Her second labor began prematurely, and she was delivered by Cesarean section—the baby was six weeks premature and had cerebral palsy. Her father is an obstetrician. So she came to me feeling that hospitals and doctors offered her nothing as far as safety. She was also a VBAC [vaginal birth after Cesarean] at a time when VBACs were new to me, and she also had a vertical scar, exterior and interior—a no-no.

Maggie has so far listed no fewer than five factors that, from a medical point of view, would define this woman as far too high risk for any midwife to take on for a homebirth: two previous problematic births, both with pathological outcomes, a father who is an obstetrician (a strong indicator for a medically oriented daughter and a potential threat to the midwife's ability to continue to practice), and a woman who wants to give birth vaginally at home, but who happens to have the kind of scar, on both her abdomen and her uterus, that is most likely to rupture during a subsequent labor. But, Maggie continues,

> What she did have going for her was God. She was a born-again Christian, and believed that this was of God's design, and so she had a lot of power from that source. So the first thing that happened was that we got close to term— 37, 38 weeks, and her baby was breech. And we kept waiting for it to turn on its own, and we did crawling and slantboarding[12] and all sorts of things but the

baby didn't turn. So we decided that the baby had to be turned. And the baby was really hard to turn, and it didn't go easily, and at one point I felt that we should stop, because it was just too difficult. But then I had this intuition that the baby could go head down, but that *I* was blocking the process.

One of the things that was happening was that the woman wanted to have a beer [to help her relax] and I wouldn't let her do that because I wanted her 100 percent present and in her body, and I wasn't willing to let her check out while I did this procedure on her. I just wouldn't allow it. [But then she began making these statements that semi-equated me with the devil, and finally I realized that my refusal was causing a lot of unpleasant tension between us. . . .]

And so I let go of my beliefs about the alcohol, and I called her husband and said, "You need to pray." I had to let go of my being righteous about my own belief system—I am not a Christian—and about religion and about alcohol, and let this woman be in her body the way she had to be in her body, and be in her beliefs the way she had to be in her beliefs. And if that meant that I had to bow my head and pray, then that's what I had to do—so it was as much about me as it was about her.

So she had a glass of wine and a half a beer, and I had a half a beer, and my partner had a half a beer, and we mellowed out a whole bunch, and she laid down on the slantboard again, and the baby just went around. So again, it was the intuition about knowing that the baby *wanted* to turn around, and looking at what everybody had been doing that was stopping that from happening.

In her willingness to compromise her own religious and health beliefs to facilitate the turning of the baby and to maintain connectedness with the mother, Maggie demonstrates the malleability of the midwife, her willingness to go the distance with the mother on the mother's terms. Maggie as practitioner-in-charge could have retained her authority to deny the woman alcohol by insisting on the authority of her "knowledge" that alcohol would be harmful. Instead, she gave up that claim altogether, gladly surrendering authority to what she saw as the higher good of connectedness and trust.

Yet another opportunity to give up authority quickly arose: hospital guidelines and many midwifery protocols state that babies must be born within twenty-four hours of the rupture of the membranes, as the danger of infection of the baby rises significantly thereafter. This rule of thumb has sent many would-be homebirth mothers to the hospital, and has resulted in many Cesareans, as it is very common for labor and birth to take far longer than twenty-four hours (indeed, as midwives know, normal labors can take up to five or six days; during that time, if left unpenetrated, ruptured amniotic sacs will often reseal). But a Cesarean was not to be Jane's fate. Maggie continues:

So she goes into labor four days later, but she doesn't just do it normally—she has premature rupture of the membranes for twenty-four hours, seventy-two hours, four days she has premature rupture of the membranes, and you better believe that intuition played a role every single day, because I had to reexamine where we were

Robbie Davis-Floyd with Elizabeth Davis

going with it all the way along. But the answer was always the same—her waters were clear, she had no temperature, and she still had God. She was filled with her faith in God that that baby was safe. And I was able to participate in that faith. . . .

So on the fourth day [after her membranes ruptured], after she is finally in labor, her backup doctor called to check on her, and someone told him that she was in labor and was out walking with her husband. . . . So now the *doctor* knows that she's in labor. And remember that I told you that her father was an obstetrician in a town about four hours away? Well *he* calls up and finds out that she's in labor, and then he starts calling every three hours. And he starts to say, "What's going on there? That baby should have been born by now."

So I have a woman who's four days with ruptured membranes, who's been in labor for about eighteen hours with contractions about five minutes apart. . . . And while I was out for a few minutes picking up food for everybody,[13] I ran into her backup doctor at the restaurant and he said to me, "I just want to know is the baby coming out above or below?" and I said—this was an intuition, come to think of it—"The baby's coming out normally."[14]

The pressure builds. Maggie is attending a woman with significant risk factors from past and now this present birth; two physicians are aware that she is in labor and are trying to monitor the situation from afar. Every midwife knows how fraught with personal peril such a situation is, and that there is also peril for the mother, as the tension induced by such pressure can easily stop or slow labor. Maggie's response at this point to "all this energy, this highly political birth," is that of guardian and protector of the natural process: she pulls the plug on the telephone. She said:

> I think that every time a midwife goes to the edge, it is the intuition that everything is all right that takes her there. I had to keep examining with this woman whether or not it was all right for us to continue, and every single time was an internal process about—we have these signs, and this is not "the rules," but I *know* the baby's all right, and I *know* that the mother is all right, so we can go on from this point.
>
> So eventually, she begins to push the baby out, and the waters broke [again— the bag had resealed] just as she began to push and there was slight meconium staining.[15] And she begins to have a slight temperature, like maybe 99, but this is all right [according to protocols] because she has begun to push.
>
> Guess what? She doesn't push the baby out in one hour, she doesn't push the baby out in two hours, not even in three hours. She takes a rest at four hours.[16] She finally gets that baby out in five hours . . . squatting . . . little by little by little by little. . . . And the baby actually breathes spontaneously and has Apgars of 7 and 8.[17]
>
> So in the end, in retrospect, it was just a challenged birth—a challenged pregnancy, a problem in late pregnancy, a challenged labor all the way along. And I couldn't have done that birth if I had followed *my own* protocols. And

there was a point where I had to say, "I am called midwife, and I am in here for whatever happens, because I have to let go. I have to absolutely let go of my desire to control this, because I can't."

Some perspective on the value Maggie places here on letting go of control is provided by an earlier study I carried out on differences between homebirthers and hospital birthers (1994). I found that the hospital birthers placed high value on control, while the homebirthers felt that giving up control was far more valuable in birth and in life than trying to maintain it—a philosophical position they arrived at through lived experience. As Liza explained it:

> I was brought up in the mainstream, and I used to knock myself out trying to control everything. Then I got sick, and I realized that I actually can't control anything or anyone. As soon as I let go of trying, and just began to surrender to what is, everything in my life started to work. I got well, I got married, I had a baby. And if the lesson needed reinforcing, labor did it. That is a force beyond control, a powerful wave that will drown you if you fight it. Better then to dive into it, to relax, let it carry you. Whenever I tried to control my labor or myself during labor, I was in agony. But when I let go and surrendered to the waves, they carried me. (quoted in Davis-Floyd 1994: 1133)

Maggie reinforces this philosophical position of surrender at the same time as she indicates how difficult it is to maintain this view in a society that supervalues control in most aspects of life:

> You know, I would never have the audacity to go to a birth and think that I could control everything that happened, for either the safety or the outcome. Sooner or later, I, along with the mother, have to give up the control. You would think after seventeen years [of attending births] I would know that, but I have to relearn that at almost every birth, over and over again.

I asked Maggie, "How do you feel about staying the course with that birth?" and she responded, "I feel that it was a great gift, a great learning, and I am so incredibly inspired by the woman, and the Goddess that she is (she would hate me for saying that)[18]—that I was able to witness that miracle."

At this point in Maggie's recounting of this birth, the question of protocols and external diagnostic technologies again came up. The high authority that Maggie placed on her inner knowing during this birth was clearly demonstrated when she said that she never made a decision based on anything that was written on Jane's chart—her blood pressure, urinalysis, information about rate of dilation and progression of labor, etc.—because, as she put it, "it wouldn't be neat, it wouldn't add up, it wouldn't follow any kind of progression that was any kind of normal anything." I asked: "So why didn't you make an effort to make this labor conform to normal by transporting her?" and Maggie answered:

> Because every time I [checked with Jane, she would tell me that she was fine and that she knew the baby was fine]. And every time I looked at her, and every time I looked inside myself, and every time I saw that—whatever it is—the place where the baby was—the baby was safe. . . . Inside my head I saw the baby safe—and this is my own metaphor, I realize, but I saw the baby surrounded by sparkling light, kind of like glittery flecks of amniotic fluid.
> Q. So your inner vision of the baby corresponded with the mother's?
> Yes.

This correspondence of Maggie's inner vision with the mother's is a prime example of the kind of connectedness that midwives see as essential for the emergence and the credibility of intuition. Our other interviewees generally agreed on the persuasive power of such correspondence of intuitions. They also agreed that, in the rare instances in which the mother and the midwife had conflicting intuitions about a potential problem during labor, clearly they were *not* connected. In such a situation, they felt that transport would be essential, as this "total lack of synergy" would seriously impede their ability to provide good, empathic—i.e., connected—care.

Maggie and I explored in further conversation the mystery of why, in some cases, she will urge a woman to transport in the face of a minimum of indicators, while in a case like Jane's she would stay home in the face of a maximum of indicators for transport. We asked her, "Is that a matter of intuition for you every time?" She replied:

> Yes. You see, I don't know about where it all goes together, because I keep charts, and I do signs, and I check dilation, I look at the color of the amniotic fluid, I take blood pressure—I do those kinds of clinical things. . . . But . . . one month I realized that I had been to five births within a month, and only one of them fit within protocols. And I had to look at myself and say, I think of myself as a conservative midwife, but what's wrong here if four out of five births are out of protocol, am I a radical midwife, am I a dangerous midwife—what's going on here?
>
> And I really had to evaluate, and look at my charts with somebody else, before I could come up with a picture of me as a midwife, and what I resolved for *me* is that *where birth is not normal, part of a midwife's job is to return it to normal*. For example, in the case of a VBAC, which is regarded medically as high risk and almost universally by midwives as not high risk, what we're doing in that case is returning birth to normal. And when we go four, five, six hours of pushing, we are also returning birth to normal, a normal that says if the woman pushes for three hours and she's exhausted, then she can take a rest, and maybe in a couple of hours, she'll get her strength up, and then she'll be able to push again—she *will* get her baby out. When we do things like that, we're returning birth to normal.

Rather than de- and reconstructing labor to fit abstract and narrowly drawn technocratic parameters of normal—a process that often results in major surgery as the final reconstructive step—what Maggie and her sister midwives do is to continually redraw the parameters, processually expanding their definitions of normal to encompass the range of behaviors and signs actually exhibited by pregnant women as they labor and birth. In short, these midwives are willing to expand protocol parameters to reflect the realities of individual labors, rather than reshaping labor to fit protocol parameters. They see a labor that is unlike other labors, not as a dysfunction to be mechanistically normalized according to the standardized technomedical system of authoritative knowledge, but as a meaningful expression of the birthing woman's uniqueness, to be understood on its own terms.[19]

Normalizing Uniqueness: The Connective Dance

The midwifery normalization of uniqueness must be understood in the context of the technomedical pathologization of uniqueness. The technocratic model of birth defines as "normal" only those births that fall within specific parameters—twelve hours for labor, cervical dilation of one centimeter per hour, steady fetal heart tones, etc. Labors that take too little or too much time, cervixes that remain "stuck" at four centimeters for hours on end, heart tones that speed up or slow down, meconium in the amniotic fluid—all are defined as dysfunctional "deviations from the norm." Aware of technomedical parameters, midwives must constantly weigh their trust in and acceptance of women's individual rhythms against the consequences of straying too far outside of the medical protocols that are regarded as authoritative in the courts.

In a recent paper, Brigitte Jordan speaks of authoritative knowledge as grounded in a community of practice, adding that within that community

> authoritative knowledge is persuasive because it seems natural, reasonable, and consensually constructed. For the same reason, it also carries the possibility of powerful sanctions, ranging from exclusions from the social group to physical coerciveness. (1992: 3)

Certainly this is true of the authoritative knowledge of the technomedical community. But midwives who act on intuition do so in *opposition* to the cultural consensus on what constitutes authoritative knowledge in birth. Their protocols are their link to that larger biomedical system of authoritative knowledge; like physicians in the hospital, the farther they stray from those parameters, the more they place themselves at risk of the powerful sanctions of which Jordan speaks.

Yet within the midwifery community, intuition does count as authoritative knowledge—to quote Jordan again, "the knowledge that *participants agree* counts in a given situation, that they see as consequential, on the basis of which they make decisions and provide justifications for courses of action" (1992: 3; emphasis in original). When Maggie shared her records with other midwives for peer review and evaluation, she was greeted with reassurance and acceptance; in spite of its devaluation, or simply nonrecognition by the larger culture, these midwives too valued intuition as authoritative.

Robbie Davis-Floyd with Elizabeth Davis

Jordan points out that "to legitimize one kind of knowing devalues, often totally dismisses, all other ways of knowing, [so that] those who espouse alternative knowledge systems are often seen as backward, ignorant, or naive troublemakers" (1992: 2). Her words capture in a nutshell what the larger technomedical culture has done, in this country and many others, to the alternative knowledge systems of midwifery. Hanging out on the ragged edge, far outside of the safety net of cultural consensus, these women of tremendous hearts find their courage not in the normalizing performance of standardized routines, but in their connectedness to the women and babies they attend. As Maggie put it:

> Mothers and midwives mirror one another. I know that I get all of my courage from the mother. And I bounce it back to her, and she gets her courage from me. . . . It's a dance—the woman has to trust her midwife, and the midwife has to trust her woman for that bouncing back.

In the eyes of midwives, birth has been made abnormal by technocratic medicine. As Maggie's story illustrates, the give-and-take of this "dance" is instrumental in midwives' ongoing efforts to normalize uniqueness in birth.[20]

Sanctioning Intuition as Authoritative Knowledge

> The midwife provides care according to the following principles:
>   Midwives work as autonomous practitioners, collaborating with other health and social service providers when necessary.
>   Midwives understand that physical, emotional, psycho-social, and spiritual factors synergistically comprise the health of individuals and affect the childbearing process.
>   Midwives synthesize clinical observations, theoretical knowledge, intuitive assessment, and spiritual awareness as components of a competent decision-making process.
> —Excerpts from the MANA Core Competencies for Midwifery Practice,
> a five-page document approved in final form by the Board of the
> Midwives' Alliance of North America, October 3, 1994[21]

Until recently, homebirth midwives' use of intuition as authoritative knowledge at births has been entirely informal, experienced in the uniqueness of the situation, talked about in wonder and awe among themselves and with the mothers[22] they attend, but not formally encoded as an official source of authoritative knowledge. With the finalization and approval-by-consensus of the MANA Statement of Values and Ethics (quoted earlier) in 1992, and the 1994 approval of the MANA Core Competencies quoted above, intuition has now received formal recognition from midwives themselves as an integral aspect of competent midwifery practice. Some new challenges have thereby arisen.

Two of the most pressing issues facing homebirth midwives in the postmodern era are those of certification and licensure. Midwives in many states have been lobbying for legalization and licensing for years, and increasingly are achieving these goals. Members of MANA are well aware that if they do not establish their own testing and certification process, others—state governments, the American College of Nurse-Midwives, medical boards—will establish one for them. So MANA has created NARM—the North American Registry of Midwives—as a separate nonprofit corporation, and empowered the NARM board to develop and implement a national certification process for direct-entry midwives, guided by a Certification Task Force of approximately forty state representatives.

This is a somewhat oxymoronic situation. MANA prides itself on its inclusivity, yet the essence of certification is some degree of exclusivity. When tests and standards are created that all midwives must meet, some will pass and some will fail, and, quite possibly, midwives who are competent at births will remain uncertified simply because they do not test well. In an effort to minimize this type of exclusionary outcome, which would limit homebirth midwifery to those who excel at ratiocinative thinking, the members of the Certification Task Force are trying very hard to create testing and evaluation systems that will be fair to all. Agreeing that written (ratiocinative) tests, while the easiest to administer, cannot provide the whole picture, task force members considered the idea of multiple options for demonstrating skill, including a simulated skills exam, in which the aspiring licensee could come to a central site and demonstrate her skills on plastic models of a birthing woman and child. When this idea was presented to the general membership of MANA, a common response was exemplified by one midwife who exclaimed in dismay, "My spiritual guides are the ones who tell me what to do at births, but they will not be there if I am working on plastic dummies!" Another midwife emphasizes intuition's central role:

> Let's decide how a midwife should be tested, and let's test her that way. Let's not kiss up to the standards of the medical profession in order to satisfy them that we are competent. Let's satisfy *ourselves* that we are competent—and we'll know that competency if our hearts are true, and if we're honest about our intuitive skills. Intuition is often what makes us smart, what makes us do the work best, what makes us able to pick up problems earlier than anyone else and therefore deal with them more effectively [Jill Breen, community midwife, quoted in Chester 1997: 3].

In response to such appeals, the task force's final certification proposal[23] is balanced between the ratiocinative and the hands-on: it requires passing a challenging written exam *and* skills evaluation by senior midwives, during which aspiring licensees can demonstrate their abilities in the physically connective context that enables them to listen to their "guides" and inner voices. The proposal's balance, as well as MANA's "Statement of Values and Ethics" and "Core Competencies," indicates the increasing determination of these midwives to honor both ratiocination and intuition as communally sanctioned and respected sources of authoritative knowledge.

Robbie Davis-Floyd with Elizabeth Davis

Robbie Davis-Floyd with Elizabeth Davis

Conclusion

In this chapter I examined the phenomenon of midwives' occasional willingness to rely on intuition as a primary source of authoritative knowledge in a society that grants conceptual and legal legitimacy only to ratiocination. We have seen that the trust these midwives place in inner knowing is a seamless part of their overall philosophy, as expressed in the MANA Statement of Values and Ethics, and as exemplified in the stories they tell about their individual experiences with intuition and birth. In contrast to the technocratic model, which charters an ever-expanding plethora of separation-based diagnostic and remedial technologies, this holistic midwifery philosophy supervalues inter- and intrapersonal connection, and charters a range of behaviors expressive of that connective "dance."

Intuition, in these midwives' view, emerges out of their own inner connectedness to the deepest bodily and spiritual aspects of their being, as well as out of their physical and psychic connections to the mother and the child. The trustworthiness of intuition is intrinsically related to its emergence from that matrix of physical, emotional, and spiritual connection—a matrix that gives intuition more power and credibility, in these midwives' eyes, than the information that arises from the technologies of separation. That midwives nevertheless carry with them and freely utilize such technologies demonstrates not only that they value ratiocination, but also that they are becoming experts at balancing the protocols and demands of technologically obtained information with their intuitive acceptance of women's uniqueness during labor and birth. We submit that their deep, connective, woman-to-woman webs, woven so lovingly in a society that grants those connections no authority of knowledge and precious little conceptual reality, hold rich potential for restoring the balance of intimacy to the multiple alienations of technocratic life.

Notes to Chapter 9

Acknowledgments. I wish to thank Sven Arvidson, anthropologists Carolyn Sargent, Ann Millard, and Gay Becker, midwives Karen Erlich, Penfield Chester, Anne Fry, Judy Luce, Marimikel Penn, and Sharon Wells for their excellent editorial assistance, and our midwife-interviewees for giving so generously of their time and experience. This is a revised version of an article that appears in "The Social Production of Authoritative Knowledge," a special issue of the *Medical Anthropology Quarterly*, edited by Robbie Davis-Floyd and Carolyn Sargent. (1996: 237–269)

1. See Goer 1995: 131–53 for complete summaries of thirty-nine medical studies relevant to EFM.
2. Non-nurse midwives in the United States used to be known as "lay midwives." But in recent years, such midwives, including those who are apprentice trained, have developed

an extensive array of skills including the ability to use various high technologies (see note 9), have banded together in professional associations, and have organized politically to create a national certification program, and to fight for state licensure. Thus many of them have come to think of themselves as professionals, and to resent the appellation "lay," which we do not use in this chapter.

3. The global scope of postmodern midwifery was evidenced by the attendance of more than 3000 midwives from forty-four countries at the 1993 convention of the International Confederation of Midwives (ICM) in Vancouver, Canada. Members of the ICM share in common a commitment to the midwifery ("with woman") approach to prenatal, natal, and postnatal care, and a growing concern for an increasingly compromised scope of practice. In Germany, for example, midwives may assist delivery but can do no prenatal care; in France they may do prenatal care but are greatly restricted in deliveries; and in the Third World the midwife's role is increasingly constrained by biomedicine (Jordan 1993; Davis-Floyd and Sargent 1997). Generally, the ICM represents midwives with professional academic preparation, but its membership is increasingly beginning to reflect a determination on the part of midwives in both developed and underdeveloped countries to ensure the continued viability of the independent midwife able to assist birth in any setting, particularly the home.

4. In Hawaiian, "mana" means "an underlying, vital energy that infuses, creates, and sustains the physical body" (*MANA News*, 1990 Vol 8:3, p.1). And as one anonymous reviewer aptly pointed out, *mana* in Greek is the affectionate term for "mother." And of course, in Hebrew and Greek, *manna* means divinely supplied spiritual nourishment.

5. Copies of the MANA Statement of Values and Ethics can be obtained from Signe Rogers, Editor, MANA News, P.O. Box 175, Newton, KS 67114. MANAinfo@aol.com.

6. Contemporary CNMs, many of whom are or wish to be in independent practice, are engaged in serious questioning of the limitations imposed by their structural subordination to physicians. Some members and officials of the American College of Nurse-Midwives are currently contemplating a focused effort to re-create nurse-midwifery as an independent primary health care profession, subject not to nursing but to autonomous midwifery boards.

7. Our collaboration emerged gradually. In 1992, Elizabeth Davis was one of my first interviewees for this study. One year later, we agreed to share data and collaborate on this chapter. We merge in this endeavor our unique perspectives. As a cultural anthropologist, I have applied symbolic, cognitive, and feminist perspectives to the study of American childbirth. For over twelve years, I have been conducting research on women's experiences of pregnancy and childbirth (1992, 1994), on the beliefs, attitudes, and training of obstetricians (1987), and on the ritual and symbolic dimensions of hospital and homebirth (1990, 1992); recently I have become interested in the emergent phenomenon of postmodern midwifery. Elizabeth Davis is an independent midwife who has been in private practice for sixteen years. She has attended more than 300 births as primary caregiver; 90 percent of them have taken place at home. Internationally known for her work in women's sexuality and reproductive rights, she has authored a number of books on birth and related topics (Davis 1988, 1994), most notably the midwifery textbook *Heart and Hands* (1987), and *Women's Intuition* (1989), and is a frequent lecturer at childbirth conferences around the world. She is the director of Heart and Hands Midwifery Intensives, an

educational program for direct-entry midwives, which she founded in 1982. She initiated the development of midwifery certification in California, and was instrumental in getting legislation passed to decriminalize direct-entry midwifery in that state. She served as chair of MANA's Education Committee, and as the first president of the newly formed Midwifery Education Accreditation Council, a national accrediting body for direct-entry midwifery education.

8. Insisting on the value of connection has many pragmatic ramifications. For example, 98 percent of American women give birth in hospitals; around 50 percent of them breastfeed their babies during the early months of life. Of the 2 percent of women who give birth at home or in freestanding birth centers—in other words, in accordance with the connection-based holistic model of birth—close to 100 percent choose to breastfeed (Arms 1994: 201). That connectedness also facilitates birth itself has been amply demonstrated by the doula studies, which show beyond a doubt that the nurturing presence of a woman companion during labor reduces length of labor, lessens perceptions of pain, and improves birth outcomes, both physical and emotional (Sosa et al. 1980; Kennell et al. 1988).

9. The importance of the web metaphor to the members of MANA as an expression of their lived experience was demonstrated during the closing ceremonies of the 1993 San Francisco conference. Four hundred and fifty midwives formed a giant circle around the edges of an otherwise-empty ballroom. They passed balls of yarn in many colors around the circle; each participant looped each color of yarn that came to her around her wrist, until all were physically connected. Then they tossed many more balls of yarn across the floor to each other, tying those around their wrists also, until all that yarn formed a giant rainbow-hued spider web that filled the ballroom floor, linking everyone to everyone through myriad connections. Spontaneously lifting the giant web into the air by lifting their arms, the midwives quickly discovered that, if one person moved her arm, the whole web would move in response. And if a ball of yarn got stuck in the middle of the floor, at least thirty people had to move in synchrony for one person to retrieve it. This of course was a perfect ritual and symbolic enactment of the high value these midwives place on human interconnectedness. (See also Carol Gilligan 1982.)

10. Interviewees Maggie Bennett, Jeannette Breen, Elizabeth Davis, and Judy Luce insisted on being identified by their own names, in keeping with their strong beliefs in the value of their work and of their intuitive experiences. All other names following quotations are pseudonyms.

11. The typical postmodern midwife carries myriad technologies with her to homebirths. A full list would take up several pages (see Davis-Floyd and Davis 1996: fn 12). Some examples: a pager and/or a cellular phone; a blood pressure cuff; a stethoscope; a fetoscope and a Doppler—an electronic amplifier of the baby's heartbeat (for monitoring fetal heart tones); urinalysis strips (to test for glucose, ketones, pH, blood, and protein); nitrazen paper (to test for leaks in the amniotic sac); culture tubes (for taking a baseline culture of the amniotic fluid); equipment for drawing blood to send to a lab for a white count (to check for infection); urinary catheter kits; a variety of herbs, tinctures, and homeopathic remedies; a birthing stool; an oxygen tank, mask for the mother, and infant resuscitation bag and mask (rarely used); syringes and drugs (injectable pitocin, injectable methergine, and oral methergine) to stop a postpartum hemorrhage; IV lines and fluids; instruments and sutures for repairing vaginal tears; a local anesthetic (xylocaine or 1 or 2 percent lidocaine) for pain relief during suturing; assorted hemostats and

Robbie Davis-Floyd with Elizabeth Davis

clamps; special scissors for cutting the cord; scales for weighing the baby and a tape measure; oral vitamin K; erythromycin ointment (to place in the baby's eyes to prevent blind-
ness from venereal disease—a requirement in most states). Most midwives carry enough
supplies with them at any one time to attend three births in a row without repacking.

12. "Slantboarding" is a midwifery technique that often proves effective in getting breech
    babies to turn before delivery. The mother must get her head lower than her pelvis. A
    bean bag chair can be used, or an ironing board (or door) can be placed against a sofa or
    heavy chair at a 45-degree angle; the pregnant woman lies on her back, head down on the
    board with her feet pointing upwards for fifteen to twenty minutes two or three times a
    day. During this time she is encouraged to relax and to visualize the baby turning. (For
    other such techniques, see Kitzinger 1991: 98, or ask a midwife!)

13. Hospital labors are usually artificially speeded up with drugs, episiotomies, forceps, or
    Cesarean section, so homebirth labors, which are allowed to take their natural course,
    tend to take far more time than hospital births do. During a long labor, it is essential for
    a mother (and indeed, her birth attendants) to keep up their strength by eating and
    drinking plenty of nutritious food and fluids. Homebirth midwives recognize that con-
    tractions that have been going on for eighteen hours and are still five minutes apart mean
    that the mother is still in "early labor"—"active labor" has not yet kicked in—and there
    is plenty of time for the midwife to go out for food.

14. Note Maggie's refusal to adopt his technomedical discourse here—a discourse that
    reduces the differences between Cesarean and vaginal birth to a matter of geography, at
    the same time as it subtly expresses the value this culture consistently places on "above"
    in relation to "below."

15. Meconium is the baby's first bowel movement. If present in the amniotic fluid, it is
    sometimes associated with fetal distress, which is usually also indicated by fetal heart
    patterns. It is generally recognized, even in most hospitals, that thin or light meconium
    staining during birth is not problematic, especially when the heart rate patterns fall
    within a normal range. Heavy, thick, and chunky meconium in the amniotic fluid is usu-
    ally indicative of fetal distress.

16. Hospital practitioners generally allow one, and a maximum of two, hours for pushing, after
    which a Cesarean will usually be performed. Homebirth midwives accept a wide range of
    pushing stages, but more than four hours of pushing is rather unusual, even at home.

17. The *Apgar score* provides a standardized means by which birth attendants can assess the
    baby's condition at birth. Signs rated at two points each on a preprinted chart are skin
    color, muscle tone, breathing attempts, heartbeat, and response to stimulus, such as a
    touch or pinprick. Babies are rated twice, at one minute after birth and again at five min-
    utes, because many babies, especially anesthetized ones, take some time to turn pink and
    begin full breathing on their own. Ten is the highest obtainable score.

18. In calling this woman a "Goddess," Maggie expresses an attitude toward women that is held
    by many midwives who tend to see the birthing woman as a powerful creatrix—a birth-
    and life-giver. Much as they interpret intuition as both spiritual and embodied, they honor
    the Goddess as a spiritual reality embodied in the earth, and as a metaphor of and for
    women's creative power, of which birth is but one expression (see for example Diamond
    and Orenstein 1990; Starhawk 1988, 1989, 1993; Diamond 1994). Spirituality is a strong
    component of independent midwifery, but there is a great deal of variation in spiritual ori-
    entation. While most midwives in MANA either actively celebrate the Goddess or are quite

comfortable with the Goddess-as-metaphor, some have a strongly Christian orientation toward birth. Christian midwives tend to interpret birth not so much as a manifestation of the woman's own personal power but of God's power flowing through the birthing woman. This is the view held by Maggie's client Jane, and the reason why Jane would not appreciate Maggie's calling her a Goddess, which for Maggie is the highest compliment she can give to express her appreciation for Jane's profound inner connectedness and strength.

19. It is important to note that this appreciation of women's uniqueness can extend even to crises and complications that midwives cannot handle at home, as is evidenced in the following story from Elizabeth Davis:

> Sometimes if a woman has had a difficult birth, part of the reason why it's been difficult is that things have come up for her that she has not worked through. . . . I think of a Japanese woman with a Chinese husband who was culturally supposed to have a son, and it was a girl, and you can bet that nothing I said or did stopped her trickle bleeding from a partially separated placenta that finally took us to the hospital. When she felt safe enough in the hospital, she staged this massive hemorrhage, and rallied her husband to her side, where he had not been since he saw the sex of the baby.
>
> So you know, the choreography of the woman's expression of need is something that's really beyond the practitioner—it's really none of your business. But it *is* your business to maintain the parameters of safety, as we say, so some part of your attention has to turn to doing as much as you can *in advance* to raise those issues, and help a woman cope with them. It's a fine line—permission to have your birth be whatever it is going to be, and the midwife's skill and also her need to have a safe outcome. I think really most of us struggle with that.

20. As one anonymous reviewer aptly pointed out, the words "normal" and "abnormal" may not even be appropriate when talking about birth from the standpoint of intuitive knowing, as the concept "normal" "has long been grounded in a worldview that is based on a ratiocinative means of reasoning and the averaging of all experiences into one standardized experience. . . . Foucault's concept of 'normalization' might be an interesting springboard here." Space does not allow us to further address the issue of midwives' efforts to normalize uniqueness versus medicine's efforts to pathologize it as "deviance," but it is an issue deserving of scholarly probing, and we call attention to it here in the hopes of stimulating further research and analysis.

21. Copies of the MANA Core Competencies can be obtained from Signe Rogers, Editor, MANA News, P.O. Box 175, Newton, KS 67114. MANAinfo@aol.com.

22. Homebirth mothers themselves often have rich intuitive experiences worthy of anthropological study in their own right, as do mothers in general, about birth, childraising, etc. We call attention to this understudied subject in hopes of generating more academic research into women's perceptions of and experiences with intuition. Additionally, we call for more research into how midwives negotiate childbirth with their clients and the role that intuition plays in these negotiations. What difference does it make, for example, when women hire midwives to save money rather than because of a shared worldview?

23. This national certification process is now in place and functioning, making national certification for direct-entry and independent midwives a reality for the first time in United States history. Several hundred midwives have taken the NARM exam; the first to successfully pass through the complete certification process was Abby J. Kinne, who was formally certified as a CPM (Certified Professional Midwife) on November 10, 1994. By May 1997, approximately 300 midwives will have become CPMs.

REFERENCES CITED

American Heritage Dictionary
  1993 Third Edition. In Microsoft Word for Windows 6.0, Windows 3.1.
Arms, Suzanne
  1994 *Immaculate Deception II: A Fresh Look at Childbirth*. Berkeley: Celestial Arts Press.
Bastick, Tony
  1982 *Intuition: How We Think and Act*. New York: Wiley.
Beth, Easton and Jean Piaget
  1966 *Mathematical Epistemology and Psychology*. Dordrecht, Holland: D. Reidel.
Clifford, James and George E. Marcus, eds.
  1986 *Writing Culture: The Poetics and Politics of Ethnography*. Berkeley: University of California
    Press.
Chester, Penfield
  1997 *Sisters on a Journey: Portraits of North American Midwives*. New Brunswick, NJ: Rutgers
    University Press.
Csordas, Thomas
  1993 "Somatic Modes of Attention," *Cultural Anthropology* 8 (2): 135–56.
D'Aquili, Eugene G.
  1978 "The Neurobiological Basis of Myth and Concepts of Deity," *Zygon*.
Davis, Elizabeth
  1987 *A Guide to Midwifery: Heart and Hands*. New York: Bantam Books.
  1988 *Energetic Pregnancy*. Berkeley: Celestial Arts.
  1989 *Women's Intuition*. Berkeley, CA: Celestial Arts.
  1994 *Women's Sexual Cycles*. London: Little, Brown, and Co.
Davis–Floyd, Robbie
  1987 "Obstetric Training as a Rite of Passage," *Medical Anthropology Quarterly*. 1 (3): 288–318.
  1990 "The Role of Obstetrical Rituals in the Resolution of Cultural Anomaly," *Social
    Science and Medicine* 31 (2): 175–89.
  1992 *Birth as an American Rite of Passage*. Berkeley, CA: University of California Press.
  1994 "The Technocratic Body: American Childbirth as Cultural Expression," *Social Science
    and Medicine* 38 (8): 1125–1140.
Davis-Floyd, Robbie E. and Elizabeth Davis
  1996 "Intuition as Authoritative Knowledge in Midwifery and Home Birth," *Medical
    Anthropology Quarterly* 10(2), pp. 237–269
Davis-Floyd, Robbie E. and Carolyn Sargent, eds.
  1996 *The Social Production of Authoritative Knowledge in Childbirth*, A special issue of the *Medical
    Anthropology Quarterly* 10 (2).
  1997 *Childbirth and Authoritative Knowledge: Cross-Cultural Perspectives*. Berkeley: University of
    California Press.
Diamond, Irene
  1994 *Fertile Ground: Women, Earth, and the Limits of Control*. Boston: Beacon Press.
Diamond, Irene and Gloria Feman Orenstein
  1990 *Reweaving the World: The Emergence of Ecofeminism*. San Francisco: Sierra Club Books.
Eisler, Rianne
  1988 *The Chalice and the Blade*. New York: HarperCollins.

Robbie Davis-Floyd with Elizabeth Davis

Fox, Renee C.

1975 "Training for Uncertainty." In *The Student Physician*, eds. R. Merton, G. Reader, and P. L. Kendall. Cambridge, MA: Harvard University Press.

1980 "The Evolution of Medical Uncertainty," *Millbank Quarterly* 58: 1–49.

Gaskin, Ina May

1990 (1977) *Spiritual Midwifery*, 3rd ed. Summertown, TN: The Book Publishing Co.

Gilligan, Carol

1982 *In a Different Voice: Psychological Theory and Women's Development*. Cambridge, MA: Harvard University Press.

Goer, Henci

1995 *Obstetric Myths Versus Research Realities*. New Haven: Bergin and Garvey.

Goldberg, Phillip

1983 *The Intuitive Edge*. Los Angeles: Jeremy P. Tarcher.

Harper, Barbara

1994 *Gentle Birth Choices*. Rochester, VT: Healing Arts Press.

Hayward, John

1984 *Perceiving Ordinary Magic*. Boston: Shambala.

Jordan, Brigitte

1992 "Technology and Social Interaction: Notes on the Achievement of Authoritative Knowledge," *IRL Technical Report* #92–0027. Palo Alto, CA: Institute for Research on Learning.

1993 *Birth in Four Cultures*, 4th edition, revised and updated by Robbie Davis-Floyd. Prospect Heights, IL: Waveland Press.

Jung, Carl G.

1971 *Psychological Types*. Princeton, NJ: Princeton University Press.

Kennell, John, Marshall Klaus, Susan McGrath, Steven Robertson, and Clark Hinckley

1988 "Medical Intervention: The Effect of Social Support During Labor," *Pediatric Research* April: 211 (Abstract #61).

Kitzinger, Sheila

1979 *Birth at Home*. New York: Penguin Books.

1990 *The Midwife Challenge*. London: Pandora Press.

1991 *Homebirth: The Essential Guide to Giving Birth Outside the Hospital*. New York: Dorling Kindersley, Inc.

Laughlin, Charles D.

1992 *Brain, Symbol, and Experience: A Neurophenomenology of Human Consciousness*. New York: Columbia University Press.

1993a The Mirror of the Brain: A Neurophenomenology of Mature Contemplation. Unpublished ms.

1993b "Fuzziness and Phenomenology in Ethnological Research: Insights from Fuzzy-Set Theory," *Journal of Anthropological Research* 49: 17–37.

Lee, Peter R.

1976 *Symposium on Consciousness*. New York: Penguin.

Leveno, K. J. et al.

1986 "A Prospective Comparison of Selective and Universal Electronic Fetal Monitoring in 34,995 Pregnancies," *New England Journal of Medicine* 315: 615.

MacCormack, Carol

1996 "Maternal Health, War, and Religious Tradition: Authoritative Knowledge in the Pujehun District of Sierra Leone," *Medical Anthropology Quarterly* 10 (2): 270–86.

Marcus, George E.
  1993 "What Comes (Just) After 'Post'? The Case of Ethnography." In *The Handbook of Qualitative Social Science*, eds. Norman Denzin and Yvonne Lincoln. Beverly Hills, CA: Sage Publications.
Marcus, George E. and Michael J. Fischer
  1986 *Anthropology as Cultural Critique: An Experimental Moment in the Human Sciences*. Chicago: University of Chicago Press.
Martin, Emily
  1987 *The Woman in the Body*. Boston: Beacon Press.
McCutcheon-Rosegg, Sue
  1984 *Natural Childbirth the Bradley Way*. New York: E. P. Dutton
Merchant, Carolyn
  1983 *The Death of Nature: Women, Ecology, and the Scientific Revolution*. San Francisco: Harper and Row.
Midwives' Alliance of North America (MANA)
  1992 MANA Statement of Values and Ethics, MANA News 10 (4): 10–12.
  1994 MANA Core Competencies, MANA News 12 (1): 24–27.
Poincaré, Howard
  1913 *The Foundations of Science*. New York: Science Press.
Prentice, A. and T. Lind
  1987 "Fetal Heart Rate Monitoring During Labor—Too Frequent Intervention, Too Little Benefit." *Lancet* 2: 1375–1377.
  1994 *Pursuing the Birth Machine: The Search for Appropriate Perinatal Technology*. London and Sydney: ACE Graphics (U.S. distributor: ICEA Bookcenter, P.O. Box 20048, Minneapolis, MN 55420).
Quinn, Daniel
  1993 *Ishmael*. New York: Bantam and Turner.
Rooks, Judith Pence
  1997 *Midwifery and Childbirth in America*. Philadelphia: Temple University Press.
Rooks, Judith P., Norman L. Weatherby, Eunice K. M. Ernst, Susan Stapleton, David Rosen, and Allan Rosenfield
  1989 "Outcomes of Care in Birth Centers: The National Birth Center Study," *New England Journal of Medicine* 321: 1804–1811.
Rothman, Barbara Katz
  1982 *In Labor: Women and Power in the Birthplace*. New York: W. W. Norton.
  1989 *Recreating Motherhood: Ideology and Technology in a Patriarchal Society*. New York: W. W. Norton.
Rubinstein, Robert A., Charles D. Laughlin, Jr., and John McManus
  1984 *Science as Cognitive Process: Toward an Empirical Philosophy of Science*. Philadelphia: University of Pennsylvania Press.
Sandmire, H. F.
  1990 "Whither Electronic Fetal Monitoring?" *Obstetrics and Gynecology* 76 (6): 1130–1134.
Sargent, Carolyn
  1989 *Maternity, Medicine, and Power: Reproductive Decisions in Urban Benin*. Berkeley: University of California Press.
Sargent, Carolyn and Grace Bascope
  1996 "Ways of Knowing about Birth in Three Cultures," *Medical Anthropology Quarterly* 10 (2): 213–36.
Schlinger, Hillary

Robbie Davis-Floyd with Elizabeth Davis

1992 *Circle of Midwives: Organized Midwifery in North America.* Independently published by Hillary Schlinger.

Sesia, Paola
1996 "Authoritative Knowledge in Oaxacan Prenatal Care: Conceptual Differences between Traditional and Biomedical Approaches." In *Childbirth and Authoritative Knowledge: Cross-Cultural Perspectives*, eds. Robbie Davis-Floyd and Carolyn Sargent. Berkeley: University of California Press.

Shy, Kirkwood et al.
1990 "Effects of Electronic Fetal Heart Rate Monitoring, as Compared with Periodic Auscultation, on the Neurological Development of Premature Infants," *New England Journal of Medicine* March 1: 588–93.

Singer, Linda
1992 "Feminism and Postmodernism." In *Feminists Theorize the Political*, J. Butler and J. W. Scott. New York: Routledge.

Sorokin, Pitirim A.
1941 *The Crisis of Our Age.* New York: E. P. Dutton.

Sosa, R., J. Kennell, S. Robertson, and J. Urrutia
1980 "The Effect of a Supportive Companion on Perinatal Problems, Length of Labor, and Mother-Infant Interaction." *New England Journal of Medicine* 303: 597–600.

Sprenger, Jally and George Deutsch
1981 *Left Brain Right Brain.* San Francisco: W. H. Freeman.

Star, Rima Beth
1986 *The Healing Power of Birth.* Austin: Star Publishing.

Starhawk
1988 *Dreaming the Dark: Magic, Sex, and Politics.* Boston: Beacon Press.
1989 *The Spiral Dance: A Rebirth of the Ancient Religion of the Great Goddess.* HarperSanFrancisco.
1993 *The Fifth Sacred Thing.* New York: Bantam Books.

Sullivan, Deborah and Rose Weitz
1988 *Labor Pains: Modern Midwives and homebirth.* New Haven: Yale University Press.

Susie, Deborah Ann
1988 *In the Way of Our Grandmothers: A Cultural View of Twentieth-Century Midwifery in Florida.* Athens: University of Georgia Press.

TenHouten, Warren
1978–1979 "Hemispheric Interaction in the Brain and the Propositional, Compositional, and Dialectical Modes of Thought," *Journal of Altered States of Consciousness* 4 (2): 129–40.

Vaughan, Frances E.
1979 *Awakening Intuition.* Garden City, NY: Anchor Books.

Wagner, Marsden
1994 *Pursuing the Birth Machine: The Search for Appropriate Perinatal Technology.* London and Sydney: ACE Graphics (U.S. distributor: ICEA Bookcenter, P.O. Box 20048, Minneapolis, MN 55420).

Weil, Andrew
1972 *The Natural Mind.* Boston: Houghton-Mifflin.

Westcott, Alan
1968 *Toward a Contemporary Psychology of Intuition.* New York: Holt, Rinehart, and Winston.

IO

STANDING BY PROCESS

A Midwife's Notes on Story-telling, Passage, and Intuition

Lucia Roncalli

INTRODUCTION: STORY-TELLING AND SUBVERSIVE POSSIBILITIES

I am a midwife, and I attend births at home. Not coincidentally, I am also a student of spirituality and comparative mysticism. Each involves risk and immersion, and each invites great trust. Each opens onto the sacred.

When I drive to a birth, it is my habit to open to the universe, and to look for the quiet center within. I ask for the humility to act from that center, and to let it manifest in all that I am about to say or not say, do or not do.

This is meditative centering. It is a way of inviting intuitional knowledge. It is also a way of praying. Like prayer and meditation, intuition involves loosening or bypassing one's everyday self. My guess is that there are as many varieties of intuitive as of mystical or meditative experience. In this chapter, I give examples of intuitive experience at play in healing and midwifery, and explore not only the revelations, but also some of the ethical riddles they pose. I also want to explore story-telling as a form of expression that may be as appropriate to this way of knowing as equations are to physics.[1]

Different forms of knowledge need different standards of rigor or precision, and many people in our culture have made the mistake of assuming that predictability

Lucia Roncalli

and a high degree of (preferably mathematical) precision are universal criteria for judging the excellence of a body of knowledge.[2]

This is not a new tendency in the West; Aristotle saw it at work in his time, and told a parable to question it. All Greek builders once used finely calibrated straight-edges—the height of precision!—to measure columns on their buildings, he began. All builders, that is, except those on the island of Lesbos. There, builders used something at once more supple, more commonplace, and more accurate. They used knotted string—not the conventionally exact "hard rule" but the more useful and appropriate "Lesbian rule," the innovation from Lesbos that made possible the graceful, soaring columns of later Greek architecture.[3]

Story-telling may be the equivalent of a "Lesbian rule" in developing intuition in oneself and even in understanding it through the canons of science. It is more common and more supple than a statistical survey or clinical study; its teaching is richer and more diffuse and thus can percolate more readily and more deeply to the soul, to surface later, transformed, unexpected and surprisingly apt, in other life situations. Story-telling is essential to clinical practice: what else is a "case history" but a special way of telling a story? And what is "anecdotal evidence" but a term for a story that teaches what the culture or a profession wants to ignore?

Story-telling is also integral to what Davis-Floyd (see chapter 9) calls "postmodern midwifery." If you ever have the chance, listen in on a group of midwives talking shop. One midwife will tell a birth story and the group listens intently, perhaps interrupting with questions: What did the mother eat during her first trimester? How was her relation to her partner? To her mother? Did she have cats in the house? What was her own birth like? What was the phase of the moon? Would it have helped to have her push on the toilet, or to use homeopathic caulophyllum, or shepherd's purse tincture? Did she already have a name for the baby?

To an outsider, these questions might seem like farfetched non sequiturs; to the midwives, each one telegraphs or occasionally opens up worlds of meaning and connection. Once the story is told, the group works it like a many-woman quilt. Each one brings her own scraps of experience, her own insight, derived from keen observation and undomesticated reflection, into how things are connected in a life, in a woman, and in a birth. The collective intelligence in such a session is staggering. I come away aware that this is a distinctive way of knowing; sometimes I label it the midwives' way, sometimes, women's way. Sometimes I simply taste it and know it, apart from any name or label. Unquestionably, these sessions "prime the pump" for us; they affirm and deepen a way of being that is rare and precious and deeply intuitive.

In my practice, as in other homebirth practices, prenatal exams begin with tea over the kitchen table and last an hour or more. One of the things this allows, in myself and in other women, is the freedom to share and validate each other's stories. Early on, I marveled at how many of these stories are "anomaly stories"—stories of synchronicity, serendipity, telepathy, clairvoyance, intuition. I saw also the special delight and relief that come of sharing these stories with others who do not dismiss them as impossible or fanciful. They are miracle stories, after all—stories that signify a universe *not* reducible to linear causality only.

Pregnant and birthing women (and their midwives) often have such experiences. (In fact, so do the dying and their families and caretakers; the passages of birth, death, and major illness destabilize the ordinary self and are especially fertile times for intuitive insight.) Experiences of clairvoyance or telepathic communication between a woman and her unborn child, or her dead mother or her present partner, hint at patterns of connection within a larger and meaningful whole. A midwifery practice like ours merely provides an atmosphere in which it is comfortable to share them. Sharing and welcoming the stories seems to open invisible channels; it's like preparing the pathway for mystery and connection to well up again later.

Telling and hearing anomaly stories generate visible relief: relief that it's not all figured out after all. Relief that we really do swim in so vast and mysteriously interconnected a reality. Relief that the story-teller isn't crazy.

Such stories are also liberating. As the authors of *Women's Way of Knowing* (Belenky et al. 1986: 23–34) discovered, there is for many women a bitter link between violence and silence, between feeling invisible to others and feeling oneself to be non-existent. Telling stories and having them really be heard can create the experience of *being* in those who wonder if they exist at all, and who therefore have hesitated to speak or act in the world, or even to feel. For this reason storytelling has been for decades at the heart of women's and other liberation movements.

Because these stories are liberating, they are subversive as well. A woman's new knowledge that she exists opens the possibility that she will act and believe freely—perhaps even differently from the norms of her culture. Anomaly stories express a reality that differs emphatically from this culture's. They are akin to the "kitchen talk" of antebellum slaves: talk that springs from and generates another reality than the dominant culture's. Though they are, in fact, as widespread as the dominant worldview, they are not able to be recognized because they lack public airplay. Women are often careful to keep anomaly stories private and untold. The flip side of such secrecy is the hidden fear that one is insane. Being open and empathically received leads to the knowledge that one is not only not crazy, but is in fact verifying with others the subtlety and meaningfulness of the non-"normal" universe revealed in our stories. The anomaly stories I hear in my practice are almost always punctuated by: "You mean other people have these experiences, too? I thought I was the only one. So I must not be crazy after all. . . . "—and the body's sudden relaxation, followed by a slow smile that turns from radiance to mischief as all the implications and possibilities dawn. Speaking and being heard, seen, welcomed, brings one in from the cold. It brings a woman in from the realm of subhuman, beast, or freak, to be included as a full human being, a canny explorer among other canny explorers, a story-teller among story-tellers.

In *Power and the Profession of Obstetrics,* William Arney (1982: 88ff) accurately notes that a "confessional style" in relation to her caregivers can be disempowering for a woman.[4] This is true if story-telling is one-sided and occurs within a context of clinical detachment and economic and gender inequality. But if a woman has been silenced most of her life, or has often had the experience of speaking without really being heard, she will be vivid with exhilaration if she has taken the risk of sharing her story and if it has been fully heard and she has been celebrated both for her uniqueness and for her common connection with others.

I have seen this truth shine in the faces of rural peasant midwives in Central America, in workshops led by nurses and midwives who genuinely admired these women's intelligence and courage and welcomed their stories, as well as in the faces of North American midwives shyly taking the floor for the first time at open sessions of MANA conventions. (See chapter 9 for a description of the Midwives' Alliance of North America.)

Intuition stories are subversive for another reason as well—they come singly. They are "anecdotal evidence"—and in our context they are not disparaged for being singular. There is no question of "washing them out" with bigger and better statistics or with reductive psychology. Karl Jaspers once wrote that a single case profoundly understood can yield as much insight as statistical knowledge of millions.[5] More than that: the "single case," especially the "single anomalous case"— the single intuition story, for example—brings possibility out into the open. It whispers to us to think again about how we are made, and about how the world is.

A Garland of Teaching-Stories

Questing for Wisdom

I took my science courses in the Ivy League. I arrived there from San Francisco in the sixties, with all that implies—a peace child in quest of wisdom. I thought, for example, that one who understands the structure of the universe must be a wise and accomplished contemplative, so I went straight to the head of the astrophysics department my first week in college, to ask him what light Einstein's equations could shed on the deepest questions about life and death. (To his eternal credit, he took the question at face value. After a long introspective silence, he ruefully confessed that a deep understanding of the physical universe had not helped him much with questions of life and death. It had not helped him to be a better husband, or father, or friend—but it had, nonetheless, afforded him some moments of surpassing beauty, moments well worth a lifetime's preparation.)

I realized one night in a physics lab that there are two paths to understanding the interchangeability of mass and energy: one is to master the equations, and one is to live that interchangeability—for example, by pursuing a yogin's training until one is able to ignite a hearth fire from the movements of one's mind. I knew that both paths were important to me, and I knew that neither would be worth anything unless it would make me better able to love.

The quest for wisdom led me temporarily out of college and into some years of hospital work. I needed to see people die and be born, to accompany them through the immense transformations of illness—then, I thought, surely I would be closer to wisdom. I gravitated to those who had died and been resuscitated—what wisdom did they have to share? Much, it turned out. My encounters with those people, and with the dying, were freighted with wonder.

I realize now that "wisdom" for me meant a particular kind of transformative and untamable experience, one in which intuition is a key element. It comes as a gift, a grace, which, like a mystic's, can be prepared for and invited, but never commanded solely by will. (Certain stories, and the wonder and possibility they open in the heart, are one mode of preparation.)

Wisdom could come, for example, as a flash of light that overtakes me in the nurses' station just as old Russian Anastasia is dying in her bed down the hall. I have nursed the comatose woman for weeks, speaking low into her ear before I bathe or turn her. I treat her as if she is here, and I find myself cringing and apologizing silently to her when others talk in her presence as if she is absent.

The flash of light brings me into sudden communication with Anastasia, though my body remains sitting quietly in the nurses' station. I am again speaking into her ear, and helping her across a kind of gulf. To my surprise, the words that come slowly out of my mouth are instructions for the dying from the *Tibetan Book of the Dead*: "Oh, nobly born, do not be afraid. The time has come to set your face toward the Clear Light of Realization. . . . Go toward the light, Anastasia. Don't be afraid of it." In a few moments, the light and the words dim, and I return to the lesser fluorescence of the nurses' station—reverent, shaken, humbled, grateful— just as the orderly who has been making rounds comes to announce that Anastasia has died in her sleep minutes ago.

Why would one prize this and other similar incidents so much, and deem them wisdom? Certainly the question of whether Anastasia shared the experience with me and/or gained anything from it must be bracketed; I can claim no certain benefit to her. But perhaps the work done by the pediatrician Melvin Morse on adult and child survivors of near-death experiences can begin to explain its immense value to me.[6] Psychological testing and Morse's open-ended interviews reveal a noticeable serenity and fearlessness in survivors whose near-death experiences involved light, even years after the event. These experiences are transformative, even for those who merely witness or assist—to share them is a privilege. It is like being given a gift from the deepest love there is—and that is its own teaching about how better to love.

One day, I realized that the mystery at the end of life I was pursuing so intently had a mirror image at life's beginning. Suddenly I knew it was time I was with people who had just completed the birth passage—that meant babies, labor and delivery, and the newborn nursery.

What confronted me in those places, however, was an ocean of unnecessary pain. I saw women laboring on their backs: the one position not represented in a comprehensive nineteenth-century study of birthing positions in primitive cultures; the one position—headstands excepted—that goes against gravity, and thus the "most unnatural position" (Engelmann 1882). I saw women whose arms were tied spread-eagle to the delivery tables, ostensibly to prevent them from "contaminating the field" of their own powerful bellies. I saw women come away from such births "unaccountably" depressed. And I saw babies sobbing disconsolately and then giving up as they lay the requisite six hours after birth in "the haven," a "scientifically" prewarmed, oxygen-enriched plastic box.

The quest for wisdom became a new fierce quest for a way of birth that didn't involve so much needless pain, a way that would honor the wild wisdom of laboring women and the uncanny sentience of the just-born. That quest led me eventually to midwifery school and then to midwifery practice.

I didn't know then that the circle would come round full again, because the labor of dying and the labor of birthing have so much in common, and because both will, if we let them, open onto the holy. I didn't know that I would eventually taste again that peculiar kind of anomalous and transformative experience that could touch both life and death with grace, which I had come to believe lay at the heart of wisdom. Nor did I realize that I would at times feel caught between two competing worlds, struggling to make coherent conversation between them.

Direct Intuition I

> intuition . . . 2a. the act or process of coming to direct knowledge or certainty without reasoning or inferring: immediate cognizance or conviction without rational thought: revelation by insight or innate knowledge
> —Webster's Third International Dictionary

A friend whose first birth I attended calls to tell me she is pregnant again. I hang up the phone and say to my sister, who is one of the most gifted scientists and one of the most gifted intuitives I know, "She's not going to have a baby from this pregnancy." Just like that: the words pop out of my mouth with authority—no drama and no wrapping-paper. "I know," my sister says.

A month later my friend calls for help because she has been cramping on and off. Anguished, she sobs, "I think I'm losing this baby. What do you think? Do you think I'll be able to keep it, or do you think it's gone, too?"

In a split second I weigh my usual open-ended answer, which would still hold out the possibility that the right combination of bedrest, herbs, pharmaceuticals, and psychological work might be effective—against what I *know*. Her question springs from a deeper place than weighed possibilities. She is asking me to give of myself, to answer naked, from my own being and my own wild knowledge, not from what I know in common with others.

"I don't think so, Michele. I have a feeling this life has already completed its purpose." She begins to cry. "You're right. That's what I feel too, but I needed to hear it from someone else. Thank you for just saying it. Now I can get ready to do what I need to do here. . . . But this really hurts, and I'm afraid I won't be able to go through it."

Something else pops out of my mouth then, a reference to her first birth, a truth about her extraordinary strength and dignity. Something, she tells me later, that enabled her experience of miscarrying to be filled not only with sorrow, but also with a kind of triumph and ecstasy for herself as a woman, connected to, and then releasing the little girl-child she had to let go.

My experience with Michele is a story about direct intuition. Just as scientific data can be classed as "hard" or "soft," intuitive experience can feel subjective or objective, filtered or direct.

Direct intuitions feel as if they come from somewhere outside myself. They are indeed immediate—so much so that I am not aware of having formulated what "I" am saying or doing. These intuitions feel not-from-me; perhaps "ex-tuition" is a better term for them. Also, they often engage the witness self: I can act from direct intuition and simultaneously watch or listen to myself, or even editorialize internally on "my" words and actions: "What a totally weird thing to say—where did that come from?"

Direct intuition tends to show up in high-intensity moments: in medical or emotional emergencies, or at those points in conversation that are especially ripe for significant breakthrough. Apart from naming it, and telling stories about it, I have not much to say about direct intuition, for "I" have not much to do with it.

Direct Intuition II: Intuitive Attunement

> intuition . . . 2d. [bergsonism]...a divining empathy . . . gives direct insight into
> reality as it is in itself and absolutely
> —Webster's Third International Dictionary

Intuitive attunement is the low-intensity version of direct intution, another form of immediate knowing that completely bypasses self and seems to come from elsewhere. It is an interactive intelligence, a "divining empathy" akin to Gardner's interpersonal intelligence (1983: 239), that comes as direct insight into another person's reality.

In my practice, intuitive attunement manifests most frequently. It is modest and undramatic and probably familiar to skilled practitioners in many fields: the question that comes bubbling out of me at just the right time during a prenatal exam and unlocks the troubling story that if untold could hold up a labor; the way my hands travel to "just the right spot—how did you know?" to soothe or provide counterpressure during a labor, or to field an emergency.

I come in on Pam, a woman in labor with whom an associate has been sitting for half a day. I am backup for this midwife; she has two women in labor and needs me here so she can go to the other woman. Pam has been stuck at five centimeters' dilation for several hours; the contractions are painful, and she is writhing and moaning, "Oh God, Oh God, Oh Godddd . . . "

I sit quietly behind Pam, legs astraddle, and synchronize my breathing with hers. "Oh good," I breathe softly into her ear, in rhythm with her. "Oh good. Oh good. Oh gooooood." She picks it up. "Oh gooooooood," her voice dips with mine into lowest abdominal registers, good primal rhythmic toning.

At something so simple and slight as the change of a single vowel, her tense body softens. We keep up the cadence, and half an hour later, she is completely dilated and easily pushes out her second son.

Later Pam tells me that her bag of waters was artificially ruptured against her will when she was six centimeters' dilated with her first child. She was plunged into agonizing contractions and had to take them on her back (Engelmann's "most unnatural position") in the hospital. Pam's body remembered, although her conscious mind didn't; her body tensed and balked at the possibility of a repeat performance in this labor. "Oh goooood" broke the hold of the past and allowed Pam to relax unencumbered into the present.

Intuitive attunement is at play 98 percent of the time intuition shows up in my practice; it will get 2 percent of the attention here because it is so seamless. It is simply there, common and nourishing, like brown rice. To write about it would be like writing about how to walk.

I don't recall having learned it; but it may be a learned awareness that has become automatic. Its origin may lie in a decision I made as a child, when I realized that a person who was causing me and others extraordinary pain had no idea of how much pain was being caused. This person's lack of awareness of something so obvious impressed me very deeply; I vowed to study the mechanism of such pain-causing in the hope that I could avoid reproducing it.

So, in addition to feeling my pain, I looked carefully at how it came to be, and at what made it better. I thought about what I as an adult might do in similar situations, should they arise. I wanted not to be unaware when I inadvertently caused pain. I also wanted to look for and gently change in myself the peculiar self-deafness I surmised to be the driving force behind the inability to recognize the hurt one causes in others. Working by analogy from my own pain, I learned deep connection to others, and possibly this has become second nature. This may disqualify it from being genuinely intuitive — otherwise we could claim bike riding and reading as intuitive behaviors. On the other hand, if it is a learned awareness rather than a learned behavior, it may be at least a close cousin in the intuition family.

Filtered Intuition

Direct intuition feels like it comes from outside; by contrast, filtered intuition feels more refracted by my insides, thus it has more potential to be affected by personal quirks and unconscious fears. Like direct intuition, it may manifest suddenly, as spontaneous image or dream, but it doesn't move as fast to bypass self; it is easier to get caught up in sticky internal debates about "Is this just my stuff, or is it actually relevant to the situation?" Therefore, it is easier to get talked out of filtered intuitions, or to talk myself out of paying attention to them.

In clinical practice, there is also the lovely dance of filtered intuition for two or more: the process of cross-checking the hunches, senses, impressions, feelings of the mother or the father or my midwifery partner with each other and with my own.[7] (See also chapter 9.) The usual rule of thumb is: if there is a clash, disregard no one's take, but give priority to the mother's (or, on occasion, to her partner's). I give the mother priority for two reasons: first, because work with the critically ill has shown that people have profound unconscious knowledge of their own bodily processes and conditions, and this a crucial resource to use in pregnancy and birth.[8] Second, filtered intuitional messages are subtle, and in this culture, women especially can be easily intimidated out of paying heed to their intuition when "the facts" appear otherwise. Therefore, I want to offer the kind of encouragement that can catalyze a birthing woman's discovery of her own innate deep knowing. In the following story, the mother's and the midwife's intuitions didn't tally. The mother was wise enough to stand by her dream-message, and her son was lucky she did.

A client eight months' pregnant calls me to the house two nights running to check her and the baby. She has had a dream in which her little son is lying deathly still, surrounded by cord and placental membranes. On exam, both she and the baby appear normal to me, but I encourage her not to dismiss her dream. The next night the feeling is so strong that she checks into the hospital on her own for testing. First she has a non-stress test, in which the baby is monitored through the normal physiological contractions that accompany pregnancy. The results show nothing wrong, so she demands an oxytocin challenge test, in which the baby is monitored while a drug is administered to strengthen the contractions to labor-strength. Because the mother is an M.D., she gets her way. The baby goes into severe distress as soon as the test begins, and an emergency Cesarean section minutes later reveals a little boy in just the position and situation of her dream. Very likely he would have been stillborn in early labor had she not followed her intuition, or had she allowed herself to be talked out of it.

Filtered Intuition and Birth as Symbolic Self-Expression

"As a woman lives, so shall she birth."[9]

Many medical conditions are a form of symbolic self-expression, and obstetrical emergencies are no exception. (The trick is to facilitate symbolic expression in other ways, so that it is no longer necessary to use literal emergency as an expressive or therapeutic form.) These births can be major opportunities for inner healing or closure,

Lucia Roncalli

and a practitioner's intuition is often a powerful ally in avoiding tragedy. It is as if the practitioner, woman (or family), and issue to be resolved form a gestalt, a flowing, moving, subtle, interconnected whole. In chapter 9, Davis-Floyd gives an example of one obstetrical emergency—a postpartum hemorrhage—that was in part a woman's expression of her need to have her husband close and attentive, and of her midwife's intuitive response.

There are some parallels with that story and the one I am about to tell. Yet it is valuable to have another example, because these situations are so common in birth. I think this is the "X factor" that accounts for the startling fact that close to half of obstetric emergencies arise in women whose prenatal status has been "normal" or "low risk."

This fact propels the movement toward more precise forms of "monitoring" to detect potential problems. It can also be used to argue that all births should occur in a fully equipped obstetrical suite.

However, from a midwife's perspective, this is a fear-based response to personal—and, if you will, to universal—process. I do not mean to minimize the risks associated with birth. But I do mean to point out that a willingness to trust intuition and to "trust process" also involves a willingness to embrace difference, the unfamiliar, and by definition, risk. It is distinct from the fear that often will short-circuit process and disallow its expression and healing wisdom. Fear breeds the "national security" mentality that leads nations to invest billions more in machines and guns—war technology—than in the effective and equally demanding technology of peace: real human contact and dialogue.

When I reentered midwifery after a long hiatus caused by major illness, I began work in a group practice. My supervisor wanted to be sure I did a home visit right away on Joy, a woman who had been having contractions and might deliver soon. It would be good for us to meet in case I'd be at her birth that weekend.

By the book, Joy is ready. The dates are close enough, she is having strong pre-labor contractions, the house is prepared, the names for the baby picked out, and she is bulky, uncomfortable, and very ready not to be pregnant anymore.

But as we visit, I am almost-seeing a cloud around her, a mix of unclarity and unwillingness, or even truculence. It seems to me that Joy will not deliver for a while. And I am sensing that the birth won't be straightforward, even though there is nothing to indicate this won't be a smooth and fast fifth baby for her.

As the new kid on the block the first day on the job, I choose not to share my impressions from that home visit with others in the practice. I visit with Joy when she comes to the clinic for prenatal checks a couple times after that, and continue to "almost-see" the same cloudiness around her each time we are together.

Two weeks later, Joy goes into labor. I attend with another midwife, Molly. Molly is a warm, funny, earthy, and implacably common sensical woman; I am very glad we are the team for this birth.

When we arrive at the house at 2 a.m., we find Joy laboring in a tub filled with hot water; she's having good strong frequent contractions that she and her husband meet with grace. Clearly they have done this a few times before. Molly and I will use the time to set up.

We lay out the oxygen and baby resuscitation mask, the suction equipment and the drugs against hemorrhage, all with great care. Together we check the oxygen tank and test the valves. Then we check again. We are matter-of-fact and even casual—after all, one always has the emergency equipment ready at a birth—but we are notably thorough. I wonder if this is Molly's usual way, and I am impressed. Then we turn to the other setup tasks: hot water for compresses when Joy comes out of the tub, set atop a pile of old towels and receiving blankets for the baby, in order to warm them; instrument packs, bulb syringe, chart, all laid out on the dresser.

The cloudiness I am almost-seeing around Joy persists until the very end of her eight-hour labor. She pushes hard for an hour—a new experience for her, as her other babies had all but flown out. Slowly a beautiful baby's head emerges. He doesn't budge with the next contraction, the one that should bring out his shoulders and body.

Molly's eyes meet mine as she checks inside Joy. "There's cord around the neck, and I can't get enough slack to loop it over the head."

"Follow it with your hands."

"It's back around the shoulder and maybe down the chest—I can't tell. And it's completely taut. I can't move it at all."

From her vantage point, Molly suddenly sees the baby's lips and facial tone relax, a sign that he is not getting enough oxygen and must be born immediately. She does the appropriate thing: clamps and cuts the cord internally, quickly unwinds it from around his neck and shoulder. Out he shoots, another son for Joy: named Vito. Limp and floppy, he needs the oxygen and resuscitation we are ready to give him.

One works in these situations in a curious mix of hyper-alertness and time dilation—by the clock, there are few minutes to work effectively, yet those few minutes have a blessed spaciousness in which much can be accomplished.

This baby is "vibrationally present" as we work to get him breathing. Vito's heart tones are strong throughout, too, but that's a bit different. There are degrees of aliveness, a spectrum of being in-the-body, and anyone who works with birth develops a visceral sense of that spectrum, and of a given baby's location on it at any given time in the process of resuscitation. One can feel a subtle shift from not-here to here, the shift that signifies that whatever remains to be done externally— even if it is several more minutes of stimulation—is really mop-up, pro forma, a matter almost of etiquette with regard to the material plane.

In fact, with Vito, no shift occurs, because he is never "not-here." I look around the room, at the tense faces of family and carefully chosen friends. "He needs you all to call him by name. Tell him you want him here. Breathe, you guys! No one's breathing. Show this baby how to breathe! He needs your help."

For a moment, the cloudiness around Joy disappears. "*Vito! I love you! Come be with us, baby! We really want you here!*"

The baby starts, and gasps, and begins to howl. Vito has to tell his story and his distress, and it takes a while. "Oh, my family—this was *so hard* to do!"

Often after a difficult birth, the mother has a profound need to go over each detail, to hear the story from others and to tell her part, to fill in the memory gaps or make sense of what she was too consumed by to understand in labor. In the hours after Vito's arrival, Joy's focus is not, as would be usual after such a birth, those tense moments before he breathed. Joy is coming to terms with pushing. "I can't believe I pushed so hard. I never knew I could push like that. It was so hard, but I did it." She repeats these sentences as if they are a mantra.

"So now you know how strong you are, Joy. Now you know that you have what it takes inside to do anything you might ever want or need to do, and no one can ever take that knowing away from you."

Joy doesn't demur, or deflect by protesting the corniness of my delivery. She looks up, still in semi-trance, and nods. "Yes. That's right. I know that now. And you're right—no one can ever take it away from me. I really know that now. I can't believe I pushed so hard. . . . "

Later, the fragments began to come together. "I kept watching myself as we set up," mused Molly. "I always lay everything out, but usually not like that. My hands kept going over and over the stuff, and I kept wondering what I was doing. I guess at some level I knew we were going to need it."

We learned that Joy decided while she was pregnant that if the baby were a boy, she would name him after her brother—the baby brother who had died before birth because he was too tangled in his cord to survive early labor.

Joy may have known subliminally by late in her pregnancy that she was going to take on the challenge of reliving and rewriting that chapter in her family's story, and she may not have been altogether willing or confident—that, at least, is my explanation for the cloudiness I had sensed in her from our first visit together.

We also learned that throughout Joy's youth and adulthood, her mother tended to emphasize what a "hard worker" Joy's sister is. But when her mother made mention of this a day or two after Vito's birth, I saw Joy look her mother in the eyes and say with calm assurance, "I am a 'hard worker,' too, Mom. You don't see it in me, but Sarah's not the only one." I believe that exchange was connected with the complete disappearance, on the first day postpartum, of the cloudiness around Joy: not only was the private challenge over; but she had come out with flying colors. She had the evidence she needed that she, too, could do "hard work, and bring forth the double gift of her own self-esteem and the transgenerational recasting of a tragic chapter in her family's history."

"No undercurrents between the grandmother and the baby?," a friend who is also an analyst quizzed me when I wonderingly described the birth to her.

"None. She's really delighted with him." Joy's mother especially glowed when she spoke of how much she treasured the early morning hours she was spending rocking Vito so that Joy could get some uninterrupted sleep.

"In this culture, we underestimate how very much children want to give gifts to their parents. It sounds as if your client set out to give her mother the gift of a Vito who made it—and luckily, that was a gift her mother could really accept and rejoice in—not all parents can accept gifts from their children. What a healing exchange!"

One of the midwives in our practice laughed knowingly when we presented the story of the two Vitos at a staff meeting. She then told a birth-story from several years earlier, in which a boy child had been prenamed for the mother's father, whose life had hung in the balance for several months before the birth. The grandfather came off a ventilator three weeks before the birth, and three weeks later, the baby went on a ventilator for exactly as many months as his grandfather had been on it. "When births like that happen, you have to accept that you are just a pawn on the board in a game that isn't really about you at all. It's not your game, and it's much, much bigger than you ever will be," the midwife twinkled, gesturing wide with her hands. "You're just along for the ride."

The MANA Statement of Values and Ethics underscores this point when it states,

> We value the art of nurturing the intrinsic normalcy of birth, and recognize that each woman and baby have parameters of well-being unique unto themselves. . . . We value skills which support a complicated pregnancy or birth to move toward a state of greater well-being or to be brought to the most healing conclusion possible. *We value the art of letting go.* (MANA 1992: 11, emphasis mine)

It takes a certain something—trust, in fact—to stand by a woman whose personal growth involves, for example, heavy postpartum bleeding or a baby seriously tangled in its cord. Neither the gift to her mother nor the gift to herself would have been possible if Joy's "long" pushing stage had been short-circuited, with whatever good intentions. I am not advocating heavy bleeding or tangled cords as a form of personal growth, nor am I advocating that drugs and technology be withheld from all birth emergencies—but I am saying that a cultural openness to psyche, intuition, body-wisdom, and process would facilitate the story-telling and play-acting, hypnotic and otherwise, that could preclude many emergencies by allowing expression of the issues that spawn them, and would meet the emergencies that do arise knowing that a willingness to hear—and respond to—their messages can be as powerful as the strongest drug against hemorrhage.[10] This willingness to stand by process is the crux of the cultural difference (and much of the animosity) between mainstream obstetrics and "postmodern midwifery." It is what the MANA Statement of Values and Ethics refers to when it states, "We value [birth] as a process larger than ourselves, [which] we may seek to know and learn from but never control" (MANA 1992: 11).

THE PRICE OF IGNORING INTUITION

Lucia Roncalli

I want also to share my hardest story with you. I ignored intuition once, because it didn't square with "objective" data and I had neither logical grounds to act contrary to the data, nor a language to talk about my dilemma. The baby died, possibly because of my choice.

I am aware that telling such a story to a non-midwifery audience risks discrediting my profession—homebirth attended by midwives is embraced by relatively few in our culture, and despite the fact that for over a century studies all over the world have shown that it is as safe as or safer than hospital birth, the idea of babies being born at home still makes many people uneasy. Therefore, I assume and rely on your familiarity with the worldview and safety statistics in chapter 9. I risk telling the story because I believe that it is time to tell as many intuition stories as possible, and to begin to explore the questions they pose. This is a story about a clash between knowledge that is legitimated by our culture and knowledge that is not, told by one who has sought and marveled at both types of knowledge for all of her adult life, and who is learning only very slowly and painfully when to abide by which kind.

The time is fifteen years ago. Annie is in labor, and I am rifling through the lab work and prenatal records in the chart, checking and rechecking vital signs, fetal heart tones, and position. I am looking for any abnormality that would correspond to the intense, nearly suffocating dread I am feeling, now for the fourth time in two hundred births.

Actually, I am not just feeling it inside me. I am seeing it in the room. It has looked the same each time I have seen it, and I call it by proper name now: Dread. It is a huge dark mound, somewhat resembling a mountain and somewhat resembling a buffalo. It has thick curly hair, and an eye—I see it in profile. It is not personally threatening, nor even monstrous. It simply is, and is with us, another presence in the room.

Dread is gendered—I think of it as male, though to call Dread "him" personifies overmuch. The other three times Dread has appeared, normal births from healthy women who have had normal pregnancies have careened off the tracks. The emergencies have been unforeseeable and bizarre. The outcomes have been good, but getting there has involved interminable moments on the razor edge between life and death.

Annie is from "the hollers" in Tennessee. Her husband is a taciturn mill worker whose employment in the Rust Belt is tenuous at best. This is their third baby. The first was born in a conventional labor and delivery suite, the second in a birthing center. Both labors were normal and short, both babies were healthy. She had episiotomies and epidural anesthesia with both. Annie passionately wants this baby to be born at home; she has been an eager student for all we have to teach about preparing for it.

For two nights before this one she thought she was in labor but wasn't. ("No, it's not 'false labor,'" we tell her, in the constant re-visioning and re-phrasing of woman-diminishing medical jargon that is second nature in our practice. "These contractions are doing real work, they're getting you closer to having this baby. There's nothing 'false' about them. But it looks like the baby is not quite ready to come tonight.")

Those prodromal nights felt OK to me; this third night doesn't. On my way to Annie's house, I stop to call my backup physician. Bill is an incomparable doctor, one who has been delivering babies for decades and still conceives of his work as a vocation to serve. When I teased him years ago about the likelihood that his colleagues would flay him for backing couples having babies at home with midwives in attendance, he looked at me in genuine surprise. "Isn't it our job to support and not to judge the choices people make, and to do our best to see that their wishes are carried out safely and well?" He assumes that his colleagues share his dedication, and he can be utterly naive about the political intrigues and power-jockeying in his profession.

"Bill, I have a funny feeling about Annie."

"She'll do fine. Her pregnancy's been beautiful. Just remind her what an extraordinary gift it is to bring life into the world."

"No, I don't mean that. She's not worried; I am."

"Is there anything unusual in her or the baby's condition?"

"No—it's just a feeling I can't shake." (In the middle of the night, from a pay phone by the side of the road, I do not want to talk to him about having just seen Dread, and all that has meant in the past.)

"I think you're nervous because this is the third time you're going out there. It sound like her labor's kicking in now, and judging by the other ones, it should be pretty smooth and quick. It's going to be fine—really."

The thing about funny feelings is that in a rationalistic culture you can be talked out of paying attention to them. And if you respect "hard data" and the "hard data" contradict feeling, then you enter Coyote territory: a subtle and unchartable realm in which cookbook rules do not apply.

You must understand, too, what homebirth means to most women or couples who choose it. It is a cherished dream involving family, freedom, privacy, and the gentlest possible beginning for a little one whose exquisite sensitivity is deeply empathized and identified with. (One midwife, Helen Swallow [1980], has called homebirth "a peak human experience," and she is right.) Transport to the hospital is disruptive and can mean considerable disappointment about letting go of the homebirth dream. Hospital staff often do not approve of homebirth and can be punitive to those who come in from home. And the hospital's technological "solutions" can cause problems that are just as serious as those they aim to solve. They can be painful, dangerous, and even life-threatening to mothers and babies (Davis-Floyd 1992; Goer 1995; Wagner 1994). Transport can also have crushing financial consequences for families without insurance. Of course, all this is worth it if a woman's or a baby's life can be saved—but transport is not something to do lightly, and unnecessary transport is to be avoided for many reasons.

Given that the "hard data" of lab work, prenatal history, and present vital signs in Annie and her baby are fine, I accept Bill's gloss and override my inner warning system. I continue on to Annie's house, and labor with her for five hours while my midwifery partner and Annie's husband sleep. The night is deep and serene, and so is our meandering conversation. Between contractions, Annie muses about God and her hopes for this child and for her life. I marvel at the composure and faith she has managed to nurture in her hardscrabble life.

When it comes time for Annie to push, we wake her husband and my partner. It takes a while for Annie to learn what pushing is all about—not uncommon in women who have previously given birth with anesthesia. We work to massage and oil and stretch the skin of the birth opening—the scar tissue from the past episiotomies is tight. For a minute before birth, we stop being able to hear the baby's heart tones—also not uncommon as the baby passes under the pubic bone. I monitor its scalp then, watching for the rosy color that signals normal circulation.

Seconds before birth, the scalp goes white. I cut an episiotomy, pull out a limp baby girl, and begin immediately to resuscitate her. She pinks up and even takes four spontaneous gasps in the twenty minutes I work on her. Yet I never feel as if she is present. Her heart tones are strong as I work on her, and she is warm and pink—but there is never any life in her flesh. As I work, my eyes meet Annie's: dark, stark, horrified. She knows.

After transport to the hospital, the baby spent several months on a ventilator, and died when her parents finally decided to pull the plug.

Autopsy results were inconclusive. Possibly she was one of the 50 percent of stillborn babies for which there is no discernable clinical or postmortem explanation. Possibly there were subtle hypoxic changes happening as she passed through the birth canal that electronic monitoring in a hospital would have detected. Possibly her life could have been saved if I had accepted the information of Dread and suggested we transport. Or—possibly there was another factor at play, one her parents could have understood and translated if I had been open with them about Dread. They may not have opted for transport and the hospital; they may have opted for prayer or something else. Then, at least, the decision about what to do and the consequences would have belonged, as they should, fully to the parents.

These possibilities still haunt me and make me want to bang pots and ring bells and shout from rooftops: *Intuitive knowledge is just as real as laboratory data! It needs to be included in clinical decision-making with just as much respect as what can be quantified! We need to develop a language to talk about these things, and talk about them well!*

I believe that very few of our stories belong only to us. In most cases, they are given to us in trust, and we are their guardians. It is our job to know when to keep them and when to let them loose in the world to do work in other lives. The decision to tell this story and contribute to a discussion of the role of intuition in practical life is one of the ways I can honor the memory of that little girl and the suffering of her family. It is one of the ways her life can make a difference in the world.

They named her the day after she was born: Charity. Charity Ann.

Riddles from the Ethical

Guardianship and Informed Decision-Making

Intuitions are like stories. Sometimes—often, if you are a practitioner—they are not just for you. Sometimes receiving intuitive insight about others' lives makes you a guardian of those insights. You have to know when to keep silence, and you have to know when and how to share them.

I didn't just make an obstetrical decision that night, in the conversation at the pay phone with Bill. I also made an ethical decision. Given the discrepancy between my intuition of danger and the externals that expressed normalcy, I chose to act upon the externals. It seemed presumptuous to me then to privilege my "personal" intuition over "objective" data. Now, it would seem presumptuous and even unethical not to take such an intimation just as seriously and at times more seriously than the lab work and vital signs. I had "lab results" from an unusual "monitoring system" of my own, but one whose accuracy rate to that point had been 100 percent. But because I couldn't point to a machine that was doing the monitoring, much less explain how it worked, I kept silent.

In choosing not to share my premonition with Annie and her husband, I departed from the norm of "informed decision-making," another value by which "postmodern midwifery" distinguishes itself from mainstream obstetrics. "We value the right to true informed choice, not merely informed consent to what we think is best" (MANA 1992: 11). Our clients and their children, after all, are the ones who must live with the outcomes of the decisions made. As midwife Judy Luce insists, the question is:

> not so much ethical issues as . . . the people who make ethical choices. Only individuals can make decisions about what is ethical for them. In fact, when these decisions are made for whole groups of people rather than by them we are faced with an ethical dilemma in itself. Rather than talk about what is "ethical," I want to talk about the efforts that women make to do what is right in their lives. Wholeness and harmony in one's life, living with integrity, being responsible, simply having one's life make sense: these are what concern women when they make choices about their childbearing. (Luce 1980)

Dread's appearance was information and I withheld it; I reverted to a paternalistic model of decision-making. Granted, the information I had was not quite the usual type of information—this is where the cultural issue of finding language that dignifies and validates intuition intersects with an issue that is even more culturally remote: the question of the influence that thoughts and attitudes have on the course of events.[11]

For example, when I "knew" immediately that my friend Michele wouldn't carry to term, I chose not to share that with her. Furthermore, I proceeded just as if she were having a normal pregnancy—this in my thoughts as well. In philosophical terms, I "bracketed" the certainty that she would not carry to term—didn't dismiss it altogether, but didn't give it any pride of place in my thoughts. I didn't share it with Michele until she was already miscarrying and asked me directly. The last thing I wanted to inject into a long-hoped-for pregnancy was the fear that it wouldn't last, because such fears find physiological and subtle pathways to materialize into events. Nor was I impelled to try and work psychically to prevent a miscarriage—and in this instance, given the sorrow but also the self- and life-affirmation of her miscarriage, I believe that was an intuitively correct decision, made and carried out without reflection.

In Joy's situation, I also chose not to share my intuitive take with her—though had I known the other midwives better, I likely would have cross-checked my intuitions with theirs—this is, in fact, something we often do in staff meetings. There is a fine line between granting further existence and momentum to a potential problem by agreeing that it exists, and allowing it the space to move and shapeshift toward resolution because one is simply willing to witness its existence and stay open to its message. Similarly, if Joy had been my client throughout her pregnancy, I would have tried to find a way gently to see if she were aware of anything corresponding to what I was picking up, and to see if she would be open to exploring that together.

Experienced human energy field healers would say that in "almost-seeing" a cloudiness in Joy, I was seeing into her aura or energy field. This raises two interesting possibilities—first, that it might have been possible to work energetically (with her consent) in her field.[12] Often such work leads to astonishing recall of suppressed memories and release of suppressed emotion—in this case, it might have eliminated the "need" for the birth emergency without eliminating the transformative experience and change in self-esteem that came about by way of the birth.

Second, human energy fields do exist—the scientific research is unequivocal about that, even if no further scientific conclusions have been drawn.[13] To see into another's field is to have access in some cases to extraordinarily intimate information. This point warrants discussion beyond the scope of this chapter, but it is worth raising because of the frequency with which midwives (and pregnant women) do spontaneously see or "almost see" human field phenomena.

In Joy's case, I sensed the likelihood of problems, but I also sensed that the outcome would be benign. I used my premonition to be vigilant as her birth attendant; I did not feel called to do more than that.

Lucia Roncalli

Dread is a bit different, for although it is my own personal image, it has accurately signaled the potential for tragedy each time it has appeared. As a practitioner, my dilemma had been this: how to say to a woman or to a couple, "Listen, I am seeing this thing/feeling this feeling and in the past, it's come before major emergencies. Even though things look OK now, I think we should consider going to the hospital." Wouldn't that be "injecting negativity" into a situation? And if the outcome were bad, wouldn't that be just as possibly the result of such a disclosure from me?

The dilemma doesn't exist in quite that way anymore. I honor the connectedness that manifests sometimes in precognitive knowledge, and speak with the authority the connectedness warrants. But it took a death, and my own "impossible" healing from a supposedly incurable disease, and subsequent training as an energy field healer, as well as a tremendous amount of reading about the cultural construction of knowledge and about human abilities regarded as normal in most societies but as "paranormal" in ours, to get to this point.

Intervention, Control, and Standing by Process

Although Dread has not appeared again at a birth, I consider the big brooding buffalo-mountain my friend, and if it shows up again, I will be prepared in ways I was not before. I am ready to engage Dread in conversation, to open toward it in silence, and let it communicate. I am also ready to ask if it has particular information or advice for me or for the mother. I am open to sharing with the parents what I feel and see.

I may check to see if it is possible to intervene on the level at which Dread and other such precognitive apparitions appear, to work with them, or with the situation in such a way as to transform the emergencies they portend.

Some practitioners disagree with me about this; they maintain that Dread and other similar phenomena are intimations of how things are; I see the possibility that they hint at how things could be, and that it might be possible to become skilled enough to intervene precognitively and psychically, or to work directly with the mother in such a way as to avert catastrophe. This could mean sending healing energy to Dread or to the situation; it could mean using Vajrayana meditation techniques for compassionate dealings with "terrifying entities" on the bardo plane.

Isn't this the same mindset as interventionist obstetrics? Isn't it just another species of the desire to control the birthing process?

Yes and no. I have no interest in controlling birth for my own convenience—I would never induce or retard a birth in order to keep institutional timetables or personal appointments, as hospitals and obstetricians too often do (Rindfuss 1977; Rothman 1982: 272–74; Davis-Floyd 1992: 95–113). Nor do I wish to have the births I attend conform to a temporal[14] or any other kind of predictable norm.

Yet—if I could control outcomes in such a way that every labor results in a calm, wide-eyed, smiling baby and a joyous, self-loving woman, I would.

Lucia Roncalli

Notice how I said it, though. I am not just talking about survival—I'm talking about radiance. And I know that the way to get there is different for every birthing woman, and will in most cases entail openness to mystery and to something else that emerges with the baby. The choice is not between high tech and no tech; the choice is between being open to process or not. And opening to process means opening to intuition.

Opening to process and standing by it cannot be categorized as either passive or directive. It is like musical improvisation: the music shapes your response, and your response shapes the music. The "given" evolves, and the best musicians, like the best birth attendants, are both receptive to what is in the instant, and unafraid to take it into another mood or key. Standing by process requires wisdom and develops wisdom—"wisdom" as I first came to know it in the hospitals: a kind of transformative and untamable experience, in which intuition and openness are key elements. It is a form of love, because it is a willingness to wait for and support and engage with what wants to emerge, without dictating the terms beforehand. This is true whether the process is birth, dying, or deep healing.

Although intuition stories show that radiant outcomes neither come from nor preclude high-tech care, the wonders and achievements of technology can make us forget how very much we do innately know.[15] Standing by process can be lonely and, especially when there are potentially formidable legal penalties for doing so, it can at times be frightening. The MANA Statement of Values and Ethics acknowledges this:

> The choices one can or will actually make may be limited by the oppressive nature of the medical, legal, or cultural framework in which we live. The more our values conflict with those of the dominant culture, the more risky it becomes to act truly in accord with our values. (MANA 1992: 12)

It takes courage—an old word whose root is "heart." Intuition and anomaly stories can teach and hearten us, encourage and remind us to "remember that we've forgotten that we remember" (Whitridge 1993) how to die and how to give birth, how to heal, how to play, and how to love. It is the difference between developing machinery to predict and flatten the sea-waves we fear, and remembering that we can develop ourselves enough to connect even with sea-waves as sentient beings in a sentient universe. We have the ability to hear what the waves whisper to us, and to whisper back, for there truly is an underlying "pattern that connects." This is the ultimate mystery, the one we truly can "seek to know and learn from, but never control."

NOTES TO CHAPTER 10

1. David Tracy has observed that when a culture's standards or criteria for what constitutes genuine knowledge change, the form of its discourse changes as well. Hume's dialogues and Kant's critiques, for example, are experiments in form as well as innovations in dis-

course. (David Tracy, book in progress; graduate seminars on modernity and postmodernity at University of Chicago, Jan.–June 1995.)

2. The work of Arne Naess is especially clear about this point (see especially *Ecology, Community, and Lifestyle*, 1989).

3. Martha Nussbaum, lecture presentations on Aristotle, Brown University, 1986. See also Nussbaum 1986.

4. Arney's excellent book (*Power and Profession of Obstetrics*) chronicles the shift in American obstetrics to what he calls the "ecological style," in which practitioners see it as their role to be concerned not only with pregnancy and birth, but also with "monitoring": a woman's complete personal history, her socioeconomic status, occupational hazards, extended family relations, and so forth, now are within the legitimate purview of her obstetrician. Arney is concerned to show the role "monitoring" has played in enabling American obstetricians to obliterate the strong boundary between normal birth, attended by midwives, and abnormal or high risk birth that necessitates obstetrical management. Following Foucault, Arney sees the emphasis on "monitoring" and the "encouragement of a confessional style in a woman's relation to her caregiver" as an insidious step toward a "lighter, more precise" form of social control. For him, visibility can only mean vulnerability to being controlled.

   The feminist and Orwellian points are well taken. Nonetheless, Arney's monocular conclusion is resonant with the tendency in Carol Gilligan's (1982) male subjects to perceive isolate autonomy as desirable, and connected relationship as threatening or even violent. From this perspective, "being seen" means the end of being autonomous, and can only hold the threat of being controlled by a maleficent other. It cannot hold the possibility delineated in this text, of being enfranchised as a full human being lovingly connected to others.

5. I read this years ago, and have looked for it since then, but am unable to locate its source in Jaspers' writings.

6. See References for Melvin Morse.

7. I mean "cross-checking" quite literally—my favorite example of this comes from a healing session I did for a woman with asthma. The session was quite profound, and the woman has not had an asthma attack in the two years since. I sensed at one point that her mother and grandmother, both dead, had appeared to help. One sat at her head and one sat at her feet, while I worked on her chest. I said nothing as this occurred—I didn't want to disrupt the work we were doing. When the session was over, the woman mentioned that her mother and grandmother had been present. I nodded. "Your grandmother was at your head, and your mother was at your feet."

   "No," she said. "It was the other way around."

   "But the woman at your head had such gnarled hands. Wasn't that your grandmother?"

   "No—that was my mother. She had rheumatoid arthritis."

8. See, for example, the work of Elisabeth Kubler-Ross and her student Bernie Siegel (1986). They use simple drawings made by cancer patients that express a startlingly precise knowledge of the location of the disease in their bodies, its advance or remission or the nearness of death, as well as the underlying issues that have catalyzed the disease and must be addressed in order for peaceful death or physical healing to occur. Pregnant women have a similarly precise conscious or preconscious knowledge of their bodies and of the little ones they carry.

9. This is a favorite adage among midwives. It also appears in Gayle Peterson's works (e.g., 1981).

10. The work of Gayle Peterson (1981) and Peterson and Mahl (1984) is an example of the latter kind of intervention.

11. Much, perhaps too much, is made of this in New Age circles. The work of Robert Jahn and Brenda Dunne (1988) stands in contrast. Although they would be the first to acknowledge that their work is pioneering and incomplete, it is flagship research, elegant and precise, on precognition and also on the influence of human consciousness on the material world.

12. See Dolores Krieger (1979) and Barbara Ann Brennan (1993, 1987) for examples of how this work can be done.

13. Harold Saxon Burr (1935, 1972), Valerie Hunt (1995), Jan Walleczek (1993), and Hireshi Motoyama (1979) are just a few who have devoted their lives to research in this area; Daniel Benor (1994, 1995) has compiled a good overview of the research of these and other scientists.

14. See Davis-Floyd, this volume, on the Friedman curve and its implications.

15. William Irwin Thompson (1991: 136) points out that many modern technologies are ersatz or degraded forms of the esoteric abilities that can be developed in yoga and other meditative disciplines: telephone conversation, for example, is the epigone of telepathic communication; cloning, of bilocation; virtual reality, of astral travel into other dimensions. We find ourselves awed and overwhelmed by technical accomplishments that seem outside our unaided powers, and forget that we possess the potential for these and much more. The key to it all is the ability—and courage—to drop or listen past the isolate self to the living process beyond it.

Thompson believes our civilization to be at a crossroads of not only historical, but also evolutionary significance. It is a true "catastrophe bifurcation," and the choice is between a path that values surveillance, mechanism, and control, and one that is comfortable with "ambiguity, complexity and women." The decision is about whether control or co-existence is the supreme value, and for Thompson the primary battlefield is not land or ecology, but the human body, especially the female human body. "We stand little chance of getting out of this century with the same human nature with which we entered it."

References Cited

Arney, William
 1982 *Power and Profession of Obstetrics*. Chicago: University of Chicago Press.
Belenky, Mary F., Clinchy, Blythe M., Goldberger, Nancy R., Tarule, Jill M.
 1986 *Women's Way of Knowing*. New York: Basic Books.
Benor, Daniel
 1994, 1995 *Healing Research: Holistic Energy, Medicine and Spirituality*, vols. I and II. London: Helix Editions Limited.
Brennan, Barbara
 1987 *Hands of Light: A Guide to Healing Through the Human Energy Field*. New York: Bantam Books.
 1993 *Light Emerging*. New York: Bantam Books.

Burr, Harold Saxon
  1935 *An Electrodynamic Theory of Life*. New Haven: Yale University Press.
  1972 *The Fields of Life: Our Links with the Universe*. New York: Ballantine Books.
Davis-Floyd, Robbie
  1992 *Birth as an American Rite of Passage*. Berkeley: University of California Press.
Engelmann, George
  1882, 1977 *Labor Among Primitive Peoples*. New York: AMS Press
Frye, Anne
  1995 *Holistic Midwifery: A Comprehensive Textbook for Midwives in Homebirth Practice. Volume I, Care During Pregnancy*. Portland: Labrys Press.
Gardner, Howard
  1983 *Frames of Mind: The Theory of Multiple Intelligences*. New York: Basic Books.
Gilligan, Carol
  1982 *In a Different Voice: Psychological Theory and Women's Development*. Cambridge, MA: Harvard University Press.
Goer, Henci
  1995 *Obstetric Myths vs. Research Realities: A Guide to the Medical Literature*. Westport, CT: Bergin and Garvey.
Hunt, Valerie
  1995 *Infinite Mind: The Science of Human Vibrations*. Malibu: Malibu Publishing.
Jahn, Robert and Brenda Dunne
  1988 *Margins of Reality: The Role of Consciousness in the Physical World*. New York: Harcourt Brace & Co.
Krieger, Dolores
  1979 *The Therapeutic Touch: How to Use Your Hands to Help or to Heal*. New York: Prentice Hall Press.
Luce, Judy
  1980 "Ethical Issues Relating to Childbirth as Experienced by the Birthing Woman and Midwife." In Holmes et al, *Birth Control and Controlling Birth: Woman-Centered Perspectives*. Clifton, NJ: Humana Press.
MANA (Midwives Alliance of North America)
  1992 Statement of Values and Ethics. *MANA News*, vol.X, no.4. (Reprinted in Frye, *Holistic Midwifery: A Comprehensive Textbook for Midwives in Homebirth Practice. Volume 1, Care During Pregnancy*. Portland, Oregon: Labyrs Press, 1995: 31–34).
Mehl, Lewis
  1982 *Mind and Matter: Foundations for Holistic Health*. Berkeley: Mindbody Press.
Morse, Melvin
  1992 *Transformed by the Light: The Powerful Effect of Near Death Experiences on People's Lives*. New York: Villard.
  1990 *Closer to the Light: Learning from Children's Near Death Experiences*. New York: Villard.
Motoyama, Hiroshi
  1979 *The Functional Relationship Between Yoga Asanas and Acupuncture Meridians*. Tokyo: IARP.
Naess, Arne
  Ecology, Community, and Lifestyle. New York: Cambridge University Press.
Nussbaum, Martha
  1986 *The Fragility of Goodness: Luck and Ethics in Greek Tragedy and Philosophy*. Cambridge: Cambridge University Press.

Peterson, Gayle
  1981 *Birthing Normally: A Personal Growth Approach to Childbirth.* Berkeley: Mindbody Press.
Peterson, Gayle and Lewis Mehl
  1984 *Pregnancy as Healing: A Holistic Philosophy for Prenatal Care,* vols. I and II. Berkeley: Mindbody Press.
Rindfuss, Ronald
  1977 "Convenience and the Occurrence of Births: Induction of Labor in the United States and Canada." Presented at the 1977 Annual Meeting of the American Sociological Association.
Rothman, Barbara Katz
  1982 *In Labor: Women and Power in the Birthplace.* New York: W. W. Norton and Co.
Siegel, Bernie
  1986 *Love, Medicine and Miracles.* New York: Harper & Row
Swallow, Helen
  1980 "Midwives in Many Settings." In Holmes et al., *Birth Control and Controlling Birth: Woman-Centered Perspectives.* Clifton, NJ: Humana Press.
Thompson, William Irwin
  1991 *The American Replacement of Nature: The Everyday Acts and Outrageous Evolution of Economic Life.* New York: Doubleday.
Wagner, Marsden
  1994 *Pursuing the Birth Machine: The Search for Appropriate Birth Technology.* Campdown, Australia: ACE Graphics.
Walleczek, Jan
  1993 "Bioelectromagnetics and the Question of 'Subtle Energies,' " *Noetic Sciences Review* Winter 1993.
Whitridge, Candace
  1993 "Fate of the Earth, Fate of Birth." A talk given at the annual convention of the Midwives' Alliance of North America (MANA).

Lucia Roncalli

CONTRIBUTORS

P. SVEN ARVIDSON. Originally from Washington, D.C. (Ph.D., Georgetown University), he is currently Assistant Professor of Philosophy at the College of Mount St. Joseph in Cincinnati, Ohio. His degrees are in philosophy, psychology, and human development. Arvidson has researched and written on the origin of organization in consciousness; the nature of marginal consciousness; the phenomenon of attention; the shape of aesthetic consciousness; the shape of mystical consciousness; the possibility of chaotic experience; and the notion of "limit" in the field of consciousness. His passions are teaching, learning, writing, and most of all his bride Julie.

MARCIE BOUCOUVALAS is a professor of Adult Learning at the Graduate Center of Virginia Polytechnic Institute and State University in Falls Church, Virginia, where she teaches graduate courses, conducts research, directs doctoral dissertations, and serves as program leader in Adult Learning and Human Resource Development. Prior to her fifteen years of service to the university, she worked for twelve years in the continuing education of physicians, community development work with both urban and rural poor, training and development efforts in the criminal justice system, and other arenas. She has been deeply involved for the past twenty years in the study of transpersonal psychology and serves as a field editor for the *Journal of Transpersonal Psychology*. She is continually refining and exploring the intuitive realm both in herself and with regard to the further evolution of the human species.

GUY BURNEKO. Raised among the broad hills, small towns, pastures, and woodlands of upstate New York and navigating thence by the stars of chaos, doubt, and imagination to further geographies and epistemologies, I make my home and work using ancient and postmodern learning as an artist would the palette. Less interested in immutable truth than in fluent and labile meaning, my thinking, such as it is, moves with serendipity, lucky finds, and the conversation of friends more than it rests on certain foundations. Thus, like galaxies pinwheeling, the turning of tides, and the vagaries of love, I am always (un)hinged on an axis of no certain nature. My pride is in a surpassing wondrous daughter, Eva; my hope is in a planet only just coming to its senses; and my joy is in the greater part of meaning. I teach now at Golden Gate University in San Francisco, where I direct the Graduate Liberal Studies Program.

ELIZABETH DAVIS, CPM, has been a midwife, women's health care specialist, educator, and consultant for the past 20 years. She is internationally active in women's rights, and is widely sought after for ability to apply principles openness and humanism to specific problems. She has served as a representative to the Midwives Alliance of North America, and as President of the Midwifery Education and Accreditation Council for the United States. She holds a degree in Holistic Maternity Care from Antioch University and is certified by the North American Registry of Midwives. She lives in Windsor, California and is the mother of three children. Her books include the classic midwifery text *Heart and Hands: A Midwife's Guide to Pregnancy and Birth*; *Energetic Pregnancy*; *Women's Intuition*; and *Women, Sex, and Desire: Exploring Your Sexuality at Every Stage of Life*. Her latest book (co-authored with Carol Leonard) is *The Women's Wheel of Life: Thirteen Archetypes of Woman at Her Fullest Power*.

ROBBIE DAVIS-FLOYD is a cultural anthropologist specializing in medical anthropology and gender studies. She is author of *Birth as an American Rite of Passage* (1992) and *The Technocratic Body and The Organic Body: Hegemony and Heresy in Women's Birth Choices* (in press); co-author (with Gloria St. John) of *From Doctor to Healer: Physicians in Transition* (1997); editor of *Birth in Four Cultures*, by Brigitte Jordan (1993); and co-editor of *Childbirth and Authoritative Knowledge: Cross-Cultural Perspectives* (with Carolyn Sargent) (1997) and *Cyborg Babies: From Techno-Sex to Techno-Tots* (with Joseph Dumit) (1997). She gives talks on gender and evolution, on ritual, and on childbirth in the technocracy across the United States and internationally. She is a Research Fellow in the Department of Anthropology, University of Texas at Austin, and a Research Associate at Rice University, Houston. Her current research project investigates the politics and professionalization of direct-entry midwives in North America. She is the mother of two children, a daughter Peyton, 17, and a son Jason, 13.

BRENDA J. DUNNE, Coordinator of the International Consciousness Research Laboratories (ICRL) and the Academy of Consciousness Studies, has been Manager of Princeton Engineering Anomalies Research (PEAR) Lab and a member of

Princeton University's Professional Research staff since 1979. Informed by her academic background in psychology and the humanities, her principal research interests address the role of consciousness in physical reality through empirical studies of human/machine interactions and anomalous information acquisition via remote perception, and the formation of a theoretical framework capable of accommodating the laboratory's experimental data. This work has been described in detail in numerous publications and technical reports, and in the book *Margins of Reality: The Role of Consciousness in the Physical World* (Harcourt Brace 1987), co-authored with Professor Robert G. Jahn, Director of the PEAR Program and Dean Emeritus of Princeton's School of Engineering and Applied Science. A Councilor of the Society for Scientific Exploration since 1986, Dunne has served as its Executive Vice-President since 1991, with primary responsibility for organizing its annual meetings and topical symposia. She is the proud mother of two and the indulgent grandmother of four. She takes almost as much pride in the Academy of Consciousness Studies, and hopes to see the Academy and its activities repeated and extended in years to come.

BOB HARBORT is Professor of Computer Science at Southern College of Tech-nology in Atlanta, Georgia. A licensed professional engineer, he also holds certification in data processing and computer systems. His Ph.D. is from the Graduate Institute of the Liberal Arts at Emory University, where he studied theories of interpretation and how they may be applied to both human and machine information processing systems.

JEREMY HAYWARD received a Ph.D. in theoretical physics at Cambridge University, followed by four years of research in molecular biology at MIT and Tufts Medical School. Realizing that science had become the dogmatic religion of our time, obsessed with removing mind from the cosmos, he looked for a more intelligent and encompassing view of life and mind. Thus he began the study and practice of Tibetan Buddhism in 1970. In Boulder, Colorado in 1974, he co-founded the Naropa Institute, an undergraduate and graduate-level college with an educational philosophy based on joining intellect and intuition—academic study and direct experience. He has written four books, including *Perceiving Ordinary Magic: Joining Science and Intuitive Insight*, and *Sacred World*, and co-edited *Gentle Bridges: Dialogues with the Dalai Lama on the Sciences of Life and Mind*. His most recent book, about to be published, is entitled *Love, Energy, Awareness: Letters to My Daughter on Freeing Ourselves from the Brainwashing that Depresses Us and Binds Us to the Dead World*.

CHARLES LAUGHLIN is a professor of anthropology and religion in the Department of Sociology and Anthropology, Carleton University, Ottawa, Ontario, Canada KIS 5B6. He has spent much of his career studying how the brain mediates consciousness and culture, and has written numerous books and articles on symbolic aspects of ritual and alternative states of consciousness. He is co-author of *Brain, Symbol, and Experience* (Columbia University Press, 1990), which discusses many of these issues. He has done ethnographic fieldwork among the So of Northeastern Uganda, Tibetan lamas in Nepal and India (for seven years as a monk himself), and most recently among the Navajo people of the American Southwest. His experiences during his work with Tibetan Buddhists and Navajos convinced him of the central importance of intuitive knowledge in the world's traditional cosmologies.

EVELYN H. MONSAY is Associate Professor of Physics and Chair of the Physics Department at Le Moyne College in Syracuse, New York. She holds a Ph.D. in Physics from Princeton University, and an M.B.A. in General Management from Syracuse University. Her graduate work was in relativistic quantum field theory, but her most recent research area has been photonics, the marriage of quantum optics and electronics. She has also held the position of program manager in a major aerospace corporation. Originally from Malvern, Pennsylvania, she now lives with her husband Tom in their ever-lively household of many cats and one beleaguered dog in central New York.

ANNE PINEAULT was born in northern New Brunswick on Canada's East Coast. Her Mic' Maq heritage led her to appreciate the importance of ecological principles applied through every area of life. On this basis she sought to develop her ideas through her talents as an artist and subsequently entered Brock University's Honors Fine Arts Programme. She is currently completing a Master's degree in Environmental Studies at York University and is employed as the Education Officer at the Niagara Regional Native Center in Niagara-on-the-Lake, Ontario. Her upcoming exhibition at the Woodland Cultural Center, a center that serves as the cultural voice of the Six Nations/Iroquian community in Brantford, Ontario, addresses issues of cultural and ecological restoration from an indigenous perspective.

LUCIA RONCALLI is a midwife and healer who travels from her home in rural Alaska to teach and lecture. She is midway through doctoral work at the University of Chicago on healing and cross-cultural spirituality; she has just begun her apprenticeship to an Inupiaq medicine woman. Lucia's household includes three boys, nine sled dogs, and a visiting ermine.

JOE SHERIDAN was raised on the shores of the Georgian Bay off Lake Huron in the midst of the Thirty Thousand Islands, where he later sailed as a deckhand on a Canadian Coast Guard search-and-rescue vessel. He was privileged to have known the area when it still supported trappers and hunters, among whom were his forebears. The local Ojibway peoples of the Wasauksing First Nation have been of inestimable importance in his outlook on what it means to be in that place. Any deficiencies in his argument are purely his own and not theirs. He currently teaches in the Faculties of Education and Environmental Studies at York University in North York, Ontario. His West Ireland ancestors, the O'Sirideains, translated their surname as "savage."

Index